T0306086

Obstacles to Ethical Decision-Making

In commerce, many moral failures are due to narrow mindsets that preclude taking into account the moral dimensions of a decision or action. In turn, sometimes these mindsets are caused by failing to question managerial decisions from a moral point of view, because of a perceived authority of management. In the 1960s, Stanley Milgram conducted controversial experiments to investigate just how far obedience to an authority figure could subvert his subjects' moral beliefs. In this thought-provoking work, the authors examine the prevalence of narrow mental models and the phenomenon of obedience to an authority to analyze and understand the challenges which business professionals encounter in making ethical decisions. *Obstacles to Ethical Decision-Making* proposes processes – including collaborative input and critique – by which individuals may reduce or overcome these challenges. It provides decision-makers at all levels in an organization with the means to place ethical considerations at the heart of managerial decision-making.

PATRICIA H. WERHANE is the Callista Wicklander Chair of Business Ethics and Director, Institute for Business and Professional Ethics at DePaul University. She is also Professor Emeritus at the Darden Graduate School of Business Administration at the University of Virginia. Her previous publications include *Ethical Issues in Business, 7th edition*, edited with Tom Donaldson and Margaret Cording (2001).

LAURA PINCUS HARTMAN is Vincent de Paul Professor of Business Ethics at DePaul University's College of Commerce. She serves as Research Director of DePaul's Institute for Business and Professional Ethics. Her recent publications include *Alleviating Poverty Through Profitable Partnerships*, co-authored with Patricia H. Werhane, Scott Kelley, and Dennis Moberg (2009).

CRINA ARCHER is a Ph.D. candidate in Political Science at Northwestern University, Senior Research Fellow to Vincent de Paul Professor Laura Hartman, and senior scholar with the Institute for Business and Professional Ethics, at DePaul University. She is the co-editor of *Second Nature: Rethinking the Natural Through Politics* (2013).

ELAINE E. ENGLEHARDT is Distinguished Professor at Utah Valley University. Specializing in practical and professional ethics, she has authored and/or edited eight books.

MICHAEL S. PRITCHARD is the Willard A. Brown Professor of Philosophy and Co-Director of the Center for the Study of Ethics in Society at Western Michigan University. His previous publications include *Professional Integrity* (2007) and *The Ethical Challenges of Academic Administration*, with Elaine Englehardt, Kerry Romesberg and Brian Schrag (2010).

Obstacles to Ethical Decision-Making

Mental Models, Milgram and the Problem of Obedience

PATRICIA H. WERHANE, LAURA PINCUS
HARTMAN, CRINA ARCHER, ELAINE E.
ENGLEHARDT, AND MICHAEL S. PRITCHARD

CAMBRIDGE
UNIVERSITY PRESS

CAMBRIDGE
UNIVERSITY PRESS

University Printing House, Cambridge CB2 8BS, United Kingdom

Cambridge University Press is part of the University of Cambridge.

It furthers the University's mission by disseminating knowledge in the pursuit of education, learning and research at the highest international levels of excellence.

www.cambridge.org
Information on this title: www.cambridge.org/9781107000032

© Patricia H. Werhane, Laura Pincus Hartman, Crina Archer, Elaine E. Englehardt and Michael S. Pritchard 2013

First published 2013
3rd printing 2013
First paperback edition 2014

A catalogue record for this publication is available from the British Library

Library of Congress Cataloguing in Publication data
Werhane, Patricia Hogue.
Obstacles to ethical decision-making : mental models, Milgram and the problem of obedience / Patricia H. Werhane, Laura Pincus Hartman, Crina Archer, Elaine E. Englehardt, and Michael S. Pritchard.
    pages   cm
Includes bibliographical references and index.
ISBN 978-1-107-00003-2
1. Business ethics.   2. Decision making – Moral and ethical aspects.   I. Title.
HF5387.W457   2013
174′.4 – dc23   2012035058

ISBN 978-1-107-00003-2 Hardback
ISBN 978-1-107-44205-4 Paperback

For our good friend and colleague, Dennis Moberg.

Contents

Notes on the authors

Patricia H. Werhane is the Callista Wicklander Chair of Business Ethics and Director, Institute for Business and Professional Ethics at DePaul University. She was formerly the Peter and Adeline Ruffin Chair of Business Ethics and Senior Fellow at the Olsson Center for Applied Ethics in the Darden Graduate School of Business Administration at the University of Virginia, where she is now Professor Emeritus. Until 1993, she was the Henry J. Wirtenberger Professor of Business Ethics at Loyola University of Chicago. She received her BA from Wellesley College, and MA and Ph.D. from Northwestern University.

Professor Werhane has been a Rockefeller Fellow at Dartmouth, Visiting Professor at the University of Cambridge, and Erskine Visiting Fellow at the University of Canterbury (New Zealand). Professor Werhane has published numerous articles and case studies, and is the author or editor of over twenty-five books including *Ethical Issues in Business*, edited with Tom Donaldson and Margaret Cording, seventh edition, *Persons, Rights, and Corporations*, *Adam Smith and His Legacy for Modern Capitalism*, *Moral Imagination and Managerial Decision-Making*, and with Laura Hartman, *Alleviating Poverty Through Profitable Partnerships*. She has written over 100 published articles and book chapters on various business ethics on such topics as employee and employer rights, mergers and acquisitions, responsibilities of multinational corporations, intellectual property, and the intersection between healthcare organizations and business ethics. Professor Werhane serves on the editorial boards of a number of journals and she is founder and former editor-in-chief of *Business Ethics Quarterly*, the journal of the Society for Business Ethics and advisory editor for *Business and Professional Ethics Journal*. She is also on the academic advisory committee for the Business Roundtable Institute for Business Ethics.

Her recent work focuses on globalization, with an emphasis on developing new models for corporate governance and corporate initiatives to alleviate poverty both in the United States and in less developed countries around the world.

Laura Pincus Hartman is Vincent de Paul Professor of Business Ethics and Legal Studies in DePaul University's College of Commerce, where she has received the university's Excellence in Teaching Award, the college's Outstanding Service Award and numerous university competitive research grants. She also serves as Research Director of DePaul's Institute for Business and Professional Ethics.

For the past two years she has represented DePaul University on the Global Projects Committee of the Worldwide Vincentian Family, a committee responsible for hands-on design and implementation of a micro-development, finance and education system for the poor of Haiti. She was named to that effort after recently returning to the faculty, having served for a number of years as Associate Vice President for Academic Affairs for the university. In that capacity, she was responsible for, among other programs, the administration and adjudication of the Academic Integrity Policy across the entire university (24,000+ students). Hartman also chaired DePaul's Task Force on Speech and Expression Principles at the request of its President, among numerous other service contributions.

Hartman has published over eighty books, cases and articles in, among other journals, *Business Ethics Quarterly*, *Business & Society Review*, *Business Ethics: A European Review*, and the *Journal of Business Ethics*. Her research and consulting efforts have also garnered national media attention by publications such as *Fortune Small Business* where she was named one of the "Top 10 Minds for Small Business," as well as the *Wall Street Journal*, *BusinessWeek*, and *The New York Times*.

She was invited to serve as the Gourlay Professor at the Melbourne Business School/Trinity College at the University of Melbourne (2007–8), an invited professor at INSEAD (France), HEC (France), the Université Paul Cezanne Aix Marseille III, and at the Grenoble Graduate School of Business, among other European universities. On behalf of the accrediting body for schools of business, AACSB, Hartman is the global coordinator of the regular, bi-annual seminar series, "Teaching Business Ethics." She received her BS from Tufts University and her JD from the University of Chicago.

Crina Archer is a Ph.D. candidate in Political Science at Northwestern University, Senior Research Fellow to Vincent de Paul Professor Laura Hartman, and a senior scholar with the Institute for Business and Professional Ethics at DePaul University. Her research focuses include democratic political thought, political temporality, and ethical and political judgment. She is the co-editor of *Second Nature: Rethinking the Natural Through Politics* (2013).

Elaine E. Englehardt is Special Assistant to the President and a Distinguished Professor of Ethics at Utah Valley University (UVU). She received her BA and MA from Brigham Young University and her Ph.D. from the University of Utah. She has taught ethics, philosophy and communication classes at UVU for the past thirty years. Her current assignments include teaching, scholarly work and federal coordination. As a Professor of Philosophy she teaches courses in Ethics and Values, Business Ethics, Communication Ethics, Bioethics, and Legal Ethics. She is a broadcast Philosophy Professor for Utah's Channel 9 (KUED).

For the past twenty years, she has written and directed seven multi-year, national grants. Four large grants are in ethics across the curriculum from the Department of Education; and three are from the National Endowment for the Humanities. She is the author of five books in ethics including: *Ethics and Life: An Interdisciplinary Approach to Moral Problems, 3rd Edition*; *The Organizational Self and Ethical Conduct: Sunlit Virtue and Shadowed Resistance*; *Interpersonal Communication Ethics: Friends, Intimates, Sexuality, Marriage and Family*; and *Principled Media Ethics*. She has additionally published numerous articles. In 2008 she became the co-editor of *Teaching Ethics*, an international journal for the Society for Ethics Across the Curriculum. Dr Englehardt is a visiting Professor in the MBA program at the Helsinki School of Economics. She also consults in ethics and ethics across the curriculum at numerous universities. Her awards include the National Outstanding Distance Education Program; *Parade Magazine*, Paul Newman Top Ten Service Project; Theodore M. Hesburgh Award; The National First Place Award for Faculty Development to Enhance Undergraduate Teaching and Learning – for the Ethics Across the Curriculum Program; Governor's Award in the Humanities; Awarded by the Utah Humanities Council for a lifetime of outstanding contributions to the Humanities; UVU Trustees award for Outstanding Scholarship; Utah Academy of Sciences, Arts and Letters, The Distinguished Service Award; and CASE Utah Professor of the Year, Washington, DC.

Michael S. Pritchard is Willard A. Brown Professor of Philosophy at Western Michigan University. His Ph.D. is in philosophy from the University of Wisconsin. His publications include, *The Ethical Challenges of Academic Administration* (2010), co-edited with Elaine Englehardt, Kerry Romesburg, and Brian Schrag, *Taking Sides: Clashing Views in Business Ethics and Society, 11th edn.* (2010), co-edited with Lisa H. Newton and Elaine Englehardt, *Engineering Ethics: Concepts and Cases* (2009), with C. E. Harris and Michael J. Rabins, *Professional Integrity: Thinking Ethically* (2007), *Reasonable Children* (1996), *Responsible Communication: Ethical Issues in Business, Industry, and the Professions* (1996) co-edited with James Jaksa, *Communication Ethics: Methods of Analysis, 2nd edn.* (1994), with James Jaksa, and *On Becoming Responsible* (1991).

In 2008 he became the co-editor of *Teaching Ethics*, an international journal for the Society for Ethics Across the Curriculum. He has served on the Executive Committee, and is a Founding Member of the Society for Ethics Across the Curriculum, 2000–8. He has also served on the Executive Committee and is a Founding Member of the Association for Professional and Practical Ethics. He has served on the Final Review Panel, EVIST Program, National Science Foundation, 1996–9, and was a consultant and presenter at the National Science Foundation program for junior and senior high school teachers, "Ethics and Values in Science and Technology," State University of New York–Stony Brook, Summer 1994–Spring 1997. He also served as Consultant and External Evaluator, FIPSE grant, "Development and Pilot Testing of a Graduate Degree Program With a Specialization in the Teaching of Applied and Professional Ethics," University of Montana, 1996–9.

Acknowledgments

The idea for this book came originally from an introduction to the Milgram experiments by Ed Freeman at the University of Virginia, and the subsequent integration of those experiments in our teaching and research. Indeed the book was initiated as an expansion of the voluminous research on the Milgram experiments, culminating in Bidhan Parmar's ground-breaking 2011 dissertation on the topic. Milgram's analysis of obedience and subsequent research of his ideas led all the authors of this volume to expand our thinking about practical ethics, asking the question Milgram presses us to consider: Why do seemingly decent people (our friends, neighbors, and colleagues) and reputable organizations engage in questionable behavior? But we soon found ourselves going beyond a preoccupation with Stanley Milgram's work.

Werhane had first addressed this question in her 2005 essay, *Why do Good People do Bad Things?* The answers, as you will read in this volume, are both multilayered and complex. Subsequently, our thinking was greatly influenced by Dennis Moberg's 2006 article, "Blind Spots," the thinking of Max Bazerman, Dolly Chugh and Ann Tenbrunsel, and by Margaret Heffernan's 2011 book, *Willful Blindness*. But our analyses and conclusions are our own.

We want to especially thank the Institute for Business and Professional Ethics at DePaul University for their support of this project. A number of people have been instrumental in creating the book, including our good friend and colleague Dennis Moberg and a former graduate student at the University of Virginia, Bidhan Parmar, who challenged traditional conclusions about Milgram's research. Nathan Shepard and Summer Brown from the Institute were enormously helpful in the project. We also want to give special thanks to Crina Archer, who not only is an author of the book but who tirelessly edited each chapter. Our grateful thanks too, to the Cambridge University Press and the patience and encouragement of Paula Parish, the general editor.

1 | Introduction

All perception is theory-laden.

(Harman, 1977, 7)

On March 14, 2012, Greg Smith, a director at Goldman Sachs, resigned from his job in Goldman Sachs' London office and went public in *The New York Times* about his dissatisfaction with the firm. Smith was clearly unhappy about the culture at Goldman. Perhaps he was disappointed at the smaller bonuses the previous year. Perhaps he disliked his boss or was unhappy that he had not been promoted to Managing Director.

We will never know why Smith came forward. Motivations matter, of course. But more important are the issues that Smith raised about the corporate culture at Goldman, which should have reverberations across the financial industry. About Goldman Sachs when he arrived there, Smith writes, "It might sound surprising to a skeptical public, but culture was always a vital part of Goldman's success. It revolved around teamwork, integrity, a spirit of humility, and always doing right by our clients. The culture was the secret sauce that made this place great and allowed us to earn our clients' trust for 143 years" (2012, A27). Today he sees a "decline in the firm's moral fiber," including a preoccupation with profits rather than client services. He writes, "Over the last 12 months I have seen five different managing directors refer to their own clients as 'muppets,' sometimes over internal e-mail." If it is true that at Goldman some managers referred to clients as "muppets," that use of language creates an image of clients as merely puppets to be manipulated by the firm. Such a view was reinforced by Lloyd Blankfein's 2008 audacious remark to the *Financial Times* that Goldman Sachs was "doing God's work" (Arlidge, 2009). The image of the sacred work of finance cannot escape the reader.

All funds, including our pension funds, depend on the trust and transparency of the industry in order for the funds to prosper for each of us. Thus a corporate culture of integrity is important, if one wants to build up a loyal workforce and clientele. According to a recent Yankelovich Monitor poll taken in 2011, more than 40 percent of Americans have lost trust in the financial industry, placing it just above corporate executives and lawyers (Schwartz, 2012). None of this may matter in the short run, but in the long run, firms with a corporate culture like the one described by Smith, whether or not this description accurately fits Goldman, is destructive to any company, its managers, its clients, its reputation, and eventually its long-term profitability. Smith (2012) writes,

> I truly believe that this decline in the firm's moral fiber represents the single most serious threat to its long-run survival. It astounds me how little senior management gets a basic truth: If clients don't trust you they will eventually stop doing business with you. It doesn't matter how smart you are . . . Without clients you will not make money. In fact, you will not exist. Weed out the morally bankrupt people, no matter how much money they make for the firm. And get the culture right again, so people want to work here for the right reasons. (Smith, 2012)

This is a book about hope. Despite the plethora of moral failures we encounter in commerce, politics and in personal lives, as the case of Greg Smith and Goldman Sachs illustrates, most of these failures are unnecessary and could be remedied or avoided altogether. It is not that there is no evil in the world. There is, and there are people and institutions that deliberately with premeditation commit crimes, violate basic human rights, and harm others. But a great deal of the time we agree with Hannah Arendt that much of what we call evil does not arise from the deliberate intention to do harm, but from the failure to think about what we are doing (Arendt, 1963 cited in 2006). Often this failure to think takes the banal form of blind obedience to some or another form of institutional or organizational authority, which is presumed to release us from responsibility for the consequences of our own actions and judgments. The authors of this book are optimistic enough to imagine that most individuals and organizations have some grasp of immorality; they are usually committed to some view of right and wrong. But often, personal, interrelational, organizational, or cultural obstacles get in the way of engaging in sound decision-making that reflects these moral commitments. This book will make some headway in outlining some of these obstacles and showing how overcoming them is difficult, but possible.

In commerce, many moral failures can be traced to narrow or blinded mental models that preclude taking into account the moral dimensions of a decision or action. In turn, some of these are caused by a failure to question managerial decisions and commands from a moral point of view, because of focused mindsets that construct a perceived authority of management whose directions one should follow without question. Examples abound. For instance, the recent failures of Johnson & Johnson, leading to recalls of baby Tylenol, baby Motrin, and hip implants, demonstrate a preoccupation with profitability that apparently sidelined the edicts of the company's credo so carefully executed in the 1980s Tylenol poisoning scares. The *Columbia* shuttle disintegration virtually repeated the causes of the earlier *Challenger* shuttle explosion in 1986. Somehow, organizational blind spots, some of which were due to failures in communication between engineers and managers that were partly responsible for the first explosion were replicated in the second tragedy. Worse, despite their expertise, engineers at NASA in both the *Challenger* and *Columbia* tragedies did not see it as within their purview as engineers to question managements' decisions to launch the shuttle spacecraft.

The "too good to be true" Bernie Madoff promises of repeatedly high returns on investments were horrendously irresponsible. Madoff's performance demonstrates what Margaret Heffernan has called "willful blindness," the almost deliberate exclusion of the moral ramifications of one's decisions and actions (Heffernan, 2011). But it demonstrated willful blindness on the part of investors as well, those who did not use their common sense in evaluating promises that consistently contrasted with market performance. The subprime mortgage crisis, blamed on banks and mortgage brokers, resulted both from irresponsible – and sometimes predatory – loan strategies and from prospective homeowners who were so preoccupied with the idea of ownership that they did not do the math on the financial effects of balloon loans. The Penn State sex abuse scandal was caused by the criminal acts of Jerry Sandusky, but a share of the responsibility also must be borne by Penn State officials who, because the abused boys were not part of the Penn State system, ignored their plight as if they did not count as human beings. Various missed whistleblowing opportunities, such as those at

Enron by insiders who knew what was going on, demonstrate that company loyalty and following the lead of persons in authority can override what individuals know is the right thing to do. Moral responsibility may be ceded because actors' perceptions of their choices are limited by their organizationally defined roles or role responsibilities. Oftentimes, these moral failures are not caused by a lack of awareness of the ethical issues, but rather, failures in a perceived ability to act. The bankruptcy of Lehman Brothers, while not the fault of CEO Richard Fuld exclusively, was exacerbated by Fuld's failure to go below the executive suite to investigate what was going on the trading floor (Cohan, 2012).

Discourse plays an important role in shaping mindsets and subsequent decision-making. On the night before the *Challenger* launch, after questions about the safety of the launch were raised by some of the engineers, the manager of the project told the lead engineer, "Take off your engineer hat and put on your management hat" (Presidential Commission, 1986). That encouragement to adopt a managerial mindset led to engineers giving in to management's decision, and as a consequence, not going above management to corporate leadership with their concerns about launch safety. The shuttle was launched the next day.

Part of the impetus for this project is a reexamination of the 1960s Milgram experiments and their later iterations. In brief, Milgram (1974) created an experiment in which a naïve participant was to teach a perfect stranger word pairs under the direction of a person in authority who continually commanded that the "experiment go on." Responding to the verbal directions of this authority figure, 65 percent of the participants delivered what they took to be the maximum shock level of 450 volts to learners who made mistakes.

While we organize and order our world through mental models, we do not often do so with the luxury of analytical hindsight. To the contrary, if we doubt whether our actions might have been different from those of Milgram's participants, we are simply asking whether we order the world in a manner so terribly distinct from others. After more than forty years since the Milgram experiments were conducted, one might expect that the human race has, if not evolved, at least learned just a small lesson from its collateral historical events. But many of the same mental models persist, attenuating our ability to "think for ourselves" with some degree of autonomy. We have shared experiences in the intervening years; yet, we recognize distinct patterns based on our particular and personal biases, mental models and social schema. Accordingly, no single descriptive analysis of ethical decision-making is possible; only vastly diverse but overlapping normative prisms exist through which we continue to view identical scenarios. Chugh and Bazerman (2007) remind us that our incomplete constructs often omit the data most necessary for *effective* decision-making. "What you fail to see can hurt you," they submit (p. 1); but our business pressures induce a polar opposite belief system. Instead, we whet and hone toward singular objectives, creating exclusionary silos when the reality of our professional dilemmas demand the broadest perspectives possible. To be our most effective, efficient, and ethical "best," we must perform the apparent and essential functions of our positions with the aim to meet bottom line objectives *and* to guard against any ethical risk or vulnerability that might threaten those objectives, at all times, and whether anticipated or incidental. But most of the time we do not.

Ariely (2008) explains the vulnerabilities and applied risks congenital in failing to attend to these silos and ethics blind spots. Vision is "one of the best things we do," he explains. "We have a huge part of our brain dedicated to vision. Bigger than dedicated to anything else... we are evolutionarily designed to do vision. And if we have these predictable repeatable mistakes in vision, which we're so good at, what's the chance that we don't make even more mistakes in something we're not as good at, for example, financial decision making."

But, are we to abandon all hope of community understanding, of victory over common biases since, as Haidt contends, "[o]ur minds were not designed by evolution to discover the truth; they were designed to play social games" (Kristof, 2009)? Ariely (2008) illuminates these visual impairments or obstructions, but also the metaphor for their subjugation. "For some reason, when it comes to the mental world, when we design things like healthcare and retirement and stock markets, we somehow forget the idea that we are limited... If we understood our cognitive limitations in the same way that we understand our physical limitations, even though they don't stare us in the face in the same way, we could design a better world. And that, I think is the hope. ...." Since these cognitive limitations are deeply rooted, they do not yield effortlessly, and we remain blind to many of them.

We will conclude that it is therefore a vital imperative to surmount the obstacles that impede effective and ethical decision-making. If we do not attend to this blindness, if we do not revisit our mental models and develop a strong moral imagination in order to challenge the intuitions that otherwise persist without question or deliberation, we are destined to accept common biases and poor decision-making. Maloney (2001, 262) cautions that one day "others will shake their heads, when reminiscing about us, and say: 'how could they have thought that?'" And what shall be our only answer? We were simply not thinking.

The book is based on a theory of social construction, the claim that human learning and interactions do not merely result from passively formed mental representations or mental pictures of our experiences, that is, representations that are derived simply from the stimuli or data to which we are subject. Rather, our minds interact with the data of our experiences, selectively filtering and framing that data though various forms of social learning mechanisms (Werhane, 1999; Gentner and Whitley, 1997, 210–11; Gorman, 1992; Senge, 1990, Ch. 10). In the process of focusing, framing, organizing, and ordering what we experience, we bracket and leave out data, simply because we cannot absorb all that we experience (Werhane, 1999; Senge, 1990). Because they are socially constructed through incomplete data, mental models or mindsets are themselves incomplete, changeable, and malleable phenomena. Still, in some contexts we can get trapped in a particular point of view that prevents us from noticing or focusing on important components of our experiences, choices, and decision-making processes.

Our thesis is that moral failures in decision-making, at least in commerce, may often be traced to narrow or compromised mindsets that preclude or dissuade the actor from considering the moral dimensions of the decision or action. Our decision-making abilities are jeopardized by such mindsets; and the manner in which we respond to authority and the perceived power it wields intensifies our inadequacies, incapacities, and vulnerabilities. This book will address these issues by analyzing many of the ways in which decision makers are precluded from including moral dimensions in their decision-making, or find themselves following along with others without daring to question whether or not what is expected in their managerial or employment role is morally appropriate.

Mental models or mindsets are both the ground of all our experiences and sources of bounded awareness (Bazerman and Chugh, 2006), blind spots (Moberg, 2006; Bazerman and Tenbrunsel, 2011), the phenomenon of unquestioned obedience to a perceived authority

(Milgram, 1974), and other impediments to ethical decision-making. In the case of Greg Smith, the prevailing corporate mindset, according to Smith, was that making money for Goldman, even after the economic downturn of 2008 and the resulting scrutiny of the firm by the SEC and the media. The bounded awareness created by Goldman Sachs' culture and acquiesced to by its leadership and management, could have caused Smith simply to go along with this agenda. But he was able, somehow, to step back from the firm and its expectations, examine it from a moral point of view, and critically evaluate its shortcomings.

In addition to bounded awareness, there are a plethora of other obstacles that thwart responsible ethical decision-making. These include inattention such that one misses the obvious, role identification that is imagined to be absolute even when faced with an ambiguous or conflicting moral issue, or pattern recognition wherein one simply applies a learned pattern to a new situation rather than imagining it might be different. Others include habits that are allowed to prevail despite new circumstances, lack of courage, and of course, obedience to whomever is perceived to be an authority figure despite moral reservations to the contrary.

How these moral failures can be reduced or overcome is an important topic of this book. Our argument is that there are important synergies for the next generation of ethical leaders based on the alignment of modified or adjusted mental models, a well-developed moral reasoning process, an understanding of the critical role of discourse in decision choices, and an application of moral imagination through collaborative input and critique, rather than "me too" obedience. We will examine and propose processes by which individuals and decision-makers throughout organizations – from subordinate roles, through middle managers, to positions of significant authority – may reduce or overcome instances involving these challenges. Appealing to a series of organizational examples we will illustrate both the blinding effect of certain mental models and how these can be revisited and revised through new thinking, challenging thought processes, regulation, and alterations of our mindsets.

Included in the discussion will be various methodologies in the literature that address these obstacles and that assist in the processes of unbinding our blinded or bounded thinking. These include: developing a strong internal sense of individual or organizational choice to combat our own blindness and organizational blind spots, a disinterested dis-engagement from one's setting, a self-improvement regimen that questions prevailing mental models and combats intentional blindness, and a development of a strong moral imagination that questions prevailing mindsets and habits, delves into fresh possibilities, and evaluates both old and new alternatives from a moral point of view.

Mental models bind our awareness within a particular scaffold and then selectively can filter the content we subsequently receive. Through recalibration using revised mental models, we argue, we cultivate strategies anew, creating new habits, and galvanizing more *intentional* and evolved mental models. This recalibration often entails developing a strong sense of self and self-worth, realizing that each of us has a range of moral choices that may deviate from those in authority, and moral imagination.

Moral imagination has been defined as "a necessary ingredient in responsible moral judgment" that can enable decision-makers in par-ticular circumstances to discover and evaluate possibilities not merely determined by those circumstances, limited by operative mental mod-els, or merely framed by a set of rules or rule-governed concerns (Wer-hane, 1999, 93). The importance of moral imagination resides in the idea that within organizations, managers who strive to success and excellence, in many cases, risk binding themselves in a cognitive trap, where only a narrow, partial perspective on reality emerges as pos-sible. In such cases, managers' interpretations of reality can become distorted such that abilities to grasp ethical dimensions are impaired and the capacity to exercise moral judgment is impeded. To ameliorate these risks, the facility to disengage from operative mindsets, evaluate their credence, and then engage in moral imagination, along with a "self-improvement regimen" are key assets.

The book begins with an outline of a theory of social construction, focusing on the critical roles mental models or mindsets play in framing and ordering all our experiences. The purpose of Chapter 2 is to fore-ground examples of mental models in business ethics – those models on which many of us, as well as key decision-makers, have relied for decades in framing our teaching and leadership. For instance, sacred to the integration of ethics throughout an organization's culture is a strong ethical tone from the very top of the firm's hierarchy. Yet, a critical analysis of that mental model illustrates vulnerabilities in its reliability. The conversation at the "top" often consists of platitudes irrelevant to the decision-making worker; leaders are not always aware of the particularities faced by regular employees; and the role modeling on which the integration depends relies on similarity, while executives simply are not sufficiently engaged with the company's workers expected to model them.

Chapter 3 focuses extensively on the question of obedience through scrutiny of the Milgram experiments and follow-up investigations. Two questions are of importance. The first, "Why did so many participants in the experiment carry out the experiment to 450 volts?" was addressed by Milgram and, later, by other researchers. The perception of authority of the Experimenter, the ability to disengage from the role as lever-pusher and discharge the responsibility to the Experimenter, the bracketing of one's role in the experiment from other roles where the participant was a good mother, teacher, nurse, or engineer, and the passivity of the naïve Teacher (what Milgram called an "agentic" state), all contributed to the high levels of obedience. The second question, one that has only recently begun to be addressed with some seriousness is "Why did a few participants disobey and exit from the experiment?" This is harder to explain, but a number of thinkers now argue that the language of the Learner, specifically when he cries at 150 volts that he wants to get out, affected the mindsets of some participants. These participants realized they had a choice to exit and that they *should* stop the experiment in order not to harm another human being. Thus a few naïve Teachers were able to construct a sense of personal choice that enabled them to discontinue the experiment despite the Experimenter's admonitions to continue (Parmar, 2011; Packer, 2008).

Mental models serve to conceptualize, focus and shape our experiences, but in so doing, they sometimes cause us to ignore data and occlude critical reflection that might be relevant or, indeed, necessary to practical decision-making. In Chapters 4 and 5, we examine how the practice of constructing mental models, defined and illustrated by example in Chapter 2, may devolve into the formation of barriers or obstacles that ultimately prevent decision-makers from reaching ethical decisions. We argue that distorting mental models are the foundation or underpinning of many of the impediments to effective ethical decision-making.

Under optimal conditions, we reach decisions through an ethical decision-making process. One formulation of this process is framed as follows. A decision-maker (1) becomes aware of a present issue; (2) gathers facts relevant to the ultimate decision; (3) identifies alternative solutions to the dilemma at hand; (4) considers stakeholders implicated or impacted by these alternatives; and (5) reaches a conclusion by comparing and weighing these alternatives, often guided by insights offered by philosophical theory and/ or external guidance, as well as by testing solution possibilities by reflecting on their likely consequences from the perspectives provided by other mental models (Hartman and DesJardins, 2008). In Chapter 4 we introduce this framework. We then examine common impediments to the initial two steps of this decision-making model, which describe the process of coming to perceive a situation or conflict as a dilemma that calls for an ethical response. We identify and analyze distorting mental models that constitute experience in a manner that occludes the moral dimension of situations from view, thereby thwarting the first step of ethical decision-making. Examples include an unexamined moral self-image, viewing oneself as merely a bystander, and an exaggerated conception of self-sufficiency. These mental models, we argue, generate blind spots to ethics, in the sense that they limit our ability to see facts that are right before our eyes – sometimes quite literally, as in the many examples of managers and employees who see unethical behavior take place in front of them, but do not recognize it as such. We then further refine this discussion by examining ethics-impeding conceptual frameworks that disable or frustrate the second step in the ethical decision-making process: gathering information. In this section, we examine situational and cognitive factors that are particularly threatening to the capacity to attend to, and seek out, critical information in decision-making settings, such as ideological worldviews; selective attention, or "bounded awareness;" and selective neglect of attention to ethics, or "bounded ethicality."

Chapter 5 turns to a discussion of mental models that prevent the execution of the remaining three steps of ethical deliberation. These steps outline the mechanisms of decision-making within a situation that has been perceived as posing an ethical challenge: imagining alternative solutions, considering the impact of these solution possibilities on affected stakeholders, and enacting a decision that accords with consciously-held values. This analysis illustrates the practice of critical reflection crucial for crafting a responsible decision that maintains fidelity to consciously held, personal, as well as corporate, values. There we continue to identify and analyze mental models that work to distort or frustrate the process of forging ethical decisions. Obstacles to enacting these three steps include such distorting mental models as the avoidance of unfamiliar people or situations; trust in intuition; the cognitive release that may come from adherence to decision rules, obedience to authority, or conformity to the behavior of peers; "confirmation heuristics," or selective attention to preferred information; dehumanizing strategies; and the "learned helplessness" and sense of invisibility that may arise when the decision-maker is repeatedly told that his or her ethical perspective does not matter.

Chapter 6 addresses how many of the obstacles to rigorous critical reflection and ethical decision-making outlined in Chapters 3, 4, and 5 can be remedied. Our mental models frame our experiences in ways that both aid and hinder perception. They enable us to focus selectively on ethically relevant matters; but, by their very nature, they provide incomplete perspectives, oftentimes resulting in unwarranted partiality, or even ethical blindness. There is no escaping from mental models, but we can try to develop constructive ways of reframing these models that resist these limitations. This reframing requires critical dialogue with others and the exercise of moral imagination.

Indiscriminate and unmindful obedience to authority, skewed intuitions, emotional attachments, and the bounded mental models that distort moral decision-making in commerce are correctable, but with difficulty. There are various methodologies in the literature that address these obstacles and assist in the processes of unbinding our blinded or bounded thinking. Bazerman and Chugh (2006; see also Chugh and Bazerman, 2007) suggest that people could learn to become more observant, and Moberg (2006, 413) contends that "ethics blind spots can be corrected by a self-improvement regimen." Bazerman and Tenbrunsel (2011, 154) argue that we need to prepare "for the hidden psychological forces that crop up before, during, and after we confront ethical dilemmas." Adam Smith's idea of impartial spectatorship, that ability to step back, disengage from the scenario and its operative mindsets, and examine our roles, motivations, desires and values, will turn out to be a useful concept in this regard. Simply asking, "Is this the right thing to do?" may help to trigger this disengagement. All of these remedies contribute to the development of moral imagination:

the ability not merely to become disengaged but to evaluate, create new mindsets, and expand one's vision and choices.

To some extent we deceive ourselves about how good we are, but our moral blindness is sometimes quite willful. Appropriately structured programs in moral education can help us develop better self-understanding and ways of making sounder decisions. In corporate settings, stricter and more comprehensive compliance programs will go a long way in solving deviant behaviors. Chapter 6 concludes with an analysis of both the promise and limitations of attempting to promote ethics in organizations through compliance measures.

Chapter 7 presents a series of contemporary organizational examples that illustrate the narrowing, compromising, or blinding effect of mental models as well as how these can be revisited and revised through new experiments, challenging thought processes, and revisions of our mindsets. Individuals can better understand the need for remedies by examining current and historical cases and practices, and their remedies. Sometimes mental models become deeply embedded and reinforced within a social structure, and flawed habits can become choices. This sort of embedded structure was part of the Penn State football scandal of 2011, this chapter's first illustration. The next example, the 2008 meltdown of Wall Street, is obviously much broader in scope than college football. In exploring various investment cases, we analyze practices and mental models that have severe financial, legal and ethical complications. The decline of ethical decision-making within investment banking and other professional lending fields is a continuing problem for individuals and investors across the globe.

"Blowing the whistle" on improper activities is examined in regard to a variety of uses particularly considering whether loyalty to the company is ethically more important than safety to a consuming public. The chapter ends with an illustration of how some best organizational ethical practices can be adopted and habituated. The Belmont Report of 1978 provides an ethical framework designed to protect participants in behavioral and medical research. It has been voluntarily adopted throughout medical research and practice and remains today the standard for research in that field. It is a model that other industries and institutions could adopt, voluntarily, that would mitigate many of the untoward practices we have illustrated throughout this book.

While questioning whether acute observation, moral disengagement, or self-improvement is always possible, we will conclude that linking the modification of mental models to an *unbinding* of awareness represents an important synergistic relationship and one that can build effectively on the lessons learned from our experience with moral imagination.

2 | The role of mental models in social construction

On Saturday, February 1, 2003 the space shuttle *Columbia* exploded on reentry. It was the second space shuttle disaster, the first was the *Challenger* explosion in 1986. The physical cause of the explosion was a "breach in the Thermal Protection System on the leading edge of the left wing, caused by a piece of insulating foam," foam that had broken off from the shuttle right after launch (CAIB, 2003, 9). On reentry this breach let very hot air melt some of the wing, penetrating the shuttle and causing loss of control and, ultimately, the breakup of the spacecraft. According to the *Report of the Columbia Accident Investigation Board* (CAIB, 2003) that analyzed events leading up to the second explosion, there were a series of incidents that led to this result, many of which mirrored incidents that led to the *Challenger* explosion. In both cases at least half of the causes of these explosions are linked to NASA's organizational structure and hierarchy.[1]

I. Introduction

We begin with the *Columbia* tragedy for a number of reasons. Foremost is that we have verifiable inside data on events within NASA that led to the explosion, data not always available in other organizations. According to the CAIB report, at the time of the 1986 *Challenger* explosion "NASA was transformed from a research and development agency to more of a business, with schedules, production pressures, deadlines, and cost efficiency goals elevated to the level of technical innovation and safety goals" (CAIB, 2003, 198). This philosophy remained unchanged after the *Challenger* disaster, despite the fact that NASA is a government research agency. Moreover, everyone at NASA

---

[1] The CAIB report also lists other cause including governmental and public pressure, budget constraints, and subcontractor frustrations. In this chapter we will focus primarily on the internal organizational causes of this disaster.

and its subcontractors, including astronauts, managers, engineers, subcontractors, and maintenance workers on the launching site, had no motives other than to create a successful launch and landing. In other words, it is impossible to find any even remotely evil intentions on the part of anyone or any organization involved in the shuttle operation, and indeed, every individual and organization who had anything do to with *Columbia* only worked for its successful completion. Thus we witnessed a tragic event created by a smart people of good will and a well-meaning organization (and sub-contractors) that is very much like a business organization. The narratives of NASA and the *Columbia* explosion, then, illustrate the overarching theme of this book: how do smart good-willed people and decent companies create or take part in a flawed system that produces untoward outcomes?

The events at NASA leading up to the explosion exemplify what happens or can happen inside complex organizations. Despite studies of the earlier *Challenger* explosion in 1986 that outlined in detail the organizational causes of that disaster (Presidential Commission, 1986), many of the organizational causes of the *Columbia* failure demonstrated that little had changed at NASA to prevent a reoccurrence. Some of these included poor communication between engineers and managers and accompanying clashing mindsets, hierarchical silos that interfered with organizational integration, faulty risk analysis, habits built from past shuttle successes (what the Report called "history as cause") and resulting overconfidence, and a complacent or "broken" safety culture, all of which created a culture that contributed to both shuttle tragedies. Worst of all, NASA did little to change these practices after the *Challenger* explosion.

Early on in the *Columbia* mission there were problems with foam debris disengaging from the shuttle, observable problems that were predicted before the first launch, but these alleged anomalies were not dealt with and were instead interpreted as "normal" and expected occurrences. Consequently, that design flaw was not addressed. Because eighty-seven missions had been flown successfully before the explosion, the risk of the debris was downgraded. Indeed, "[so] ingrained was the agency's belief that foam debris was not a threat to flight safety that ... after the *Columbia* accident, the Space Shuttle Program Manager still discounted the foam as a probable cause, saying that Shuttle Managers were "comfortable" with their previous risk assessments" (CAIB, 2003, 196). Because of these successes NASA and its subcontractors became overconfident and complacent habits were the result.

There was also a lack of communication between engineers and managers, and between levels of hierarchy at NASA, that created a loss of information between the silos as well as silence among dissenters that further undermined what was supposed to be a good safety system. Engineers could not *prove* the debris would cause malfunction; even after the fatal blow to the wing during the last launch, managers assumed it would not. Engineers "were accustomed to turning their analysis over to managers and letting them decide, and did not have the quantitative data that would empower them to object further" (CAIB, 2003, 201). This lack of communication within organizational hierarchy and between sub-contractors and NASA was directly related to the fact that, after ground control discovered that foam debris had damaged the left wing during that fatal launch, the Debris Assessment Team were not given images of this damage, which hindered both their assessment and their recommendation for a viable solution for the shuttle's reentry.

Despite the fact, again proven after the *Challenger* disaster, that the shuttles in this program were all experimental vehicles, thus each launch and each element of every launch was at high risk, there was also a philosophy at NASA that the shuttle was an operational not an experimental vehicle. Even after the failure of O-rings during the *Challenger* launch, this mindset remained, interfering with a sound risk analysis of the dangers inherent in this experiment. Finally, there was a sense of invincibility at NASA – a "can do" attitude that they were and could be successful. "NASA made many changes after *Challenger*. The fact that many changes had been made supported a belief in the safety of the system, the invincibility of organizational and technical systems, and ultimately, a sense that the foam problem was understood" (CAIB, 2003, 199).

The *Columbia* disaster, like that of the *Challenger*, should not have occurred and could have been prevented, but only if NASA, its organizational structure, communication mechanisms, and its managers and engineers changed the structure of the organization and the operative mindsets. As this case illustrates, the ways in which we socially construct our experiences through fallible and incomplete mental models, or mindsets, can either broaden or distort our perspectives. The latter can create "blindness" to the very data or information one needs to avoid difficulties, negative outcomes, or even tragedies such as *Columbia*.

This chapter will outline a theory of social construction, the resulting work of mental models. It will then illustrate with examples of problematic mental models in business – those models on which many, including key decision-makers, have relied for decades in framing decision-making and leadership. As illustrated by the *Columbia* tragedy, we will argue the underlying structure of human experience can create these problems and, alternately, can avoid them. The theory we propose defends the thesis that we do not simply and passively form mental representations or pictures of our experiences, representations that are derived merely from the stimuli or data to which we are subject, which then result in human learning and interactions. Rather, our minds interact with the data of our experiences, selectively filtering and framing that data though various forms of socially learning mechanisms or mental models (Werhane, 1999; Gentner and Whitley, 1997, 210–11; Gorman, 1992; Senge, 1990, Ch. 10). That is, we socially construct our experiences. In the process of focusing, framing, organizing and ordering what we experience, we bracket and omit data, simply because we cannot observe or absorb all that we experience (Werhane, 1999; Senge, 1990). Thus, as we will illustrate, often data important to a particular decision-making context are distorted or left out, resulting in morally questionable or even tragic decisions and behavior.

II. Mental models and social construction

By *constructionism* or social constructionism, we shall mean various sociological, historical, and philosophical projects that aim at displaying or analyzing actual, historically, situated social interactions or causal roots that led to, or were involved in, the coming into being or establishing of some present entity or fact (Hacking, 1999, 48).

We begin by outlining a version of social constructionism and mental models that is suited to this undertaking. Its origins may be traced to Immanuel Kant's critique of a *tabula rasa* construct of the mind (Kant, 1787, cited in 1965). Kant's thesis is that our minds do not mirror experience. This thesis, Kant argued, does not explain how each of us has different experiences but can communicate and understand each other. Rather, Kant argues, our minds project, constitute and/or reconstitute phenomena, the raw data of all experiences, into structured, ordered coherence and thus to knowable experiences. Kant concluded that all human beings order and organize their experiences through identical sets of formal concepts. While the content of our experiences may be quite different for each of us, the ways in which we structure and order these experiences is the same, universally for all human beings.

Today many thinkers challenge both whether and how minds are hard-wired as proposed by Kant. Nevertheless, the mentally constitutive interaction between the perceiver and the perceived that, according to Kant constitutes what we call "experience," is retained and explained within a social constructionist perspective, by the thesis that each of us perceives, frames, orders, and organizes the data of our experiences through a lens, from a point of view or within a set of frames, each of which, a social constructionist will argue, unlike Kant, is socially acquired and developed. These lenses, perspectives, and frames are conceptual schema or mental models that serve as selective organizing, filtering, and focusing mechanisms, through the use of which we construct meaning. Mental models, then are "mental representations, cognitive frames, or mental pictures through which all human beings interact with experience, developing narratives, observations, and scientific content, which is then called 'knowledge'" (Werhane, 1999, 53; Gentner and Whitley, 1997, 210–11). Various scientific methodologies are themselves mental models through which scientists discover, predict, and hypothesize about what we then call reality. In the social constructionist paradigm such mental models frame all our experiences. They schematize, and otherwise facilitate and guide the ways in which we recognize, react, and organize the world. How we define the world is dependent on such schema and thus all realities are socially structured. In the socially constructed paradigm, the multivariate mental models or conceptual schema are the means and mode through which we constitute our experiences. Because these schema are socially learned, fragile, transient and changeable, each is always incomplete or unfinished, such that one never gets a totally holistic world view (Werhane, 1999; Gorman, 1992; Senge, 1990).

Because all mental models or mindsets are incomplete, we can engage in second-order studies, evaluations, judgments, and assessments about our own and other operative mental models. Of course this is highly complex since the act of reflection is itself a further of framing or reframing. This insight is analogous to the physicist Werner Heisenberg's (1959) realization in his study of subatomic particles that one cannot eliminate the observer from her effects on the observed at least when examining small data. How subatomic particles interact "on their own" is impossible to determine, since the mere act of observing affects their motion and direction.

Many philosophers argue that mental models or conceptual schema are semantically based (e.g., Johnson, 1993; Rorty, 1993; Putnam, 1990; Anscombe, 1976; Wittgenstein, 1953). Whether human beings conceptualize or deal with the world non-linguistically is not a topic for this book, but as Hilary Putnam and Richard Rorty argue, *"[E]lements of what we call 'language' or 'mind' penetrate so deeply into what we call 'reality' that the very project of representing ourselves as being mappers of something 'language-independent' is fatally compromised from the start"* (Putnam, 1990, 28; cited with approval in Rorty, 1993, 443; emphasis, Rorty's). Language shapes our perspectives in such profound ways that it is difficult to imagine how we would conceptualize or socially frame experience purely non-linguistically, because the very acts of describing and explaining such concepts and frames employ language. This leads Rorty (1993, 443) to conclude that the notion of reality as "something outside all schema" or observers makes no sense.

Still, there is a difference between claiming that one cannot get at reality, or the world, or even experience, except through some mental model, and concluding that reality or experience *itself* is merely created or solely socially constructed. Although Rorty is agnostic on this, we conclude that the contention that the incomplete and disparate ways in which we present and distill experiences are socially constructed is different from arguing that experience or reality itself is socially created. The latter is a form of strong constructionism. "Strong social constructionism claims not only that representations are socially constructed, but that the *entities themselves* to which these representations refer are socially constructed" (Goldman, 2010). A strong or universal constructionist would argue that " ... every object whatsoever, is in some nontrivial sense socially constructed. Not just our experience of them, our classifications of them, our interests in them, but *these things themselves*." (Hacking, 1999, 24; emphasis added.)

Ian Hacking and others contend that strong social constructionism is not tenable because it then creates a form of regress regarding the status of the constructionism thesis itself. Moreover, the Wittgensteinian argument that essence is expressed but not created through grammar challenges universal constructionism. Wittgenstein claimed that how we conceive of the world is conceptually dependent, that is, "[e]ssence is *expressed* by grammar" (Wittgenstein, 1953, 371; emphasis added). But as G. E. M. Anscombe has pointed out, this is quite different from concluding that "essence is *created* by grammar" (Anscombe, 1976, 188). When essence is merely *created* by the use of grammar, we may call it lying, fantasy, storytelling, or mythmaking. Within any belief system we are generally concerned to distinguish fantasy and myth from "the real," "the true," or "the facts," even though each may be socially structured.

This conclusion is a weak constructionist conclusion, that we do not construct reality or the data of our experiences; however, we cannot get at that data except through socially constructed language and framing models. These framing perspectives or mental models construe the data of our experiences, and it is the construed data that we call "facts." What we often call reality, or the world, is constructed or socially construed in certain ways such that one cannot get at the source of the data except through these construals.

A socially situated model of social construction

We have argued that social constructionism is the idea that all the data of our experiences are framed in some manner of other. These frames or mental models are socially learned, incomplete, and changeable or revised when one comes into contact other mental models. Hacking adds two important points. First, according to Hacking and others, we are born into and depend on a world that is historically situated; linguistically, socially, and culturally defined; and usually in some process of evolution or change. These particular sets of embedded historical, political, economic, and social narratives are narratives that we neither created nor chose. These narratives define our early mental models and roles, as children, as women or men, as tribal members, as worshippers, as citizens (Hacking, 1999; MacIntyre, 1981, 199, 201; Sartre, 1956). These narratives and the language in which they are embedded are the background for individual experiences. They provide the initial conditions for the conceptual schema that frame all our experiences, and they often direct, influence, or confine the range of mental models we learn and adapt. Nevertheless, background narratives themselves function as revisable mental models that are neither static nor incommensurable with each other. Thus, none of us is identified merely with our socially connected selves; neither are we merely determined by our background historical social narratives. We are at once byproducts of, characters in, and authors of, our own stories (e.g., Werhane, 1999; Johnson, 1993, 153; Sartre, 1956).

Hacking's second point is that social constructionism is an inter-active phenomenon. That is, as social linguistic beings each of us is constantly interacting, thus affecting and affected by others' mental models. These in turn are historically and culturally situated and at least partly constructed from this situational context. Out of these interactions we often come to consensus on our views, say, about the scientific method, the validity of historical models, the social construc-tion of race, gender, ethnic origin, sexual orientation, and the meanings of terms such as child abuse, serial killers, homelessness, etc. This is what Amartya Sen (1993) calls "positional objectivity."

Positional-dependency defines the way in which the object appears "from a delineated somewhere" (Sen, 1993, 127). That is, any person in that position will make similar observations, according to Sen. Sen assumes that from a certain point of view we are able to observe and process the same data similarly. We would add that the parameters of positionality are not merely spatial but involve shared mental models and similar or identical historical and cultural contexts.

Positionally dependent observations, beliefs, and actions are central to what we call knowledge and practical reason. The nature of objec-tivity in epistemology, decision theory, and ethics has to take adequate note of the parametric dependence of observation and inference on the position of the observer (Sen, 1993, 126). However, a positionally objective point of view could be mistaken if it did not account for all available information. Almost any position has alternatives; almost every position has its critics. We would qualify that as well. Allegedly positionally objective phenomena are still phenomena that have been filtered through the social sieve of a shared mental model or narrative, neither infallible nor complete.

For example, recall the familiar case of the Ford Pinto. Managers at Ford each had access to much of the same data about the Pinto and approached the Pinto accidents from a positionally dependent point of view. Ford's decision not to recall the Pinto, despite some terrible accidents, could be defended as a positionally objective belief based on the ways in which managers at Ford processed information on automobile crashes, due to a shared organizational mental model on risk assessment. Outsiders, however, for example, Pinto owners, might have processed the same information differently; for instance, if they operated under a belief system that placed safety concerns ahead of economy. These two perspectives are analogous to the views of the Copernicans and Ptolemaists, who at least initially processed the same data about the universe, but each processed it differently, resulting in different conclusions and thus conflicting positionally objective points of view.

According to Sen (1993), in addition to taking positionally objective points of view, we are able to engage in "transpositional" assessments. A transpositional view is a constructed critique of a positionally objective phenomenon, and no positionally objective view is merely relative or immune from challenge. This assessment compares various positionally objective points of view to determine whether one can make coherent sense of them and develop some general theories about what is being observed. From a transpositional point of view, mental models themselves can be questioned on the basis of their coherence or their explanatory scope. Transpositional assessments are constructed views, because they too depend on the schema of the assessors. Although the challenge could be conducted only from another mental model, the assessment could take into account a variety of points of view. Revisions of the schema in question might produce another mental model that more comprehensively explained a range of phenomena or incidents. In short, studying *sets* of perspectives can show how certain events are experienced and reported and even bring into view the mental models or narratives at work in shaping the narratives about these experiences. Although one can never begin with a pure unconstituted data, nevertheless one can, at least in principle, achieve a limited, dispassionate perspective.

But if a transpositional assessment is a possibility, why, then, do we observe so many instances when people fail to critique their situation from a more dispassionate or alternate perspective? As Dennis Gioia, the recall coordinator at Ford during the Pinto era, later recalled, "My own schematized . . . knowledge influenced me to perceive recall issues in terms of the prevailing decision environment and to unconsciously overlook key features of the Pinto case, mainly because they did not fit an existing [Ford] script" that bracketed the consideration of individual safety in driving a Pinto (Gioia, 1992, 395). Gioia admits he was so engaged in thinking from an organizational point of view that he failed to consider the possibility that human beings drive Pintos and thus are in mortal danger. This seems a logical question, but Gioia admits that the dominant Ford organizational script created a blind spot, a fatal one. Thus, mental models can become implicitly habitual or block obvious implications, and, as we shall demonstrate, flawed decision-making is the result.

III. Individual and organizational sensemaking

One version of social constructionism is what Karl Weick and others call "sensemaking." "Sensemaking involves the ongoing retrospective [and prospective] development of plausible images that rationalize what people are doing" (Weick, Sutcliffe and Obstfeld, 2005, 409). Sensemaking is in part habitual, describing the implicit ways in which we socially frame and order our experiences. But according to Weick *et al.*, sensemaking can also be proactive, when one deliberately reframes or reorders one's experience in an effort to give meaning or new meaning to those experiences. It is one of the ways one can order or reorder and shape organizations, as well as one's personal experiences. "A central theme in both organizing and sensemaking is that people organize to make sense of equivocal inputs and enact this sense back into the world to make that world more orderly" (Weick *et al.*, 2005, 410). Sensemaking can also be actively retrospective, as illustrated by Dennis Gioia's critical reflections on his decisions as Ford's recall coordinator. One can look back at the ways in which one has framed or interpreted an experience, and reinterpret that experience or test new perspectives on those mindsets. Similarly, in an organization, one can redefine that organization, create or change its mission or reinterpret its purpose, thus changing its identity. But organizations can also fail to be either proactive or retrospective.

Let us give examples of static reactive and proactive sensemaking. In the 1980s, Johnson & Johnson set the "corporate ethics bar" high when the company and its CEO, James Burke, withdrew its Tylenol capsule from the market permanently after several random poisonings

of the capsule. For years J&J was held up as an exemplar of supereroga-
tory moral behavior. Yet in 2010, the company had to recall several of
its most popular drugs including baby Tylenol, baby Motrin and its hip
implant (Abelson, 2010). One could speculate that J&J came to habit-
ually rest on its reputation. What was once a dominant credo in the
organization became a neglected assumption, and they allowed quality
control, a critical component of drug and medical devise manufacture,
to deteriorate. What was once a precedent for corporate behavior
became a complacent assumption that everything at J&J, just as it was
supposed to be at NASA, was fine. It is as if they assumed that, since
their quality control was exemplary in the 1980s (or, in NASA's case,
because eighty-seven launches had been successful), it would continue
to be so without reevaluation, either retrospectively or proactively.
This phenomenon is what Phil Rosenzweig (2007, 50–64) and others
call "The Halo Effect." In this case, having established that the company had performed magnificently in the Tylenol scare, J&J assumed
it would perform consistently in the future. This assumption helped
the company to retain its mission while simultaneously failing to link
it to performance. One could contend that in the Tylenol case, the
random poisoning of capsules proved not to be a result of poor quality
control or the actions of a disgruntled employee, while the latest recalls
are directly related to poor quality control. So these incidents are only
peripherally connected. But that is a poor excuse for inadequate quality
control in a pharmaceutical company known for excellent products.
Thinking about this case through the lens of sensemaking, habitual
behavior dominated J&J's culture, rather than engagement in proactive sensemaking that might have reexamined quality control processes
and considered new regulatory procedures.

The J&J case illustrates another form of sensemaking and social
construction. When a certain mindset becomes both habitual and
ingrained, it is tempting to apply this framework across diverse settings, some of which are inappropriate. An example is CEO compensation. It is often argued that CEOs deserves large compensation because
of their input in increasing economic growth and return on investment
for their company (Reich, 2007; Kay and Van Putten, 2007). Yet, in
2006, Pfizer CEO Henry McKennell was asked to step down, in part
due to poor earnings, and in part because of shareholder anger at his
hefty compensation package. Still, he received a full retirement package of approximately $200 million ("*Pfizer's Ex-Chief...*", 2006).

In 2010, after J&J's recalls and lowered share price, CEO William Weldon's total compensation package for that year was valued at $28.7 million (Loftus, 2011). In other words, the common-sense management rule of compensating growth-producing managers and downgrading or firing those who do not add value was a mindset ignored when applied to these and other CEOs and their compensation. The implicit operative mental model in these examples was that CEOs deserve large compensation packages *despite* their performance, a mindset that seems to be habitually operative with many corporate compensation committees today.

By contrast, the corporate environmental sustainability movement offers an example of proactive organizational sensemaking. Although there was public interest in environmental sustainability in the 1960s, most American companies viewed this as an externality, something they needed to tend to only if forced by regulation. But public interest grew, schools were teaching students about its importance, and Northern European companies in particular began to internalize "green" thinking as significant for the planet and as a competitive advantage. This strategy spilled over both to governmental policies and U.S. companies, and today green thinking is seldom thought of as an externality, even by companies that do not adopt green standards explicitly. For example, a few years ago General Electric began to respond to public and governmental interest in environmental sustainability. General Electric adopted what they call "ecomagination" as part of their overall strategy. The company describes its integration of environmental concerns into their mission:

When we first conceived of ecomagination a little over five years ago, our vision was to create a program that would be consistent with GE's mission to earn the best possible returns for our shareowners by solving big problems like improving energy efficiency and reducing environmental impact. Since 2005, we have invested heavily in harnessing the power of our technology and industrial capabilities to reduce our environmental impact. (*"Ecomagination . . . "*, 2008, 2)

This proactive sensemaking also illustrates Hacking's point that socially constructed mental models develop out of contextual interactions between individuals or organizations and their communities or other organizations. In this instance, the "on the ground" green movement, changes in government regulation, and corporate responses influenced each other and created interactions that change the mental models around environmental sustainability.

Organizational sensemaking in context

As the previous example illustrates, "[n]o organization can properly be understood apart from its wider social and cultural context" (Scott, 1995, cited in 2001, 151). An institutional theory of organizations argues that organizations, like individuals, are created and determined by their social and political contexts. Moreover, according to this theory, while it is true that human beings construct institutions, "institutions . . . are socially constructed to make life stable and meaningful, and they both constrain and enable action . . . [Thus] human action is largely conditioned by institutions" (Van de Ven and Hargrave, 2004, 259; Scott, 1995, cited in 2001). However, these contexts are not fully determinate of all organizational behavior and can and should be continually evaluated and revised. Organizations are created by, made up of, and decisions made by, individuals or groups of individuals who have flexible mindsets and thus can change the direction of the organization. The danger is that if managers are indoctrinated in certain organizational mindsets, they may accept those mindsets as determinate and thus fail to engage in proactive sensemaking to anticipate media influences, new regulatory forces, public changes in mindsets, or unforeseen pressures from the public.

Revision can occur at the macro level as well. Organizational retrospective sensemaking can consist of reevaluating organizational behavior as a learning experience, or it can be a rationalization for continuing to operate under the same mental models. For example, since the spread of advanced capitalism globally, most developed Western industrial nations and the global companies that originate in these countries imagine that their economic policies, corporate procedures, and Western-framed understanding of free enterprise are the best, or minimally, the least worst, economic models for every country on the globe. This presumption is not altogether bad because free enterprise has been a successful economic model in many parts of the world. That has become the dominant script in the West.

But, Javier Santiso, formerly a researcher at the Organisation for Economic Co-Operation and Development (OECD), has suggested another futuristic, data-driven, and not improbable mindset, a mental model that is a result of the current global economic crisis. Santiso suggests that the 2008–10 global economic and financial crises illustrate the growing questionability of recommendations given by the developed OECD countries to the allegedly developing countries. While the developed countries have prescribed lowering debt, financial stimuli, and eliminating unemployment, in 2010 most of the OECD countries had massive debt, large unemployment, and stagnation of economic growth. In the meantime, The BRIC countries (Brazil, Russia, India, and China) and other countries in the emerging market economies accounted for a third of consumer demand worldwide. And Chile surpassed all the other "developed" countries in the lowest debt, least unemployment, and greatest economic growth. Santiso cites massive trade between the BRIC countries and between these countries and less-developed communities that is not dependent on the developed nations at all. Thus, Santiso concludes, the dependence on the so-called developed nations for advice, expertise, and trade is decreasing rapidly (Santiso, 2010a, 2010b). Yet the OECD countries still imagine that their advice ("do what we say, not what we do") should be taken seriously, even though the economic conditions that supported their positive mindsets about Western versions of capitalism and the egoism of companies in developed countries are in question.

Although his data is virtually ignored by developed nations such as the United States and by most multinational global corporations, Santiso suggests that all of this evidence challenges traditional Western economic sensemaking. To acknowledge this data would require developed nations, such as the United States, and global companies to change the dominant mindsets, which presume that their forms of free enterprise will work successfully everywhere in every economic circumstance and that developing countries and their small enterprises could succeed without interventions. But such change would require rethinking and proactively regenerating of Western models about development, dependency, and the place of OECD countries in the global economy (Santiso, 2010a, 2010b). Such reinvention would take innovative proactive sensemaking that may undermine a traditional Western economic mindset that imagines that the so-called developed nations and large multinational corporations have the answers to development.

To conclude these sections, social construction is not an idiosyncratic phenomenon. It entails an ongoing interactive process where individuals are born into a historically and culturally situated social system from which they learn ways to frame and later to critique that system. Similarly, corporations are initially started with certain goals in mind and certain products and services to be delivered, within a defined cultural and politically defined context. Those initial starting points can become implicit habits within the organization, proactively changed through redefined sensemaking, or challenged by other mindsets that may or may not be adopted by the organization or its constituents. In the next section we shall return to the *Columbia* narrative and present some difficult examples.

IV. Problematic examples in business

This chapter has argued that mental models are ubiquitous socially constructed frames for all our experiences. Mental models are constructed from their social, cultural and historical contexts and, because they are incomplete and changeable, they also are capable of reconstructing or making new sense of those contexts. Still, sometimes individuals or organizations become so embroiled in a particular set of narratives, some flawed, that they fail to compare these narratives with other accounts or evaluate their implications. An organization and its managers can also get mired in one mindset and thus fail to anticipate new markets, technological advances, or even public policy. Alternatively, a company may rest on its reputation and fail either to be retrospective or proactive. In this section we will present some other problematic examples that occur in commerce. In Chapters 4 and 5, we will analyze cognitive and situational factors that make us vulnerable to these various forms of flawed decision-making.

Leadership mindsets: Leader-and-follower

Allegedly, sacred to the integration of ethics throughout an organization's culture is a strong ethical tone from the very top of the firm's hierarchy. Yet, a critical analysis of that mental model illustrates vulnerabilities in its reliability. The conversation at the "top" may consist of platitudes irrelevant to a decision-making employee; leaders are not always aware of the particularities faced by regular employees, while at the same time, executives may have different managerial mental models than those workers who are expected to conform to them. Discontinuity between a leader's and an employee's mental models, in turn, can result in untoward consequences. For example, the explosion of the *Challenger* shuttle in 1986 and the later *Columbia* explosion were, in large part, due to many miscommunications between engineers and managers at NASA and, for *Challenger*, at Morton-Thiokol, the chief contractor for the shuttle. In the case of *Challenger*, although many engineers were worried about the overheating of O-rings on the shuttle in early launches – a problem persistently brought to the attention of NASA by one of the leading engineers on the project, Roger Boisjoly – this problem was not attended to. By the seventeenth successful launch, the overheating was classified as "normal" by NASA, since no shuttle had exploded (Presidential Commission, 1986, 33). Many of the design engineers gave up asking questions of NASA's leadership. But it was those same unredesigned O-rings that were partly responsible for the *Challenger* explosion. Engineers on both shuttle projects were risk adverse, that is, their operative mental modal was that if one could not reasonably assure that the launch was safe, it should not be launched. In the case of *Columbia*, engineers had qualitative data that foam debris could interfere with the shuttle trajectory almost from the first launch, but they could not back this up with solid quantitative data. The managerial mindset held by NASA and its subcontractors, on the other hand, presumed that if the engineers could not prove that the shuttle launch *was* at risk, then the launch should go forward. Data on such a risk analysis could not be amassed on such short order either on the evening before the *Challenger* launch, or before reentry of the *Columbia* shuttle into the atmosphere. Before launch of *Challenger*, the NASA manager of the project told the leading engineer to "take off your engineering hat and put on your manager hat" (Presidential Commission, 1986, 94). That same mindset was operative after *Challenger* as well. Preceding the fatal *Columbia* launch, most of the NASA managers wanted proof from the engineers that the foam debris *was* a threat, data that could not be amassed. Neither party understood the mental models of the other, particularly in analyzing the risk of anomalies such as foam debris. Because they were the designated leaders, in both instances management won out. No engineer "blew the whistle," none tried to stop the *Challenger* launch, no one spoke up about the questionability of the foam debris, and we all know the ghastly results.

As we suggested, it a widely believed platitude that leadership begins only at the top of the organization, and without that leadership economic and moral failures can persist. Yet, a critical analysis of that mental model illustrates vulnerabilities in its reliability, as the *Challenger* explosion demonstrates. Let us look at a positive example that challenges that leadership assumption with the success of an aggressive middle manager.

In 1994, Jan-Kees Vis, a middle manager at Unilever, a multibillion Dutch-British company that produces food and cleaning products, was at a social function and engaged his new boss in a conversation about environmental sustainability. Vis proposed that Unilever should begin measuring its social and environmental impacts quantitatively, in the same way it currently measured its profitability, with the aim, of course, to improve its social and environmental imprints. The typical response of an executive to a middle manager might have been, "I will look into it," or "Good idea, and I will find one of the senior officers of the company to spearhead this initiative." Instead, Jan-Kees Vis's boss responded, "You are Unilever, and I am Unilever. If you think more should be done, then do something about it." Thus began Unilever's initiative, headed by Vis, to engage in institutionalizing quantitatively driven, "Triple-Bottom-Line" reporting throughout the company, a project that is ongoing (Gorman *et al.*, 1998). Vis is still a middle manager at Unilever, and Unilever is considered to be a leader in developing triple-bottom-line thinking that measures quantitatively and equally corporate social, environmental and economic outcomes. Currently, Unilever is pursuing the goal of doubling its business by 2020, while at the same time, cutting its environmental impact in half (Wright, 2012).

The young and disadvantaged as leaders?

There are two other leadership mindsets that should be challenged. The first assumes that children and teenagers can seldom serve as good leaders. The second pervasive mindset is that poor people, particularly in less developed countries, are incapable, ignorant, and unable to assume leadership positions. Yet, in New Delhi, as well as in other large cities in India, children, usually boys with little or no education, flock to cities from small villages looking for work and excitement. There is little in the way of public services to help these boys; they are usually homeless and scrape by from meager earnings on the streets. However, some find night shelters where they are provided beds and basic sustenance. In 2000, the National Foundation for India began the Children's Development Bank (Eliason, 2009). The CDB is a bank owned and run by children under the oversight of an adult banker. The CDB trains children from the shelters in the rudiments of banking and helps to set up small kiosks in the shelters where the *children* run the bank. They collect earnings from the working children, set up banking accounts, and provide each child with his own bankbook. Every evening, the children who have worked on the streets deposit money at the kiosk, managed by another child from the shelter, and that bank manager, in turn, deposits the money in the CDB. Interest is paid on the deposited money, and children can withdraw money from the bank in the shelter; when they are eighteen years-old they have to close this account. To date, over 1,300 children are served by the CDB bank in Delhi, and almost 10,000 across India. The CDB has opened branches in Nepal, Bangladesh, and Afghanistan.

This story belies our Western mindsets about teenagers and about poor semi-literate people, and because it reveals an extraordinary trust that has developed in the shelters among the children and the child-bankers. If children between the ages of eight and eighteen can become bankers and be trusted with other people's money, without written contracts or draconian laws, perhaps the mindset that cannot imagine this possibility is flawed. The CDB has set up such a model (Sinha, 2008).

Similarly, the idea that poor people, even adults, cannot achieve economic success is a mindset that is slowly being eroded by self-directed economic development projects in many of the poorest countries in the world. The Grameen Bank is one such example. Bangladesh is one of the poorest and most corrupt countries in Asia (Transparency International, 2011). It is overpopulated, with 160 million people in a country the size of Iowa, and has little in the way of natural resources. Every year, at least a quarter of the country floods. Grameen Bank of Bangladesh is a for-profit bank created in the 1970s by Muhammad Yunus to provide small loans to impoverished women living in remote villages in that country. Its mission is to eliminate poverty by empowering its borrowers, mostly women, through microcredit. The Bank calls itself a development bank because, although it is a for-profit bank and has never lost money, it reinvests all its earnings into new loans or other ventures such as Grameen Industries (whose earnings are also reinvested in loans and other ventures that produce jobs or in other ways help poor women to become self-sufficient). As well, the Bank does not pay out dividends (Yunus, 1999, cited in 2003). To date the Grameen Bank and its companies have taken over four million families and several thousand beggars out of poverty in Bangladesh. As of June 2010, it had 8.28 million borrowers, 97 percent of whom are women (Grameen Bank, 2011). With 2564 branches, GB provides services in 81,362 villages, covering more than 97 percent of the total villages in Bangladesh. One-hundred thousand of these borrowers are beggars, and to date about 20,000 of these beggars are now self-employed and off the streets.

Reiterating or misapplying mental models

Versions of the Grameen model have been adopted in several places around the globe. However, microfinancing schema are not universally successful. The 2011 scandal in the Indian microfinance sector over hard-sell lending and tough collection practices demonstrates that "business as usual" assumptions and methods can backfire in poor countries such as India (Bajaj, 2011; Chandavarkar, 2011). Eighty-eight suicides in one South Indian province, a community revolt against forcing the poor to repay micro loans, and a tough government crack-down against abusive micro lending practices appear to suggest the Grameen model for microlending cannot be adapted universally. A number of high-flying Indian banks that entered the micro-lending market are now nursing their self-inflicted financial wounds.

However, there may be other reasons for this failure in India. Bajaj (2011) and Chandavarkar (2011) have blamed the failure on what they term a single-bottom line focus on profit to the exclusion of other social and environmental goals by the banks organizing these loans. That may be true, but it has to be remembered that Grameen is a for-profit bank; although its first priority is poverty reduction, not profitability, Grameen seldom loses money. We would suggest another possibility. What the failed Indian microlenders allegedly tried to do was to adopt the Grameen model. However, they did not adopt the Grameen model and mindset in its entirety, a model that has proved successful in North and South America and other parts of Asia. The model entails a number of key elements. First, money is lent by and large to women, because global data shows that women are more likely to repay their loans, particularly married women with children. (Note that this evidence is not taken into account by dominant bank practices, which, due to a narrowly defined mindset, would be very unlikely to lend to women, particularly to poor women with children.) Second, the loans are offered to *groups* of women so that, if one falters in repayment, the others can exert pressure or assistance. Third, these loans are given *only* for projects that will generate income. In India many loans were used for new saris or house repairs, thus not providing income to repay the loans. Fourth, the loans are micromanaged. Every two weeks a bank manager appears, not merely to collect interest on the loans but also to check on the progress of the project and assist when there are difficulties with project development, with the goal that every loan will be successfully paid back *and* create income for the borrower's family. Fifth, every borrower is giving a savings account, and part of the payback must include a small bit for that account. This creates an ownership commitment on the part of the borrower so that she sees that she is invested not merely in earnings but also in savings. Each of these steps is critical if microlending is to be successful, but many steps were not followed by Indian microlenders. Loans were made without a commitment as to how they were to be used and without micro-oversight by bank managers (Bajaj, 2011; Chandavarkar, 2011). Perhaps the banks' mindsets were too bottom-line oriented, or perhaps they thought that these borrowers were like the middle-class male borrowers who had collateral for their loans, people with whom they dealt with regularly at the bank. In any event, their narrow focus, however construed, neglected key elements for success both for the lenders and the borrowers. The failed Indian banks tried to apply a traditional banking mindset to a new set of borrowers, with predictably poor results.

Notice that in these cases, Indian banks misconstrued the Grameen microlending model, applying the model only partially and half-heartedly, and as a result, these loans failed. On the other hand there are instances when applying the same mental model across different contexts leads to failure. For example, we have all read with horror the Ponzi scheme of Bernie Madoff who apparently absconded with at least $50 billion in client assets. In an effort to be successful, he violated the trust of friends, family, colleagues, and religious institutions. But there is another spin on the story. Many of those who invested in Madoff's scheme were in some way connected personally. These personal connections contributed significantly to his success. Many of these friends and relatives assumed that because Madoff was so personable and so friendly, he was also trustworthy in business. But that "trust" entailed taking one mindset, the mindset of personal relationships or golf partnerships, and imagining that that same mindset applied to money and business as well.

The example illustrates the fallacy that what works well in one personal or organizational setting will work equally well in another disparate setting. Some years ago Chevrolet successfully marketed a small car, the Nova in the United States. It was such a successful auto that it exported it to Spain. It did not sell well, and according to some sources the problem was that in Spanish "no-va" means "no go" (Erichsen, n.d.). Whether or not that was the problem, the naming illustrates that what works in one setting cannot always be universally successful. Thus prospective creative sensemaking that evaluates context, as well as product quality, is critical in every new market a company enters. In all these cases – India's microlending, Madoff's investors, and Nova – the lack of studying the context in each case, a paucity of imagination, contributed to failures.

V. Learning from history

The Johnson & Johnson Tylenol case demonstrated that corporate history can play a critical role in broadening one's scope and analysis of present situations and preventing a "silo" mentality that brackets previous learning experiences. The British Petroleum (BP) spill might have been at least partly caused by the same mentality. The massive 2010 BP oil spill caused millions of gallons to flow into the Gulf of Mexico. The long-term damage to the environment will not be known for several years. It is universally agreed, by BP officials as well, that this deep-water spill was and is an environmental disaster for which BP and others are responsible. The cost of this disaster will be several billion dollars to BP alone, as well as the other companies engaged in the construction of the oil rig.

What is interesting for our purposes is that BP seemed to have forgotten their history, in particular, the questionable safety history of their company. In March 2005, the BP refinery in Texas City experienced one of the worst oil refinery disasters in recent history. Due to several malfunctions the plant suffered massive explosions and fifteen people died. Eventually BP was fined £53 million, the largest fine (to that date) ever levied against a refinery (Clark, 2009). The plant was an old one that BP had inherited when it purchased Amoco. After the purchase, according to reliable sources such as the U.S. Chemical Safety Board, BP engaged in massive 25 percent cost cutting including drastic personnel reductions (U.S. CSB, 2007, 20). Between 1994 and 2004 the plant had suffered eight small blowdowns. Many of the now small staff of engineers and managers was working long shifts, some without any days off. Safety measures were cut back, and often staff was too tired to implement those that remained. We would suggest that BP employed a silo mentality in forgetting the importance of safety in its Deepwater oil rig. They seemingly had not "translated" the Texas City disaster in their risk analysis when drilling in the Gulf of Mexico. Obviously, these are different kinds of operations (different "silos"), but still there was much to be gleaned from Texas City that could have been – but was not – a "lesson learned" for best corporate practices.

Another example is the *Columbia* Shuttle explosion. After the 1986 *Challenger* explosion, a lengthy report was published detailing the organizational and physical failures that played a role in that tragedy (Presidential Commission, 1986). It appears, however, that NASA "forgot" the history lesson from *Challenger* that warnings should be heeded and explored (Aerospace Guide, 2003). During launches prior to the 2003 *Columbia* explosion foam insulation had broken off from the shuttle. The trouble with the foam insulation became so common that it was declared as an insolvable problem. And, as we outlined in the beginning of the chapter, organizational failures such as weak safety processes, organizational hierarchies and silos, poor communication, and faulty risk analyses all contributed to the disaster, just as they had to the earlier *Challenger* fiasco.

Margaret Heffernan (2011) blames these incidents on what she calls "structural blindness." That is, she argues, BP's leaders were interested in global growth and profitability. That mindset was so built into the dominant managerial thinking at BP that they ignored problems like safety. Moreover, because of that ingrained mindset, managers tended to focus on growth, cost centers, and profitability and did not familiarize themselves with the local issues and idiosyncrasies of each cost center. So the fact that Texas City was an old refinery with safety issues when BP acquired the plant was ignored, as were the risks of not having secondary safety mechanisms in place at Deepwater (Heffernan 2011, Ch. 9). In the case of *Columbia*, NASA forgot the lessons from

Challenger: that warning signs are just that – warnings of trouble despite previous successful launches.

"The Rashomon Effect"

Named after a Japanese Academy Award-winning film, *Rashomon*, the Rashomon Effect exemplifies how one set of events can be interpreted differently, even contrarily, by two or more contradictory mental models. For example, in a 2011 class action suit heard by the Supreme Court, 1.5 million women sued Wal-Mart for allegedly discriminating against women for unequal salaries, promotion practices, appearance, and treatment in the workplace. In a five–four decision the Court ruled against the suit, claiming that Wal-Mart had no official discriminatory policies, local stores were granted discretion in employment decisions, and that the 1.5 million women in the suit did not have enough commonality in their claims to justify one large suit rather than smaller, more focused, individual suits (Martin, 2011). The defenders of the suit, including Justice Ruth Bader Ginsberg, claimed that all of these practices were illustrative of a general corporate unwritten practice of ignoring discrimination on the local levels that was a sign of systematic toleration of discrimination at the corporate level.

Interestingly, neither party denied that discrimination took place in at least some Wal-Mart stores. They agreed, or at least did not disagree, on that data. Rather, each interpreted the data differently to defend their arguments either in favor, or defending the dismissal, of the lawsuit. Each party looked at the data employing different mental models so each reached a different conclusion. And each of the sets of mental models was itself narrowly construed. The organizers of the class action suit were taking a big risk by bundling so many different kinds of claims in one suit. The opponents and the majority in the Supreme Court followed only the letter of the law, forgetting that the suit was about people who were mistreated. The losers were the women.

Following orders

Readers will remember the WorldCom bankruptcy when the head of internal audit, Cynthia Cooper, uncovered a massive accounting fraud and "blew the whistle" on senior management, Bernie Ebbers and CFO Scott Sullivan, forcing the company into bankruptcy. What is less well known is the story of Betty Vinson, also an accountant at WorldCom. Vinson uncovered the financial irregularities (the company was booking ordinary expenses as capital expenses, thus appearing to be more profitable than they were), a fraud that was conducted over several financial quarters. Vinson reported the irregularities to Scott Sullivan, objecting to this unacceptable accounting practice. Sullivan is quoted as saying, "Think of it as an aircraft carrier . . . We have planes in the air. Let's get the planes landed. Once they are landed, if you still want to leave, then leave. But not while the planes are in the air" (Sack *et al.*, 2009). Vinson did not report these irregularities, not even to Cynthia Cooper. Eventually after the fraud was uncovered, Vinson was fired and went to jail for a few months.

The Betty Vinson case, like the NASA shuttle disasters, illustrate how many of us will go along with someone in authority when asked to do so, even when one knows that what they are doing is questionable or wrong. Betty Vinson may have assumed that because Sullivan was a senior executive and corporate leader by title that he knew something she did not about accounting. Of course, he did not. Later, in Chapter 3, we will discuss the reasons for this sort of behavior through examining the Milgram (1974) experiments and other causes.

VI. Conclusion

We have argued that social construction is a universal phenomenon that describes the framing interactions between individuals, organizations, and the data of experience, through incomplete mental models. Thus, if we are not incorrect, social construction is inescapable. Problems arise however, when the mindsets individuals or organizations adopt are reactive, when they become habitual responses to whatever is experienced, when they fail to account for changing data and contexts, when they miss, misinterpret or are inattentive to important evidence, or when they deliberately skew their interpretations. In Chapters 4 and 5 we will discuss in detail the cognitive and situational factors that are often the basis of these problems, including what Bazerman and others have called "bounded awareness," the failure to imagine that one's particular point of view is just that, a point of view, which often leads to ignoring important data if it challenges one's mental models (Bazerman and Tenbrunsel, 2011). Reviewing the examples we have presented in this chapter, the *Challenger* and *Columbia* cases illustrate how the managers at NASA exhibited bounded awareness. The Morton Thiokol engineers who were fearful of the launch, at least twenty-four of them, went along – they obeyed their leaders despite the risks of a shuttle failure. They lacked courage and implicit in their thinking was that leaders must be obeyed. Similarly, at MCI World-Com, simply obeying orders of the CFO landed Betty Vinson in jail.

Several examples epitomized how becoming mired in one mindset, "blindly," leads managers to simply miss what should be obvious. Ford managers, almost willfully, refused to put themselves in the shoes of Pinto drivers, despite the virtually charred Pintos that were brought back to the company. Johnson & Johnson was mired in the glory of its 1983 Tylenol decision, and could not retrospectively see how that might apply to twenty-first century quality control. Similarly, many corporate boards have blind spots when thinking about executive compensation, ignoring the appropriate rationale for high pay, the same rationale they apply in evaluating other managers and workers. On a more macro level, the 2008 financial crisis has failed to change Western free enterprise mindsets that imagine that their mental models are the "right" ones in any context, despite the global threat of financial failure.

The mental model that presumes that leadership must come from the top of an organization was questioned by several examples. While *Challenger* illustrated the failure of middle managers and engineers to take a leadership position and their tendency to merely go along with senior management decisions even when they are questionable, Unilever's triple-bottom-line thinking exemplified how sound leadership can come from the middle of an organization. And apparently no-one told Cynthia Cooper that senior executives should be obeyed even when their accounting practices did not meet accounting standards. Her courage as an internal auditor to take on MCI/WorldCom illustrates how effective middle management can be. The Children's Development Bank demonstrated leadership by poor, half-educated young teenagers. CDB and the Grameen Bank of Bangladesh brought into question a prevailing Western myth that the poor are deservedly so because of lack of education, laziness, or ignorance.

That irrational mindsets can block common sense is a frightening but real, and indeed common, phenomenon. The Madoff case offers an unfortunate example of how preoccupation with one idea, for example, making money, leads to such irrationality. The promise of a return of 15 percent per year contradicts sound financial acumen and market trends. Most of Madoff's victims were intelligent people. Simply using what they knew – that all markets are volatile and subject to fluctuation – should have made them wary of Madoff's promises. Similarly, in any pharmaceutical, quality control is key to successful products and profitability. J&J simply deprioritized that critical element of its operations. It developed a "blind spot" that should have been right in front of its thinking to other contexts. Part of the cause of corporate error is a form of ahistoricism. BP had forgotten the lessons from its Texas City blast. NASA forgot its *Challenger* history and the *Rogers Report* that outlined the organizational causes of the explosion.

One of the questions this chapter did not resolve was whether and in what ways one should take one set of mental models that work well in one context and apply it wholeheartedly to another context. The Grameen Bank's microlending model has been successful globally, but only when it is fully adopted. Yet, Chevy's Nova problem was imagining that a name works well in any context, despite different meanings in different languages, just as assuming that someone who is a good friend and golf companion will also be honest in business. So not every mental model is adaptable without alteration to a new setting. Indeed most are not. Thus each trial application demands individual attention to the particulars of each situation and the operative mental models that may or may not yield satisfactory outcomes. That is, each case requires moral imagination.

Karl Weick, as we read earlier in this chapter, argued that important to management decision-making is sensemaking – organizing and making sense out of the data of our experiences or reinterpreting more logically what may appear as chaotic ideas or confusing situations. We want to argue further that what is required in many of the situations we have described is a more disinterested and imaginative perspective that gauges, evaluates, and revises even those mental models that initially appear appropriate to the situation at hand. We call this process "moral imagination." For example, the construction of the Deepwater platform followed standard practice. But the dominant mental model operative in that practice was cost-savings and profitability. What were not included were secondary safety measures that were appropriate for deep water oil drilling. In the *Challenger* and *Columbia* disasters, the fact that no explosions had occurred after several launches led to the

logical and dominating, but erroneous, predictions that this pattern
would be repeated on future launches. Madoff's good golf game was
used the basis for the prediction that he was trustworthy in other
respects, at great cost to investors. Indian micro lending failures were
due in part to not thinking thoroughly about the risks and successes
of micro lending to people without capital or banking experience. In
all these cases, and others, simply stepping back from the situation
and imagining how it might be interpreted from other perspectives,
or what other models might be applicable when taking into account
other points of view, would have been propitious.

Moral imagination "is the ability in particular circumstances to discover and evaluate possibilities not merely determined by that circumstance, or limited by its operative mental models, or merely framed
by a set of rules or rule-governed concerns" (Werhane, 1999, 93).
Engagement in moral imagination, both individually and as an organization, involves (or can involve) a number of steps. First, one needs
to step back from the context, take a more disengaged perspective,
and examine operative mental models, either as an individual or in an
organizational setting. For example, in the case of Madoff's clients,
individual clients needed to ask whether and in what circumstances
15-percent steady annual return was possible in fluctuating markets.
Then one needs to challenge those mental models, imagining how these
situations would be interpreted from other perspectives. Is being the
head of an organization a guarantee of sound judgment as in MCI and
Challenger? Does being the leader of an organization guarantee good
leadership, or do we need to change that flawed mental model? Does
the organization have any "blind spots" created by the operative script,
such as cost containment or profitability? In the Deepwater BP case, BP
needed to question its preoccupation with short-term costs, its operating mental model both in Texas City and at Deepwater, to imagine the
risks entailed if the platform exploded from the points of view of the
rig workers and the thousands who live and make livings on the Gulf.
This sort of "out of the box" thinking may lead to coming up with
other mental models and alternatives, for example, checking Madoff's
returns against other well-known financial analysts, placing safety as a
first priority, heeding danger warnings from previous shuttle launches,
etc. For J&J it would have meant thinking beyond the company credo,
the dominant mental model throughout J&J's history, to its implementation through quality control. All of these models present moral

decisions, many of which are linked to financial decisions that call for moral evaluation. When critiquing our own and others' points of view we are often able to come up with alternates that can unearth new, heretofore unthought-of perspectives that may prevent poor choices, choices that are viable but flawed.

Engaging in moral imagination also helps to evaluate whether and in what ways a current operating procedure, such as the Grameen model for micro lending, is a worthwhile model in contexts other than Bangladesh, or whether, as exemplified in leadership models, one model does not fit all circumstances. Then, having explored new perspectives, one needs to test them as viable moral and fiscal alternatives. Cynthia Cooper realized that MCI's financial modeling, which involved questionable accounting practices, was just wrong. Whatever the MCI leadership defended was not necessarily correct, legally or morally defensible, or indeed, in the long term, viable. This insight led her to revamp the financial statements and "blow the whistle" on the financial cover-up created by MCI's corporate leaders, her bosses. Finally, ahistoricism, like narrow thinking, can lead to bad outcomes as well. Moral imagination can encourage us to compare our new conclusions with similar situations or with historically past situations within one's organization and perhaps, then, avoid a wrong decision or a fiscally and morally unacceptable outcome.

The engineers and managers involved in the *Columbia* disaster did not intend to participate in the commission of a grave ethical failure that, had the lessons of the *Challenger* explosion been heeded, could have been averted. Nor could it be said that executives at BP or Ford's Pinto division made a conscious decision to bring about the deadly disasters for which they, nonetheless, must bear responsibility. We have proposed that these examples bring to light the dangers of failing to acknowledge and interrogate the socially constructed mindsets that organize our experiences. As the cases explored in this chapter demonstrate, moral imagination animates the process of ethical decision-making, allowing other perspectives, decision possibilities and creative solutions to come into view. Conversely, when moral imagination is not activated, the operative mental models framing the decision-maker's perception in a given circumstance may remain below the register of conscious awareness and, therefore, be left unchallenged.

In Chapters 4 and 5, we will examine impediments to the development and practice of moral imagination in decision-making contexts. Applying the lessons of social construction theory and the mental models approach to ethical decision-making, we will analyze distorting mental models that blind decision-makers to their capacity for imaginative moral reasoning and effective moral agency at various stages in the process of forging an ethical response to a specific moral dilemma. Before turning to this wide-ranging analysis of ethics obstacles, Chapter 3 will focus in on a particular obstacle to ethical decision-making that is often at the root of ethical failures in commerce – obedience to authority – by way of a re-examination the Milgram (1974) experiments and related lines of research.

3 | *The Milgram studies: Obedience, disobedience, and ethical challenges*

The person who, with inner conviction, loathes stealing, killing, and assault may find himself performing these acts with relative ease when commanded by authority. Behavior that is unthinkable in an individual who is acting on his own may be executed without hesitation when carried out under orders... [I]nhumane policies may have originated in the mind of a single person, but they could only have been carried out on a massive scale if a very large number of people obeyed orders.

(Milgram, 1974, xi–1)

I. Introduction

After the September 11, 2001 tragedy and the failures of Enron, World-Com, and other companies during that same year, *Time Magazine* (Lacayo and Ripley, 2002) recognized and lauded three *Time* "Persons of the Year." These included Cynthia Cooper, the head of internal audit at WorldCom who blew the whistle on what turned out to be $70 billion in accounting fraud; Sherron Watkins, who unsuccessfully warned Kenneth Lay, the CEO of Enron, of the fraud being committed by the CFO, Andrew Fastow, and others; and Coleen Rowley, the FBI agent who, before September 11, repeatedly warned, without success, of the suspicious behavior of Zacarias Moussaoui, who turned out to be one of the conspirators in the bombings. For obvious reasons, *Time* neglected to mention a failed whistleblower and accountant at WorldCom, Betty Vinson, who despite moral reservations, went along with the CFO's creative accounting procedures even when she knew them to be fraudulent (Sack *et al.*, 2009). Each of these four women differently exemplifies the various ways in which individuals relate to authority.

In Chapter 2 we have argued that all of our experiences are socially constructed by incomplete mental models, some of which can create

43

biases or blind spots that can lead to fatal errors in judgment. Some of these errors in judgment are caused when people obey a person or organization that they perceive to be in authority, even when they are asked to engage in absurd, unethical, illegal, or even harmful behavior. One of the most disturbing studies of obedience is the 1960s Milgram experiments, which, taken together with the many follow-up experiments and studies that they inspired, demonstrate that obedience to authority is a pervasive mental model. We learn as children to obey our parents, then our teachers and coaches, and this followership habit has a tendency to reappear in adults, particularly when, in difficult situations, we try to transfer responsibilities to others, often others we perceive to be in authority. For example, as we discovered in the *Challenger* and *Columbia* disasters, engineers and managers built up habits of analysis and mindsets about leadership that contributed to their failure to blow the whistle concerning anomalies in the shuttles: they were not encouraged to question those problems. Many working on the shuttle went along with test results even when they were flawed. In the case of the *Challenger*, no one would disobey the leadership decision to launch, even when the engineering analysis demonstrated the many risks facing this particular launch.

In this chapter, we will examine in more detail the Milgram (1974) experiments, the well-known studies that tested whether or not naive participants would engage in unconscionable acts if encouraged or told to do so by a person in authority. We shall also present some new analyses of the original experiments that help to explain not only why so many people obeyed the person in authority in the experiments, but also why some were disobedient. In Chapter 2 we argued that the use of language in various formats, including conversation and discourse, shapes our perspectives and thus our mental models. As we shall see, the ways our mind interprets a discourse affects human choices and actions as well. It will turn out that most disobedience and exits from the Milgram experiments occurred when the teacher administered the 150-volt shock. And it was what the learner said when at 150 volts he cried, "Get me out of here," and in later iterations of the experiment adds, "My heart's starting to bother me," that was most decisive in the choices of those few naïve participants who exited the experiment before the final instruction to administer 450 volts.

II. The Milgram experiments

In the late 1960s a young psychologist at Yale University, Stanley Milgram, began a set of experiments that have come to be called "the obedience experiments." Milgram (1974) was struck by the fact that so many German citizens went along with Nazi behavior before and during the Second World War even when they knew atrocities were being committed to their Jewish neighbors and friends. He also wondered why ordinarily decent human beings who became guards at the concentration camps turned into monsters in their treatment of inmates, while carrying on seemingly exemplary family, religious, and neighborly lives outside their work. Thus motivated, Milgram created a set of experiments to test whether and how ordinary human beings would react to authority.

The experiment and its variations were fairly simple. Milgram and his associates solicited participants randomly by placing a newspaper advertisement and selecting from those respondents. Each participant would receive $4.50 for spending a few hours at Yale (and later at an off-site location of lesser prestige) in an experiment allegedly on investigating pedagogical methods. The first set of experiments, involving forty participating subjects, was set up so that what appeared to be a random drawing of who would be the "Teacher" and who the "Learner" was rigged so that a test participant was always the Teacher. Unbeknownst to the test subjects, the Learner was an actor, always a male, and his reactions as the experiment was carried out were scripted to be the same for all participants. The Teacher was instructed to read sets of word pairs, and the Learner was told to remember them. When the Learner made a mistake, the Teacher was to give the Learner an electric shock. The shock level began at 15 volts, and each time the Learner made a mistake, the Teacher was instructed to increase the level by 15-volt increments up to 450 volts. In the first set of experiments the Learner was in another room behind a closed door but his reactions to this treatment were loud enough for the Teacher to hear them clearly. The Teacher watched while the Learner was strapped in his chair, although the restraints were part of the experiment staging; the Teacher could easily escape to set up the prerecorded responses to the shocks that, in reality, he did not experience at all. Before each iteration of the experiment began, the Teacher was given a sample shock of 40 volts to understand and feel what was at stake. In the room with the Teacher was a person of authority, the Experimenter, also an actor, usually a tall man dressed in a white lab coat. If the Teacher hesitated or raised questions about following the instructions to shock the Learner each time he made a mistake, the Experimenter insisted that the experiment continue, following script established in advance. At 75 volts, the Learner began to groan, at 120 volts he complained of having heart trouble and being in pain, and at 150 volts he said, "Get me out of here!"

Milgram asked his colleagues and other experts to estimate how many participants would continue to the end of the experiment, shocking a stranger with 450 volts. Most estimated that it would be around half of one percent: this estimate was profoundly incorrect. Although the Experimenter made clear that the $4.50 was theirs no matter what they did, over half of the participants carried out the experiment to the end, despite the protestations of Learner. In the first group of forty subjects, twenty-five continued to give shocks up to 450 volts. In other words, over half of the participants gave extreme electric shocks to perfect strangers simply because they were told to do so and were instructed by the Experimenter that "the experiment must go on." Sometimes the Experimenter was asked if he would take responsibility in case something harmful happened to the Learner, and the answer was always in the affirmative. At the end of each iteration, the Teacher was carefully debriefed and told that the Learner was an actor and, thus, was not really getting shocked. Whether there was permanent mental damage to these participants was never fully determined.

Milgram altered the experiment by holding the next series away from Yale, fearing that the prestigious reputation of the university was influencing the results, but even when the experiment was moved to a simple store-front building in New Haven and in Bridgeport, Connecticut the results were virtually the same. Milgram also tried several other variations of the experiment. In one version the Teacher could not see OR hear the Learner. In this scenario, the obedience increased slightly. In a second version, the Learner was placed in the same room with the Teacher, resulting in a decrease in obedience; only sixteen out of forty participants delivered shocks to the full 450 volts. A third version further investigated the impact of the physical proximity of the Learner to the Teacher by requiring that the Teacher place the hand of the Learner on a plate to administered the shock in each instance of an incorrect answer. Under these conditions, obedience decreased the number of obedient subjects to twelve out of forty.

In yet another set of iterations of the study, Milgram altered the experiment by introducing two other Teachers (also actors) to the scenario. When these actor-Teachers protested and exited the experiment before completion, most naive participant-Teachers joined with their peers in dissent, with only four out of forty participants continuing to administer shocks to 450 volts. Similarly, when the actor-Teachers encouraged obedience and completed the experiment, almost all of the naive participants followed their lead. To measure the effects of the Experimenter and his comments, in another variation, the Experimenter left the room and gave orders remotely. In this situation, many of the Teachers "cheated" and gave the lowest shocks to the Learner rather than follow the instructions to ramp up with the shock level with each wrong answer.

Milgram and his colleagues tried to explain the variations in obedience by examining the social and educational background of the participants, but it turned out that there was no correlation between any specific criteria such as social class or education and the obedience or disobedience of the Teachers. Moreover, they could detect no gender differences. Women were not "kinder and gentler" than their male counterparts.

III. Later studies

The original Milgram experiments have been highly criticized for duping innocent participants into thinking they were participating in a learning experiment. As a result, today institutional review boards do not permit such lack of transparency in experiments with human subjects. It is tempting, then, to explain the outcomes of the Milgram experiments in terms of the 1960s culture, but similar outcomes have been verified in a number of more recent experiments inspired by Milgram's research. Notable experiments that escaped institutional review board scrutiny include the 1971 Zimbardo prison experiments, and a 2010 French experiment mimicking a reality television show. Another significant contribution to this line of research is the 2006 Santa Clara replication of The Milgram experiments, which altered the study design to reduce the risk of harm to the participants.

In 1971, Philip Zimbardo, a former student of Milgram's and
a professor of psychology at Stanford University, tried to replicate
the Milgram experiments, this time in a prison scenario. Zimbardo
(1973) recruited several Stanford undergraduate student volunteers
who seemed to be mature student leaders. In the role-playing experiment, which was filmed, ten participants were to be prisoners and
eleven were to be guards in a replica of a prison that Zimbardo and
his colleagues set up in the basement of Stanford's psychology department. The experiment was originally scheduled to go on for two weeks,
and Zimbardo himself played the role of prison superintendant. After
about one day, the prisoners and guards displayed an unsettling identification with their roles. The guards started to harass the prisoners,
covering their heads with paper bags and calling them by their prison
number, not by name. After making the prisoners anonymous, the
guards began to deny them privileges, waking them up during the
night, failing to empty their latrines, making fun of them, and requiring various arbitrary requirements. The prisoners became dependent
on the guards and initially developed highly deferential behaviors.
On the second day, however, some prisoners revolted and the guards
responded by putting them into "The Hole," a place of solitary con-
finement for disobedient prisoners. Other prisoners went along with
their roles, but displayed passive aggressive prisoner behavior and later
reported they had begun to hate the guards and their treatment. As one
of the prisoners said in a post-experiment interview, "if we had gotten
together then [during the revolt] I think we could have taken over the
place. But when I saw the revolt wasn't working, I decided to toe the
line. Everyone settled into the same pattern. From then on, we were
really controlled by the guards" (Zimbardo, 1973, 43). Finally, on
the sixth day of the experiment, Zimbardo's fiancé visited the prison
and, distressed by the abuses she witnessed, appealed to Zimbardo
to see that his experiment had devolved into a psychological danger to the participants. The experiment was halted, and the participants were debriefed. Later, reflecting on the experiment, Zimbardo
writes,

[After the sixth day,] [w]e were no longer dealing with an intellectual exercise in which a hypothesis was being evaluated in the dispassionate manner dictated by the canons of the scientific method. We were caught up in
the passion of the present, the suffering, the need to control people, not

variables, the escalation of power and all of the unexpected things that were erupting around and within us. We had to end this experiment. (Zimbardo, 1973, 45)

Although one participant suffered from a mental breakdown during the experiment, there is no evidence that the study resulted in any long-term harm (Alexander, 2001).

Two other recent studies have attempted to replicate the Milgram experiments in different ways, each confirming Milgram's original conclusions. The first, conducted in 2006 by Jerry Burger at Santa Clara University, carefully chose the participants, being sure to fully inform them of the point of the experiment. Because of institutional review board restrictions, Burger (2009) stopped the experiment at 150 volts, the point where the Learner begins to complain to get out, but recorded those participants who clearly *would* have gone further in shocking the Learner had the experiment been allowed to continue. The 150-volt moment was chosen because, in Milgram's study, many of the minority subset of Teachers who did refuse to complete the experiment stopped at 150 volts. Burger also improved the gender ratio in his choice of participants (there were very few women in the original experiments), and chose some participants who were older than fifty years, the age cutoff for Milgram's participants. Still Burger could not correlate gender or age differences with those who did or did not proceed after 150 volts. Burger writes, "I found no effect for education, age, or ethnicity on participants' behavior in the study. In short, I am as confident as a psychology research can ever be that my findings can be legitimately compared with Milgram's" (p. 10). Assuming that most of Burger's participants who were willing to go past 150 volts would have continued to 450 volts, Burger's results were very much like Milgram's forty-five years earlier. In other words, the vast majority of participants shocked a perfect stranger when the Learner could not accurately learn fairly random word pairs.

In 2010, a group of social scientists partnered with a French television station and documentary film team to replicate Milgram's study in the context of reality television game shows (Beauvois *et al.*, 2012). The participants responded to an Internet ad calling for contestants to participate in a reality show called "Game of Death." In order to eliminate the motivation of monetary reward, contestants were told the show was a pilot program to test the game show, and no prizes would be given. The naive contestants were instructed by a female game show host (a confederate of the experimenters) to give shocks to their rival contestants (also confederates of the experiment) when they could not correctly answer questions. The rival contestants were on stage with them, and could be heard but not seen by the naïve contestants. As in Milgram's original experiment, the confederates were not actually shocked, but performed a script in which they exhibited terrible pain in reaction to the shocks. The contestants were urged on by the game show hostess and an audience encouraging them to continue to administer the shocks if they hesitated. Unlike Burger (2009), who restricted his replication of the study to the 150-volt shock level, the designers of the French version included the full 450-volt range in their experiment. The study's authors argue that "transposing the experiment into a televised game setting requires the use of violence equivalent to that frequently implemented in some of these games" (Beauvois *et al.*, 2012, 2). In this reality television game setting, 82 percent of the contestants obeyed the commands of the game show presenter and continued to deliver shocks to the 450-volt level. According to the documentary producer, "They [the participants] are not equipped to disobey. They don't want to do it, they try to convince the authority figure [the hostess] that they should stop, but they don't manage to" (*"French TV . . . "*, 2010).

Milgram's findings regarding obedience to authority and responsibility-shifting have remained valid over time, even in variations such as a mock prison or a television game show. Milgram's experiments have been replicated cross-culturally, and still, the results are remarkably consistent (Blass, 1991). While obedience may or may not be a genetic trait, we appear to have a human propensity to develop mental models that enable us to relinquish our decision-making capacity to others, and consequently, to release ourselves from responsibility for our actions, when confronted with authority figures. When this propensity is not curbed by conscientious effort, it may blind us to the need to interrogate the mental models that shape our perception of reality. The choices embedded within the conceptual frameworks that we adopt when we conform to peer pressure or obey authority figures may conflict with our values, and yet, obedience and conformity studies demonstrate that these choices will appear to be the only ones available to us. When showing footage of deeply conflicted volunteers continuing to obey Milgram's experimenter to students in the classroom, they are often puzzled by the subjects' decision to remain in the room and continue with the experiment. They ask, why do the subjects not simply refuse, or leave? The lesson taught by these studies is that the subjects are not making an affirmative decision to remain; in fact, they are *not making a decision at all*. It is that omission or failure to decide that has consequences, and that itself constitutes a kind of choice. If we fail to acknowledge the vulnerability of our decision-making processes to unconscious cognitive biases and situational factors, the option to refuse to conform to peer pressure, or to disobey an immoral command from an authority figure, may not register as an alternative resolution; it may not appear as a choice at all.

IV. Explaining the experiments

It is significant to note that the obedient subjects in Milgram's experiments did not fail to see that their situation involved ethical issues; indeed, many expressed grave ethical concerns, even while continuing to obey commands that violated their conscience (Packer, 2008; Parmar, 2011). All subjects exhibited signs of strain. According to Milgram,

[t]he cries of pain issuing from the learner strongly affected many participants, whose reaction to them is immediate, visceral, and spontaneous... Administering shocks to the victim is incompatible with the self-image of many subjects... a powerful source of strain." (Milgram, 1974, 155–6)

For example, one participant who continued the experiment to 450 volts said, early on, "I can't stand it. I'm not going to kill that man (Learner) in there" (p. 73). Another who stopped at 150 volts said to the Experimenter, "Surely you've considered the ethics of this thing" (p. 48). Arguably, the subjects had access to adequate information to form an ethical decision, including knowledge of the Learner's weak heart, the cries of pain of the Learner, the labels on the shock generator that warned of danger when administering high voltage, and the absence of significant risk in their own disobedience. If we allow that many, if not all, of the participants were morally conscious, decent human beings, why, when they appeared to realize that shocking the Learner was truly harmful, did the majority omit to seek alternatives courses of action that would not violate their values?

We may gain some insight into this question by considering the case of Betty Vinson. Vinson, the WorldCom employee who was convicted for her role in inflating that company's profits using fraudulent accounting practices, knew that her decisions led to acts that were both wrong and illegal. However, by all accounts, Vinson was deeply troubled by the unethical behavior at WorldCom. She voiced discomfort to her superiors, repeatedly considered resignation, and communicated her unease to her colleagues; meanwhile, however, urged by the CFO Scott Sullivan, Vinson continued to participate in the massive accounting fraud, a decision that would eventually result in a felony conviction and prison sentence (Pulliam, 2003). Several factors contributed to Vinson's ethical failure. As Milgram's experiments demonstrate, it is difficult to follow one's conscience when pressured by authority figures. Many of Milgram's subjects, like Vinson, continued to obey despite voicing strong moral objections to the orders they were given. These subjects, though unable to develop a mental model that would rationalize their unethical behavior, also appeared unable to muster the resources to follow their conscience.

Milgram interpreted these results by focusing on the high level of obedient participants. He argued that it was likely that these Teachers moved into what he called an "agentic state," whereby they transferred their ability to make choices, to exit the experiment, and the responsibilities for the outcomes of their inflictions of shock onto the Experimenter. In Milgram's interpretation, the obedient participant adopted the mindset of the Experimenter, and no longer depended on himself or herself for decision-making. The language of the Experimenter reinforced this agentic state. When he says, for example to a participant, "The experiment must go on," implying that science will suffer if the participant disobeys, he reinforces his authority and often undermines the Teacher's ability to see herself as capable of making her own choice to exit.

There is another small, but important, element in the set-up of the experiment. According to recent studies, under the proper setting such as a laboratory or in a hospital, we tend to look up to that person and imagine that she is a person of authority and an expert in her field if she is dressed in what we imagine to be proper attire for her role. A white coat, worn in scientific or medical scenarios signals an expert and garners both respect and behavior. (Note that if it is someone painting your house, the white coat will not work this way.) The presence of the Experimenter in a white lab coat added luster to his authority and may have affected the level of obedience of the naive participants, just as the title "CEO" can have sway over behavior and affect judgment regardless of whether the bearer of this title (or the wearer of the white coat) actually wields the authority presumed (Blakeslee, 2012, D3).

Milgram cites the tendency of many subjects to shift the focus of agency from themselves to the Experimenter, which he terms the "agentic shift," as a possible explanation. "Specifically, the person entering into an authority system no longer views himself as acting out of his own purposes but rather comes to see himself as an agent for executing the wishes of another person" (1974, 133). Using the metaphor of a toggle switch to describe what is commonly referred to as cognitive release, Milgram proposes that people have a high propensity to respond to social situations that render them "open to regulation by a person of higher status" by switching off their sense of responsibility for their own actions, thus seeing themselves as a mere agent or automaton for another. For example, one participant who eventually went on to administer 450 volts asked the Experimenter, "You accept all responsibility?" The Experimenter responded, "The responsibility is mine. Correct. Please go on" (p. 160). Most of Milgram's obedient subjects were not even consciously aware that they had shifted their decision-making capacity to another, in order to release themselves of conscious responsibility for their actions. Another participant transferred responsibility to the Learner as well as to the Experimenter:

Of the learner he says, 'He agreed to it, and therefore must accept responsibility'" The experimenter has 'the biggest share of responsibility. I merely went on. Because I was following orders . . . I was told go to on. And I did not get a cue to stop.' (p. 50)

Just as there were no cues or gatekeepers to stop participants in the Milgram experiment from ceding responsibility to authority, in analyzing the Enron scandal, as the corporate legal expert John Coffee (2006) argues, there were no gatekeepers or stopping rules to prevent Enron's runaway behavior. Auditors and stock analysts who were *supposed* to be independent and disinterested did not play their roles as gatekeepers to oversee Enron's failure. Nor did the SEC do due diligence. Coffee sees the Enron scandal as more than a company failure; it was a failure of the U.S. economic system's gatekeepers to adequately carry out their professional duties. Perhaps what the Milgram experiments and data

from Enron and other corporate scandals imply is that human beings
need explicit rules and gatekeepers in order not to behave unethically
or refrain from committing atrocities or fraud. This role of a "stopping
rule" was evident in the formulation of the experiments in which the
Teacher was placed in a room with other Teachers who were actually
experiment confederates. Recall that when some actor-Teachers urged
continuing the experiment, the participant-Teacher was likely to go
on to administer 450 volts. On the other hand, when the actors urged
the Teacher to stop the experiment, thus acting as informal gatekeepers, the level of obedience when down and thirty-six of the forty participants refused to carry out the experiment (Milgram, 1974, 113–22).

As Albert Bandura (1999) argues that, whether or not they experienced moral distress, many participants were morally disengaged from
their responsibilities for the pain the Learner was feeling. Participants
were particularly inclined to moral disengagement when the Learner
was not visible to them. That distance, even when only consisting of
one room, seemed to have undermined many participants' awareness
that the Learner was a suffering human being. Others, in following the
lead of the Experimenter, were able to mentally transfer their responsibilities for harming the Learner onto the Experimenter. Even though
they were pushing the levers that administered the shock, and express-
ing awareness of the Learner's suffering, they were able to separate
their actions from themselves. In other words, they took themselves
out of the experiment and its outcomes as moral agents despite their
physical participation in the event. However, when the Learner was
in the same room as the Teacher, this proximity worked to decrease
the level of obedience. The presence of the sufferer helped to mitigate
responsibility transference in many cases. But notice that this mitiga-
tion only occurs when a participant recognizes the sufferer as an equal
human being (Packer, 2008; Bandura, 1999). As we learned from the
Abu Ghraib torture events in Iraq, prisoners in that situation were
considered not merely enemies, but lesser or unworthy human beings.
That degraded status made carrying out the torture easier. Moral disengagement can also produce positive outcomes, as seen in the cases
where the few Teachers disengaged from the experiment rather than
from their responsibilities as lever-pushing moral agents, and realized
that they had a choice to disobey and withdraw. We shall return to the
notion of moral disengagement in Chapter 5.

Steven Gilbert (1981) suggests that one ways to account for the high level obedience is the small increments in which the shocks were delivered, an increase of 15 volts each time. One could imagine that participants did not think that these small incremental changes were enough to qualitatively matter. The problem was, of course, that each 15-volt increase built up to 450 volts.[1] Recall our Chapter 2 discussion of the slide from exemplary ethical behavior to ethical failure in the case of Johnson & Johnson. Perhaps at J&J the presence of the credo, so forceful in their 1982 decision to recall Tylenol capsules, gradually faded in importance in small increments, so gradually that by 2010 when the recalls of their medicines and implants began, the company's managers were able to separate the edicts of the credo from their increasing pressure to be very profitable.

Neera Badhwar (2009) suggests that one of the reason that ordinarily decent people like those chosen for the Milgram experiments are able to compartmentalize their virtues. Thus one can be a good mother, and fine teacher, good citizen, but follow orders and engage in behaviors that contradict one's everyday good behavior. This is a form of silo mentality we discussed in Chapter 2, and it does account for some of our blind spots. To take an example from commerce, in Chapter 2 we read about the recent problems at Johnson & Johnson including their recall of about 99,000 hip implants. We might speculate that the manufacturers of the implants thought they were making implant devices, which they were. But what they were producing were faulty implants, apparently due to insufficient quality control. Perhaps the manufacturer, in haste to produce and distribute these devices, lost sight of the fact that eventually these would be implanted in human beings, and neglected to factor in this highly important aspect of their project in their mindsets. As a consequence, something like Six Sigma quality (where no flaws greater than one in six million are to be tolerated) was not instituted. The distance from the manufacture of a

---

[1] One is reminded of the well-known folk tale about the boiling frog. As the adage goes, one drops a frog in boiling water he will immediately jumps out; if one puts a frog in cold water and gradually heats it to boiling the frog will not jump out of the pan. As Paul Krugman (2009) points out, "[r]eal frogs will, in fact, jump out of the pot – but never mind. The hypothetical boiled frog is a useful metaphor for a very real problem: the difficulty of responding to disasters that creep up on you a bit at a time."

mechanical device to human implant that may have produced moral disengagement.

Whether we privilege agentic shift, the absence of gatekeepers or "stopping rules," moral disengagement, incrementalism, compartmentalism, or a combination of these factors in our explanation of Milgram's results, we are faced with the unsettling conclusion that our capacity to make ethical decisions is highly vulnerable when we are pressured to obey by figures of authority. Yet, it is important to recall that not *all* participants succumbed to this pressure. In the next section, we consider the phenomenon of disobedience, as revealed by Milgram's study.

V. Disobedience, discourse, and the 150-volt moment

Our conceptual scheme(s) and forms of language mediate even our most basic perceptual experiences. (Putnam, 1990, 28)

Many of the studies of the Milgram experiments concentrate on the strong level of obedience to the instructions of the Experimenter, the person in authority or perceived to be in authority by the participants. That is because of the large numbers of participants who followed the protocol to 450 volts. However, recent reexaminations of the audio and videotapes of the experiment have discovered another aspect of the experiment, those who disobeyed (Parmar, 2011). In each iteration of the experiment there were a small number who disobeyed, refusing to carry on the experiment after a certain point. For instance, when the Experimenter pressed one participant who exited after 150 volts that "It's absolute essential to the experiment that we go on . . . you have no other choice," this Teacher responded, "If this were Russia maybe, but not in America." Another, an engineer who also exited at 150 volts, responded to the same dialogue, "I *do* have a choice. Why don't I have a choice? I came here on my own free will" (Milgram, 1974, 51). Moreover when the engineer was asked who was responsible for administering the shocks he responded, "I would put it on myself entirely" (p. 51). In responding to the Experimenter's assertion that "you have no other choice," a Teacher who exited at 210 volts said, "I think we are here on our own free will" (p. 85). Interestingly, the participants who exited early showed anxiety prior to exiting, but after they made that choice they exhibited no more strain. According to

Milgram, "[d]isobedience is the ultimate means whereby strain is brought to an end. But it is not an act equally available to all..." because many cede their responsibility (p. 157). These disobedient Teachers realized that they were merely participating in an experiment and thus, were not compelled to engage. Participants who took this view of the situation reacted negatively to the commands of the Experimenter. Each of those who exited displayed a strong sense of their ability to make personal choices that were not dictated by the Experimenter. Each was able to disengage from their assigned role in the experiment and understand that they were hurting another person for no explainable reason, or at least, no reason that adequately justified the harm.

As Dominic Packer (2008) has shown, the 150-volt moment in the experiment is especially important, because it is at that point where at least one-third of all Teachers who disobeyed exited the experiment. While, statistically speaking, this subset is a relatively small number, it is important because at no other moment in the experiment does one find a cluster of disobedient participants. According to Packer, this 150-volt moment of disobedience is important because it is at 150 volts that, for the first time, the Learner protests to the experiment and his incarceration and cries, "Get me out of here. I won't be in the experiment anymore! I refuse to go on! Get me out of here" (Milgram, 1974, 23). The Learner repeats this later in the experiment as well, but it is when this protestation is heard for the first time, according to Packer, that the mindsets of at least one-third of the disobedient participants change. It is at the 150-volt moment that these few participants,

... responded to what they perceived as the learner's right to terminate the experiment, more specifically, we can infer that these participants believed that the learner's right to end the experiment trumped the experimenter's right to give orders to the contrary. (Packer, 2008, 303)

It is the changing discourse of the Learner, from cries of pain to a plea for his rights as a human being, that affected the participant's mindset, helping them to disengage from their roles as participants or from their identification with the Experimenter's thinking, and to exit the experiment. Those that disobeyed were a very small number; the one-third that disobeyed at 150 volts constitutes approximately

3.5 percent of all participants (p. 302). Nevertheless, the clustering of disobedience at this point in the experiment, however small, suggests that language, conversation and discourse can affect our mindsets and thus our decision-making and behavior.

The role of discourse is illustrated in the *Challenger* case. On the evening before the launch, engineers on the project objected to the launch because they did not have information that would support its success, given bad weather and rough seas for landing. The managers on the project questioned these objections because it was their mindset that if the possibility of failure could not be supported by good evidence, one goes ahead with the launch. Thus the question of whether to launch became morally ambiguous. The engineers and managers participating in the project had access to the same data, but each interpreted it differently. Finally, one of the senior managers told the head of the project, "Take off your engineering hat and put on your management hat," thereby sanctioning the launch (Presidential Commission, 1986, 94). This discursive act reframed the situation, making it clear that management thinking was and should be the authoritative mindset. No engineer tried to resist this discursive reframing; they submitted to the mindset declared authoritative by management leadership, and the *Challenger* was launched the next morning.

In support of the role of discourse in ethical decision-making, experimenters recently have examined the role of morally oriented conversations, as well as contemplation, in promoting or discouraging ethical decisions, in particular the decision about whether or not to tell the truth in situations where the better pay-off for the participant is to lie (Gunia *et al.*, 2012). The participants were undergraduate students, not always a reliable source for data to explain management decision-making (because they are not managers). Still, the authors found that "[c]ontemplation and moral conversations had strong effects: both led to more ethical decisions [not to lie] than immediate choice and self-interested conversations" (Gunia *et al.*, 2012, 22). This data supports findings from other new studies of the Milgram experiments that discourse can change the mindsets and choices of participants (both positively and negatively), depending on how participants internalize and interpret the conversation (Parmar, 2011; Packer, 2008). Applied to business ethics, corporate discourse at any level can affect the behavior of managers and employees, as we learned from the

Challenger case. Although in the *Challenger* case the outcome was to "obey authorities" to disastrous outcomes, Gunia *et al.* (2012) and Parmar (2011) have shown that discourse can have positive effects of changing behavior positively. The biannual conversations about the Credo at J&J enriched its narrative about Tylenol and corporate culture for many years before their recent problems. One wonders whether or how that dialogue changed (or was played down in importance in corporate discourse), in the years leading up to the recent ethical failures.

In his yet-unpublished study of the audio tapes of the first iteration of the Milgram experiments that involved forty participants, Parmar (2011) demonstrates how the discourse in the Milgram experiments between the Experimenter, Learner and Teacher affected the behavior of the Teacher in some cases, reinforcing role identification as Teachers for some in the experiment, ("the experiment must go on") and/or in triggering disobedience for others. Parmer argues that disobedience is triggered when participants realize that they have a choice to exit, although this occurs rarely. Although there was a low rate of disobedience, what is to be learned is that the language we use can affect our own and others' mindsets and choices both destructively and positively.

Thus discourse, the primary way humans communicate and think, is critical to forging and unsettling the mental models through which we perceive the choices available to us in any particular context. The expressions of the Experimenter were instrumental for many participants who disengaged from their responsibilities as moral agents and transferred that responsibility to the Experiment. Many also displayed "silo mentality," the ability to bracket their role responsibilities as Teachers in this experiment from their responsibilities as parents, employees, and citizens. This same silo mentality was exhibited during the Second World War by ordinary allegedly decent human beings who disengaged or bracketed what was going on by the Nazis. On the other hand, disengagement can work positively. Those few disobedient participants disengaged from the experiment, stepped back to question the role of the authority and the importance of this project, and exerted their capacity to imagine and enact a choice possibility that was not embedded within their immediate context. How to encourage this form of disengagement is important in corporate decision-making as well, to avoid a "me too" mentality that perpetuates thoughtless conformity and sometimes, untoward consequences for the company and its stakeholders.

VI. Conclusion

New studies of the Milgram experiments demonstrate that in this morally ambiguous situation, in where there are many ways to react, a few individuals disobeyed when, through the cries of the Learner, they acknowledged the Learner's right to exit the experiment. Thus, we surmise that in organizations, obstacles to sound decision-making, many of which we will discuss in Chapters 4 and 5, may be surmounted or averted when employees go above and beyond what seems to be demanded in their roles to seek alternatives to decisions that will ultimately be bad for the organization (Ghoshal and Bartlett, 1995). While this sort of deviation is often identified with whistleblowing, a response to ethical challenges that we will discuss that in Chapter 7, many times it is simply the courage to dissent to operational behaviors that can change organizational outcomes. But that courage is difficult to find, as many of us identify with those in authority, and succumb to exhortations that guide our decision-making and encourage disengagement from personal responsibility even when we are the actors accountable for the choices we make.

Returning to the whistleblowing examples with which we began this chapter, each of these women exemplifies a different form of obedience or disobedience. Betty Vinson was an obedient participant in the WorldCom scandal. Vinson was a senior accountant in the corporate accounting division at WorldCom. She repeatedly called to the attention of the CFO, Scott Sullivan, and others that WorldCom was booking ordinary expenses as capital expenses, thus making their profitability appear larger than it was. This practice is forbidden both by the standards of good practice in accounting and by law. We might call this a possible, but failed, "150-volt moment," because Vinson knew these practices were wrong in every way. Nevertheless, Sullivan justified this bad behavior by emphasizing to Vinson that the company was in crisis. When Vinson threatened to resign, he said to her, "We have planes in the air. Let's get the planes landed. Once they are landed, if you still want to leave, then leave. But not while the planes are in the air." When Sullivan used this analogy, it made

Vinson see herself as a team player first, and that conversation persuaded her to ignore problematic accounting practices that she knew were morally and legally wrong. Vinson accepted Sullivan's authority and transferred her responsibilities to him, failing to inform outside auditors or the Board of the ethical failures (Sack *et al.*, 2009).

Sherron Watkins raised questions about Enron's practices and reported her concerns to the CEO, but she did not go to the Board or the public when her efforts were rebuffed. Although she was clearly aware of the unethical and illegal practices at Enron, and the improper account of Andrew Fastow, the CFO, she did not take action but merely continued at Enron until it went bankrupt in 2002 (Lacayo and Ripley, 2002).

In early May 2001, Minneapolis FBI agent Coleen Rowley flagged Zacarias Moussaoui as a person of interest, suspected of involvement with terrorist activities. Her superiors thwarted her efforts to pursue the lead further. We now know that Moussaoui was indeed part of terrorist group responsible for the 9–11 bombings. In May of 2002, after the 9–11 tragedies, Rowley reported to the FBI Director that her questions about Moussaoui had been repeatedly ignored by the Bureau. Her whistleblowing to the director has led to reforms in the FBI and CIA and to the formation of the Transportation Security Administration. Although there are still grave difficulties with the exchange of information between the vast numbers of government agencies working on these issues, Rowley's actions triggered a new awareness of the problems of communication and information sharing in this country (Lacayo and Ripley, 2002).

Finally, Cynthia Cooper, the former head of internal audit and the whistleblower at WorldCom, was moved to action at the "150-volt moment" when she realized that the WorldCom accounting practices were fraudulent and that no one inside the company was going to change them (Mead *et al.*, 2005). She "exited the experiment," unlike the other whistleblowers, Watkins and Rowley. When Cooper noticed the quarterly miscounting of ordinary expenses and capital expenses, she first reported these errors to the CFO. When Sullivan ignored her requests to "clean up" the audit, Cooper stepped out of her role as head of internal audit. She and her audit team first reworked the Arthur Andersen external audit of the Company (not part of their jobs at WorldCom – indeed they were not supposed to touch the external audit), working nights and weekends without pay in order to secure the data needed to demonstrate the fraud. She then went to WorldCom's board audit committee. When she was initially ignored, she threatened to go to the SEC with her information. The result, as we know, was the uncovering of massive accounting miscalculations leading to over $50 billion in unaccountable revenues. Like the participants in the Milgram experiments who refused to carry on with the experiment, Cooper refused to back down from what she knew was right. Her strong self-identity and good audit skills strengthened her choices prevented her from not deviating from the expected role behavior at WorldCom.

The role of discourse in moral choice has implications for organizing, and for the (in)visibility of choice. Organizing has been defined as the process of creating interlocking routines that unequally distribute different behaviors and choices among the participants (Weick, Suttcliffe, and Obstfeld, 1995). When ordinary organizational actors such as Cynthia Cooper go above and beyond their roles and engage in extra role behavior, they can help their organizations adjust to changing circumstances. When researchers assume that these individuals are mostly rational about their behaviors, they miss the ways in which actors, such as Sherron Watkins and Coleen Rowley, were blind to certain options. The inter-related role system that constitutes organizing requires certain personal choices and actions to be highly visible and others to be invisible to their stakeholders. Understanding the discursive processes by which personal choices are constructed and distributed can help organizations more consciously attend to these choices and act more effectively to reduce risks to their stakeholders.

4 | Obstacles to ethical decision-making in the perception of ethical context

I. Introduction

In Chapters 4 and 5, we examine how the construction of mental models, defined and illustrated in Chapter 2, may devolve into the formation of barriers or obstacles that ultimately prevents decision-makers from reaching ethical decisions. While mental models serve to conceptualize, focus, and shape our experiences, in so doing, they sometimes cause us to ignore data and occlude the critical reflection that might be relevant or, indeed, necessary to practical decision-making. We argue that distorting mental models are the foundation or underpinning of impediments to effective ethical decision-making. Chapters 4 and 5 conceptualize ethical decision-making as a multi-stage process, and investigate the many ways in which this process is thwarted by obstacles such as bounded awareness (Bazerman and Chugh, 2006), blind spots (Moberg, 2006), conformity (Asch, 1955, 1951), obedience to authority (Milgram, 1974), and others.

We construct mental models – and become habituated to the experiences they enable – because they embody our history and our experiences; they are inherently (tautologically) familiar; and, somehow, they benefit us. Yet, mental models, even – and sometimes, especially – those that make us feel comfortable, happy and productive in our roles as employees, managers, and leaders, can devolve into barriers to ethical decision-making when they discourage attention to the fundamental vulnerabilities of our own processes. In this chapter, we propose a broad conceptual division of the ethical decision-making processes into five steps in order more precisely to identify the interference of distorting mental models in the development of conscientious and responsible resolutions to ethical challenges. We then examine common impediments to the initial two steps of this decision-making model, which describe the process of perceiving a situation or conflict as a dilemma that calls for an ethical response. In Chapter 5, we will turn to a discussion of mental models that prevent the execution of the remaining steps of ethical deliberation, the practice of critical reflection crucial for crafting a responsible decision that maintains fidelity to consciously held, personal values.

II. Ethical decision-making as a process: A mental models approach

Under optimal conditions, we reach decisions through an ethical decision-making process. Broadly speaking, one formulation of this process is framed as follows. A decision-maker (1) becomes aware of a present issue; (2) gathers facts relevant to the ultimate decision; (3) identifies alternative solutions to the dilemma at hand; (4) considers stakeholders implicated or impacted by these alternatives; and (5) reaches a conclusion by comparing and weighing these alternatives, often guided by insights offered by philosophical theory and/or external guidance, as well as by testing solution possibilities by reflecting on their likely consequences from the perspectives provided by other mental models (Hartman and DesJardins, 2008).

Certainly, these steps may occur in a different order, depending upon the circumstances. For example, examining a dilemma from the viewpoint of impacted stakeholders might raise new facts, or bring to light previously unconsidered ethical issues that reframe the dilemma altogether. It is important to recall that other models of ethical decision-making are possible and, in addition, that this approach will not guarantee one single and absolute answer to every decision. In any given situation, it is impossible to gather *all* facts to assess their relevance, or to consider how one's decision might impact each and every potential stakeholder, individually. Rational decision-makers may disagree at each stage of the process, from the relevance of particular data and the relative importance of particular stakeholder groups to the application or significance of a theoretical insight or the appropriate conclusion. But this analytical approach, which conceptualizes ethical decision-making as multi-step process, provides a helpful beginning in the development of responsible, reasonable, and ethical decision-making. Decisions that follow from such a process of thoughtful and conscientious reasoning will be more accountable and responsible, and will be more likely to be consistent with the decision-maker's deeply held values, than those that do not.

Though these five steps appear both burdensome and cumbersome, since they are likely to be applied in a traditional, fast-paced business environment, it is their habit-forming nature through repetition and reinforcement that tends to create an ethical corporate culture. Mental models that interfere with this process influence our choices in ways of which we are not aware, and thereby subliminally induce or persuade us away from this intentional choice-making toward behaviors inconsistent with our own values (Banaji *et al.*, 2003). The problematic mental models discussed in the previous chapter and again explored in greater depth in the current and following chapters create sub-optimal conditions for ethical decision-making at each phase of the process, by impeding our awareness of the ethical dimensions of our decisions, blinding us to significant facts, distorting our views of others, limiting our capacity to imagine alternative resolutions, and discouraging us from reflecting on the value commitments and likely outcomes of alternatives. To the extent that we fail to interrogate our mental models, we increase our vulnerability to problematic mindsets and miss opportunities to strengthen ways of framing experience that promote our capacity to forge ethical decisions and guide our behavior by their light.

Deciding to "do wrong," or failing to make an ethical decision at all

To be sure, the risk of moral failure is not eliminated by the critical and intentional practice of ethical decision-making. Unethical decisions are sometimes the outcome of a conscious, deliberate, and reflective choice to "do wrong." Bernie Madoff's admission of guilt to securities fraud, investment adviser, fraud, mail fraud, wire fraud, three counts of money laundering, false statements, perjury, false filings with the U.S. Securities and Exchange Commission (SEC), and theft from an employee benefit plan offers an egregious example of such a deliberate moral failure (Department of Justice, 2009). In his statement to the court, Madoff explained,

Your Honor, for many years up until my arrest on December 11, 2008, I operated a Ponzi scheme through the investment advisory side of my business... I am actually grateful for this first opportunity to publicly speak about my crimes, for which I am so deeply sorry and ashamed. *As I engaged in my fraud, I knew what I was doing was wrong, indeed criminal.* I cannot adequately express how sorry I am for what I have done. I am here today to accept responsibility for my crimes by pleading guilty and, with this plea allocution, explain the means by which I carried out and concealed my fraud.... (Jones, 2009, emphasis added)

Deliberate unethical and illegal behavior is surely responsible for a portion of corporate malfeasance. In this vein, a recent theory has gone so far as to propose that the global financial crisis was due in large part to rapid changes in corporate organizational practice that have facilitated the rise of "dark leadership," specifically "corporate psychopaths" who were attracted to the financial sector and who ruthlessly pursued personal greed above all else (Boddy, 2011, 2010).

However, as the examples from Chapter 2 demonstrate, most unethical decisions are not the culmination of deliberately unethical choices, such as those made by Madoff, nor are they made by the small percentage of amoral psychopaths that may occupy corporate leadership positions. Instead, they result from a failure to engage in ethical deliberation. There is no evidence that the many Madoff's investors who enjoyed an abnormally consistent and high rate of return, or the regulatory agencies that failed to discover the fraud, were parties to Madoff's scheme, or indeed were motivated by corrupt or predatory desires for personal profit at all costs. Yet, when these same investors neglected to question how Madoff was able to produce such returns or when the SEC did not pursue warnings about the Ponzi scheme, they too became implicated in the ethical failure (SEC, 2009). Identifying mental models that disable or discourage ethical deliberation is crucial, as Campbell *et al.* (2009, 1) point out, because "[t]he daunting reality is that enormously important decisions made by intelligent, responsible people with the best information and intentions are sometimes hopelessly flawed." When narrowly framed mental models create obstacles to the ethical decision-making process, we may fail to become aware that a situation has moral dimensions, or fail to attend to data, points of view, alternative solutions, and foreseeable consequences crucial to forging an ethical response.

A mental models approach to ethical decision-making

It is important to emphasize that the dangers that certain mental models pose to ethical decision-making cannot be mitigated or overcome by imagining that we could somehow free ourselves of the need for mental models altogether. Without mental models to mediate and shape our experiences, we would be incapable of having experiences at all. As Werhane writes:

The most serious problem in applied ethics, or at least in business ethics, is not that we frame experiences; it is not that these mental models are incomplete, sometimes biased, and surely parochial. The larger problem is that most of us either individually or as managers do not realize that we *are* framing, disregarding data, ignoring counterevidence, or not taking into account other points of view. (Werhane, 2007, 404)

While all experience and reflection is conditioned by our mental models, our mental models do not *determine* our thoughts and perceptions. Because our mental models are "not genetically fixed or totally locked in during early experiences," we are capable of altering, expanding, affirming, resisting, or imaginatively transforming them (Werhane *et al.*, 2011a; Werhane and Moriarty, 2009; Werhane, 1999). Indeed, practicing ethics requires this capacity to shake loose the hold that a particular mental model may have upon our thinking, so that we might become attentive to our habits of mind that disable or discourage us from posing the critical questions necessary to ethical judgment. Becoming aware that we are dependent upon particular mental models in troubling ways entails the facility and courage continually to seek out information, alternate viewpoints, and theoretical frameworks that challenge this dependence. All mental models are incomplete; those models that devolve into impediments to ethical deliberation do so when our reliance upon them encourages us to lose sight of this partiality. Mental models may become distorting to the extent that they shape experience in such a way that their framing effects are rendered unavailable to critical evaluation.

Our mental models enable particular, partial modes of experience and, thereby, organize our perception of a situation in a way that makes some thought and practices possible, while occluding others. We adopt, construct and allow habituation to these schemas because the orientations they provide are experienced as beneficial in some way. When mental models become distorted, it is often because they have become rigid and determinative. The partial perspective has come to be experienced as the whole picture, and the framing model is no longer in view. As we will see in the discussion of theoretical and practical strategies to discourage ethical failure in Chapters 6 and 7, to bring one's mental models into view often requires that we consider conflicting, opposed, or simply unfamiliar ways of orienting ourselves to the situation at hand.

It may help to shift from metaphors of pictures and (distorted) frames, to the metaphorical language of medicine. Paradoxically, if one considers that mental models impede healthy, critical ethical deliberation and action, their antidote requires *further* experimentation with mental models, which in turn may endanger the health of ethical decision-making process if they are allowed to come to dominance. Yet, like a vaccine that spurs the body's immune system into action, exposing oneself to new, unfamiliar, and even disorienting mental models can activate ethical thinking, and foster an active relationship to the construction of experience.

Risks and promises of ethical decision-making

The medical metaphor reminds us that ethical decision-making may be an uncomfortable process to the extent that it requires that we expose ourselves to unfamiliar, even conflicting, ways of seeing the situation at hand and our own roles within it. Ethical decision-making has further risks or vulnerabilities, as well. It does not result in certain or precise knowledge, but in contestable claims, as others might disagree not only with our judgment about the best course of action, but with the selection of facts, points of view, and alternative solutions that we have considered in the deliberative process. As many corporate whistleblowers can testify, choosing to act ethically may alienate the decision-maker from her or his friends and colleagues, and put the decision-maker's financial, and even physical, security in jeopardy. In an extreme example of the risks of taking ethical action in the workplace, Jeffrey Wigand claimed that, in addition to losing his job and coping with media campaigns maligning his character, his family received death threats as the result of his decision to blow the whistle on his former employer, the Brown & Williamson Tobacco Company (Brenner, 1996). In addition to the risks to security posed by others who may disagree with or feel threatened by our ethical choices, we are also exposed to accountability for the unintended consequences of our decisions when we act under the umbrella of ethics. Ethical decision-making involves acknowledging responsibility for the outcome of what we say and do, which in turn gives rise to a duty to "evaluate the implications of our decisions, to monitor and learn from the outcomes, and to modify our actions accordingly when faced with similar challenges in the future" (Hartman and DesJardins, 2008, 56–7).

However, as the discussion of impediments to ethical decision-making processes in this chapter and the next will show, the risks that ethical action may pose to one's economic security, social status, community identity, or self-esteem must be weighed against the startling evidence that the failure to challenge entrenched mindsets in a vigorous practice of ethical deliberation has been linked to moral failures that endanger our economies, social institutions, communities, and the relative autonomy that we prize as individuals.

To be reminded of the high stakes of overcoming impediments to ethical deliberation, it is instructive to return to our discussion of the famous 1960s Milgram experiments from Chapter 3. Milgram's objective was to find out why "ordinary people, simply doing their jobs, and without any particular hostility on their part, can become agents in a terrible destructive process" that "relatively few people have the resources needed to resist . . . " (Milgram, 1973, 76). Milgram's studies, and other psychological, sociological, and neurological investigations that followed in their wake have contributed significantly to our comprehension of moral failure. Neera Badhwar (2009, 268) argues that the post-war generation of studies exploring the effects of authority and peer pressure on ethical behavior has led to the fundamental, and previously unknown, discovery that "we are capable of succumbing to morally trivial situational pressures." However, the insight that the capacity for ethical action is universally vulnerable to factors unrelated to the actor's consciously and deeply-held value systems is still difficult for most of us to accept, particularly about ourselves. While each of the mental schemas raised in this chapter constitute experience in a manner that exacerbates these vulnerabilities, we begin with a discussion of mental models that constitute experience in a manner that occludes the moral dimension of situations from view, thereby thwarting the first step of ethical decision-making. We then further refine this discussion by examining ethics-impeding conceptual frameworks that disable or frustrate the second step in the ethical decision-making process: gathering information.

III. Obstacles to awareness of ethical situations

Acknowledging that a problem in our ethical decision-making structures exists is the first step in making responsible choices that reflect our personal value commitments. However, egregious moral failures in the corporate environment often follow from a managerial failure to bring ethical considerations to bear on business decisions. Consider the extent of self-preservation and denial demonstrated by the claims of Enron CEO Jeffrey Skilling and its Chairman Kenneth Lay when they claimed that they did not know of the wrong-doing taking place within their firm. The judge in that case included in his jury instructions the explanation that "knowledge can be inferred if the defendant deliberately blinded himself to the existence of a fact" (*US v. Lay*, 2006, quoted in Heffernan, 2011, 2). In the next section, we will investigate mental models that limit our ability to see facts that are right before our eyes – sometimes quite literally, as in the many examples of managers and employees who see unethical behavior take place in front of them, but do not recognize it as such. In this section, we take a step back to scrutinize the psychological biases that encourage us to obstruct or block ethics from our mental models altogether. Why might decision-makers be motivated to blind themselves not only to ethically relevant facts, but also to the relevance of ethics to their judgments of their own behavior and that of others? What psychological tendencies and contextual factors encourage us to become bystanders, rather than moral actors, in situations that call for an ethical response?

Moral self-image

When it is in our interest of self-preservation to avoid recognizing our own or those of another unethical behavior, we tend to overlook those flaws (Gino *et al.*, 2009; Moberg, 2006). This willful or motivated blindness is not so different from concluding that our own contributions to a group effort are more significant or burdensome than those of another's. Studies that show a high propensity to overclaim credit when assessing one's own role in group endeavors (Bazerman and Moore, 2008), for example, reveal that we are more aware of the sacrifice we have made or time we have taken in our efforts than the contributions of others. Similarly, we tend to justify our own behavior while judging others more harshly; we naturally understand our own motivation while do not have equivalent insight into the origins of others' behavior. In fact, research demonstrates that we all believe ourselves to be moral – even those who have demonstrated themselves to have lied or are convicted felons (Baumeister, 1998; Allison *et al.*, 1989). In maintaining this belief structure, this mental model, we construe our experience in a manner that serves to strengthen this self-perception, and remain blind to evidence that might serve to disprove it. We develop blind spots that prevent us from assessing our experience from an ethical perspective that is guided by the values that we consciously hold dear.

As the paradigm for ethical decision-making outlined previously suggests, a certain type of ignorance can account for poor ethical choices; yet that ignorance can rise to the level of willful or intentional choice when it is motivated by a desire to sustain a moral self-assessment. We make rationalizations to ourselves based on our entrenched mental models or messages that "no one will ever know," "no one is really going to be hurt," or that it was someone else who was careless; we say that we are only doing that which anyone else would do under this circumstance. Chance and Norton (2009) explain that we engage in these explanations to ourselves and to others because we do not want to be perceived as – or feel like – unethical or immoral individuals. Their research indicates that subjects routinely opt for these conclusions:

- "I read *Playboy* for the articles."
- "I'm not selfish, I just prefer not to play the Dictator game."
- "I'll pick the fat-free yogurt tomorrow."

We become skilled at such rationalizations of behavior that violates our consciously held values, because the positive self-perceptions they enable have benefits. As Chance and Norton point out, psychologists link a strong moral self-assessment with a higher sense of self-worth, and this, in turn, is correlated with lower levels of depression. In short, self-deceiving justifications allow us to do what we want, while protecting us from the "psychological cost" (2009, 17) that behavior might impose on self-assessments of moral character. However, the mental models fostered by moral self-deception carry other costs. The motivation to preserve a moral self-image encourages a reliance on distorted mental models that impede ethical considerations from view. If we become habituated to believing that we are moral, regardless of what we do (or fail to do), this self-image allows us to bypass ethical decision-making.

The Jayson Blair reporting scandal at *The New York Times* offers an example of the distorted effects of this myth at the level of corporate

culture. Over a six-month period in 2003, Blair fabricated or pla-
giarized more than thirty news stories (Mnookin, 2004). An internal
inquiry later found that "various editors and reporters [had] expressed
misgivings about Mr Blair's reporting skills, maturity and behavior
during his five-year journey from raw intern to reporter on national
news events" (Barry *et al.*, 2003, para. 7). Despite its reputation for
a strong commitment to journalistic excellence, these misgivings went
unheeded, and many of the paper's editors and Blair's colleagues were
caught unaware by the exposure of his fraudulent reporting. Werhane
and Moriarty (2009) attribute this moral failure to the widespread
belief within the corporation that such unethical behavior "couldn't
happen here." Acculturation to a high moral self-perception – a sense
that "we are *The New York Times*, after all" – generated a distorted
mental model, an ethical blind spot that hid Blair's dishonest behavior
from view.

Blind spots and mental models

Ethical blind spots prevent us from interrogating our mental models,
and therefore pose an obstacle to taking the first step toward responsible, conscientious decision-making. Moberg (2006) links these blind
spots to mental models through his concept of common perceptual
frames. He explains that these frames can create blind spots, defined
in much the same way that we define mental models: "those defects
in one's perceptual field that can cloud one's judgment, lead one to
erroneous conclusions, or provide insufficient triggers to appropriate
action" (2006, 414). However, though a significant hurdle when unac-
knowledged, Moberg explains optimistically that they can be overcome, parallel to the metaphor on which they are based; "blind spots
are similar to those that afflict drivers of motor vehicles. Once one is
aware that they exist, it is possible to develop alternative interpretive
and action strategies."

An example of an ethical blind spot in connection with others occurs
when a parent is told that her or his child has cheated in school. The
parent's first instinct may be to deny the claim and defend the child.
However, if an effort is made to review the facts involved, the evidence collected and to consider, perhaps, the pressures exerted on
the stakeholders, the correction to which Moberg refers may occur.
The parent often will engage in a more conscious focus on her or his

value structure and reach a different rational conclusion. Yet, without the recognition that ethical deliberation, rather than a presumption of morality, is called for, the parent may fail to move on from first instincts. What obstacles prevent us from moving past cognitive biases toward a high moral self-image, and a distorted moral image of others?

Situational factors may exacerbate motivated self-deception about ethical behavior. Using the vocabulary of frame theory, Moberg (2006) argues that sound moral judgment is particularly vulnerable in work organizations. In organizational settings, we tend to partition our use of moral and competency frames. When judging ourselves, we are likely to presume a positive moral assessment and, therefore, invoke competency criteria when called upon to evaluate our behavior. He refers to this tendency as a "personal ethics blind spot." Personal ethics blind spots are strengthened by mental models that assume that moral frames are "private," and therefore not appropriate to workplace judgments. The resulting dominance of competency frames in the workplace can lead managers and employees to fail to trigger moral frames when confronted with situations that call for both ethically responsible and competent resolutions.

Elizabeth Doty (2007), an organizational consultant, conducted in-depth interviews with thirty-eight business people from a broad range of professions about their negotiation of the tension between personal values and the demands of the workplace. She writes of her own experience navigating this tension while working for a luxury hotel chain. At one point, she was asked to provide attractive female staff and low-cut costumes for an all-male corporate event. After complaining to her boss privately, the request was retracted; but it left Doty with "lingering concerns":

I wasn't naïve. I told myself that ethical bumps in the road were part of the game of business. Our hotel managers sometimes secretly canceled guests' discount-rate reservations on oversold nights. I myself had concocted the "right" numbers on sales forecasts, and then convinced my boss in his staff meeting that I really believed them. For four years I'd been able to persuade myself that one had to expect such practices even in first-class operations. And it almost worked this time, too; by the final night of the annual meeting, I'd nearly stopped fuming over the costume incident. I even allowed myself to feel some pride in how well the event had come off. (para. 3)

Doty describes the trade-off between her personal unease regarding the unethical behavior in which she had participated and the pride that she felt about achieving her workplace tasks with competence as a "devil's bargain." In Moberg's terms, we might say that Doty cultivated a personal ethics blind spot by persuading herself that competency frames, rather than moral frames, were the appropriate perceptual apparatuses to utilize in the "game of business."

Personal ethics blind spots and bystander effects

Personal ethics blind spots are significantly affected by how others behave. Social psychology studies have repeatedly demonstrated that we are less likely to act if we are surrounded by other non-actors (Hudson and Bruckman, 2004; Latané and Nina, 1981; Darley and Latané, 1968). Analyzing their seminal investigations into bystander inaction, Latané and Darley (1969) proposed that, when there are multiple non-interveners observing a critical situation, individual inaction typically does not betray "apathy." Rather, each observer looks around at the reaction of others for assistance or confirmation in constructing his or her interpretation of the situation. "Until someone acts," they explain, "each person sees only other non-responding bystanders, and is likely to be influenced not to act himself." As a result, "all members may be led (or misled) by each other to define the situation as less critical than they would if alone" (p. 249). Group behavior affects individual action because we look to the behavior of others for cues to tell us which mental models to engage in a particular context. In organizational settings, this "bystander effect" serves as a deterrent to potential whistleblowers (Dozier and Miceli, 1985). When one's colleagues and managers do not appear to notice wrongdoing, or identify unethical behavior as such, it may be difficult to perceive ethical problems as existing at all.

Like all of the mental models that impede ethical decision-making, the bystander model has benefits as well as costs, and does not inherently impede responsible decision-making. Making the choice to intervene in order to prevent wrongdoing or harm can be dangerous, especially when that action is taken alone. In many urban neighborhoods with high rates of gang violence, for example, police and prosecutors face high barriers in seeking cooperative witnesses due to fear of retaliation. The National Alliance of Gang Investigators

Associations reports "the mere presence of gangs in a community . . . creat[es] a generalized fear of intimidation that hinders witness cooperation" (Anderson, 2007, 1). This generalized fear is reasonable; in Los Angeles alone, 778 cases of witness intimidation were documented over a five-year period. Typically, corporate whistleblowers are not faced with threats of physical intimidation but harassment, intimidation and job loss are real concerns. Reviewing a random sample of 200 complaints, the National Whistleblower Center found that more than half of those who chose to speak up were fired, while most of the remaining employees reported being subject to unfair disciplinary action or other forms of harassment (Brickey, 2003). Another watchdog group, the Government Accountability Project, discovered that ninety percent of whistleblowers are subject to some form of retaliation in the workplace.

In addition to reasonable concerns for self-preservation, the determination that others who are qualified or better situated can be trusted to intervene effectively might be a conscientious choice in a particular context. Trust in the others is a social value; indeed, trust is a necessary component of all social activity, and mutual trust is especially important to economic relationships (Werhane *et al.*, 2011b; Fukuyama, 1995). It would be arrogant, not to mention impossible, for each of us to claim full responsibility for all of the problems in the world, or even the workplace. Often, however, taking up the role of a bystander in a crisis is not the result of a deliberate and reasoned choice to protect oneself or to trust in others, or of an apathetic disinterest in the moral dimensions of the situation, but from a failure to perceive the situation as a crisis that calls for ethical decision-making.

The apparent inability of News Corp. Chairman Rupert Murdoch to perceive his responsibility for wrongdoing taking place within his own corporation illustrates how complex and hierarchical structures can lead the most powerful members of organization to develop mental models in which they see themselves as mere bystanders, free from accountability for the behavior of their employees. After public outrage exploded over allegations that hacking into the cell phone messages of private citizens – including the messages of a missing teenage girl who was later found murdered – was accepted practice at one of his newspapers, Murdoch was brought before Parliament and interrogated surrounding his claim that he was unaware of the malfeasance. Murdoch explained that he may have "lost sight" of the paper because it was "so small in the general frame of the company" (Hutton and Morales, 2011). Murdoch did not deem this blindness an ethical failure; instead he saw it as a justification for his assertion that, as Chairman, he bore no responsibility for the criminal activity at his paper. When asked who was responsible, Murdoch placed the blame squarely on his underlings, pointing the finger at "the people who I employed, or maybe the people they employed" (Williamson, 2011).

Significant evidence suggests that organizational hierarchy and organizational complexity can exacerbate this blindness to ethical problems. However, hierarchy within an organization does not *necessarily* impede ethical responsibility; to the contrary, a tiered division of responsibility may promote good behavior by establishing clear expectations of the rights and duties that attain to specific roles. Yet, strong role identification in a hierarchical organization risks devolution from a mental model that encourages moral responsibility to a distorting mental model that, in addition to relieving leaders like Murdoch of a sense of responsibility for their employees, also habituates employees to blindly obey superiors. Milgram (1974) proposed that the high levels of obedience to unjust orders in his studies could be explained by the participants' displacement of the responsibility of moral judgment to the experimenter. This tendency to defer moral responsibility to perceived authorities is aggravated by "chain of command" structures (Kilham and Mann, 1974). In the *Challenger* and *Columbia* disasters, discussed in Chapter 2, hierarchical leadership structures discouraged engineers from effectively communicating risk factors to managers, with deadly results.

Werhane and Moriarty (2009, 9) remind us that "[m]any managers conceive of good leadership as being primarily about motivating employees to do what they want them to do," but the truth revealed by obedience studies "is that individuals will often carry out instructions that are absurd, immoral, dangerous, or life-threatening when given by a person in authority." As Johnson (2009, 265; quoted in Tepper, 2010) writes: "Examine nearly any corporate scandal – AIG Insurance, Arthur Andersen, Enron, Health South, Sotheby's Auction House, Fannie Mae, and you'll find leaders who engaged in immoral behavior and encouraged their followers to do the same." The challenge is that hierarchical leadership models may create corporate cultures that align responsibility with the competent fulfillment of role duties, but which then also can inhibit the triggering of moral frameworks. These corporate cultures may then condition employees to be passive bystanders, rather than moral actors, and ill-prepare them to perceive ethical crises or wrongdoing as problems that call upon them to intervene.

Self-sufficiency

By definition, ethical blind spots make us doubly blind; we not only fail to perceive ethical problems and situations, but we remain unaware that that we have done so. Admitting that our view of the world is not only partial and subject to bias, but is deeply dependent upon the views of those around us – from peers and colleagues, to authority figures and even advertisers – is difficult. Although this admission is fundamental to the ethical decision-making process, it can also leave decision-makers with a sense of disempowerment. In his seminal study of American democracy in the early nineteenth-century, Alexis de Tocqueville (2000, 508) observed that democratic citizens "form the habit of thinking of themselves in isolation and imagine that their destiny is in their own hands." Today, self-sufficiency remains an exceptionally prized social value, particularly in Western societies (Markus and Kitayama, 1991). The presumption of self-sufficiency allows us to believe that we are the masters of our own circumstances, fully in control of our thoughts and actions. Acknowledging that cognitive biases and situational factors impact direct our decision-making to some extent – even any extent – can put our capacity for effective action into question, raising the concern that we may be victims of forces beyond our control. However, holding fast to the myth of self-sufficiency can be deeply ineffective and unproductive; not only do we remain vulnerable to unconscious bias and social cues, but we become complicit in our own vulnerability.

John Gaventa (1982) identified self-sufficiency preferences as an explanatory factor in his study of quiescence among certain groups of unionized coal miners in Appalachia. Despite mounting evidence that key members of the union's leadership was guilty of corruption, bribery, intimidation, the dissemination of misinformation and even murder, a few small regions continued to support the leadership against reform advocates. In fact, support of demonstrably corrupt union leaders among rank-and-file miners *increased* in these regions, while declining among much of the rest of the Appalachian mining community.

Why did some miners maintain and deepen their support for union leaders as these same leaders were increasingly revealed to be acting against the miners' professed interests? Gaventa's study of the power relationships between the union elites and the rank-and-file miners led him to theorizes that the "sense of powerlessness" generated by the historical and present-day conditions of the mine workers had led "to a greater susceptibility to the internalization of the values, beliefs, or rules of the game of the powerful as a further adaptive responses – that is, as a means of escaping the subjective condition of powerlessness, if not its objective condition" (p. 17). Without the resources to resist or exit a situation in which they had little opportunity for effective, self-directed action, the miners adapted by supporting the oppressive regime and internalizing its values, an adaptive strategy that allowed them to deny that they were victims of a campaign of manipulation and coercion.

Heffernan (2011) finds similar dynamics occurring in the wake of the discovery that a corporation had knowingly allowed its mining operation to contaminate the town of Libby, Montana with asbestos. Although a small group of locals sued the corporation, the majority of Libby residents refused to accept the truth about the contamination and actively opposed efforts to bring the extent of the harm to light. The people of Libby, Heffernan writes, are known for their stoicism: "They don't whine and they don't want to think of themselves as victims" (p. 105). However, this valorization of self-sufficiency led Libby's residents to a double tragedy. Like the Appalachian miners studied by Gaventa, they were first victimized by powerful organizations and then, in their refusal to accept the truth of their situation, they became "victims of their own blindness" (Heffernan, 2011). Unable to see their dependence on others, they unwittingly became participants in their own victimhood.

Mental models that discourage us from considering whether and how we might be dependent upon others can pose a particular danger in commerce, as studies have shown that profit-centric thinking strengthens the self-sufficiency model. Vohs, Mead, and Goode (2006) conducted experiments to test the psychological effects of economic motivation. They found that when subjects were prompted to think about money, they were more likely to prefer "to play alone, work alone and put more physical distance between themselves and a new acquaintance" (p. 1154). After playing games in which some participants were led to profit considerations and others were not, those who had been thinking about money were less likely to provide help to student confederate, donate to a charity, assist a stranger or select a leisure activity that involved other people. Vohs *et al.* term this effect a "self-sufficiency pattern," which suggests that "money evokes a view that everyone fends for him- or herself" (p. 1156). The relationship between profit-thinking and self-sufficiency preferences need not lead us to conclude that profit motivation inherently leads to unethical decisions. However, if we remain unaware of the bias toward individualism and against interdependence, which is triggered by considerations of profit, this mental model may blind us to the ethical issues at stake in our decision-making practices, double-blinding us to the fact that our self-sufficiency is merely a presumption or preference at all.

Slippery slope

Blind spots to ethical issues are easier to develop when the adoption of problematic mental models occurs over time. In other words, one is less likely to produce strong cognitive conflicts if the disengagement from deeply held moral beliefs takes place over an extended period of time. Bandura (1990) uses the term "gradualistic moral disengagement" to describe the strategy used by terror group leaders to socialize new recruits to violence. Rather than trying to persuade recruits to abandon the moral probation against the killing of civilians, terror groups tend to undermine the moral judgment of recruits gradually, first requiring only very minor criminal acts, and slowly disconnecting the recruits from all ties to non-criminal society before revealing the more extreme terror tactics of the organization. By the time new members are fully exposed to the commitment to violence, they have likely developed mental models that preserve their moral self-images by rationalizing their criminal behavior and disengaging from their previous value systems. Although we have been presenting ethical blind spots, and the moral self-assessments, bystander roles, obedience patterns, and self-sufficiency illusions that support them as obstacles to the first step in the ethical making process (awareness of an ethical issue), the failure to take this first step towards ethics may often be the culmination of long process of moral disengagement.

Questions of adaptation to gradual shifts to a model and the failure of decision-makers to notice these gradual changes over time fall under the umbrella term "change blindness" (Gino *et al.*, 2009; Gino and Bazerman, 2006). Historically, we have recognized both the inherent risks involved in gradual shifts – also referred to as a slippery slope – as well as the non-trivial implications of awareness or preparedness for these shifts in connection with integrity and value consistency. Bazerman and Chugh (2005) offer the example of the Arthur Andersen auditors who did not notice the ethical depths to which Enron had fallen in terms of its decisions. Other stumbling blocks are less intellectual or cognitive than they are a question of motivation and willpower. As author John Grisham explained in his book *Rainmaker*, "Every lawyer, at least once in every case, feels himself crossing a line he doesn't really mean to cross. It just happens." Arguably, this sensation applies to decision-makers well beyond the legal profession; sometimes it is simply easier to do the *wrong thing*. Unfortunately, we do not always draw the lines for appropriate behavior in advance and, even when we do, they are not always crystal clear. As Grisham suggests, it is often easy to do a little thing that crosses the line, and the next time it is easier, and the next easier still. One day, you find yourself much further over your ethical line than you thought you would ever be. You may find yourself failing to see that you are called upon to engage ethics in your decision-making at all.

IV. Obstacles to gathering facts relevant to ethical considerations

If our mental models are disengaged from moral frames altogether and the first step in the process of ethical decision-making is bypassed, a likely byproduct will be a failure to take the second step: to seek out salient information. The information-gathering stage also may be impeded by problematic moral frameworks or by conceptual schemas that lack a moral dimension. When our mental models – regardless of their moral content – reassure us that our picture is complete and that we have no need to seek out additional facts, when they block relevant information from our perceptual field, or when they prompt us to disregard significant information that conflicts with their framework, they thereby distort our assessment of whether we have adequate knowledge. In this section, we examine situational and cognitive factors that are particularly threatening to the capacity to attend to, and seek out, critical information in decision-making settings.

Ideological worldviews

The term "ideologue" often is used pejoratively to refer not only to a deep conviction in the explanatory power of a particular model, theory, or systems of ideas, but also to a conviction that will not admit the possibility of facts or experiences that challenge the validity of the belief system. The political theorist Hannah Arendt described ideologies as those "'isms' which, to the satisfaction of their adherents, can explain everything and every occurrence by deducing it from a single premise" (Arendt, 1951, cited in 1973, 468). Referring to ideological believers in the "domino theory" that drove U.S. foreign policy during much of the Cold War period, she writes, "[t]hey needed no facts, no information; they had a 'theory,' and all data that did not fit were denied or ignored" (Arendt, 1969, cited in 1972, 39). When we become dogmatic in our conviction that a particular theory or belief system is capable of accurately accounting for any and all real-world possibilities, the need for an open and critical fact-gathering process is blunted. Rather than examining and testing our ideas to see if they correspond to factual reality, ideologues test the validity of the facts by determining whether they fit into the picture of the world generated by their preferred system of ideas.

Typically, mental models are not ideological, in Arendt's sense of the term. Most of us invoke plural, diverse and even conflicting mental models to constitute our perceptions across and within particular domains of experience, rather than allowing a particular theoretical framework or system of ideas to dominate our worldview. Ideologues provide an example of an extreme form of mental modeling in which experiences that cannot be fitted within a preconceived worldview or theory are ignored or rejected. Their extremism serves to remind us of the dangers of mistaking mental models, which are inherently partial and incomplete, for reality itself. Consider Reverend Harold Camping's widely publicized (and just as widely dismissed) prediction that the Rapture would occur on May 21, 2011, launching an earth-bound judgment day. When the date arrived with no accompanying apocalypse, Camping admitted to being "flabbergasted" (Cane, 2011). This was not the first time that Camping's prophesies had failed to materialize. A prediction that scheduled the end of the world for 1994 had also proven inaccurate, a disappointment that he attributed to calculation error (James, 2011). Subsequent to the missed 2011 Rapture event, Camping proclaimed a new doomsday date six months down the line (McKinley, 2011). Evidently, even repeated exposure to facts that contradicted his ideology did not shake his conviction in its truth or in his own ability to distinguish ideology from other details.

To many of us, Camping's consistent refusal to accept that his system of ideas had been proven false appears to lack logic. However, Margaret Heffernan (2011, 57) reminds us that peculiar ideas, such as those of apocalyptic prophets, are not the only objects of ideological commitment, "[W]hen ideas are widely held, they don't stand out as much; they can even become the norm. We may not see them as ideology and we don't see their proponents as zealots. But appearances can be deceptive." Heffernan raises Fed Chairman Alan Greenspan's zealous advocacy for market deregulation as an example of *ideology hidden in plain sight*. She is not alone. The financial crises in 2008 led many commentators to charge that Greenspan's ideological commitment to deregulation had contributed to the collapse of the mortgage market (Schneiderman, 2011; Suttell, 2011; "*Greenspan Admits...*", 2008). Testifying before Congress in October of 2008, Greenspan was pressed to consider whether his economic philosophy had prevented him from confronting and assessing important facts:

Representative Henry Waxman (CA): "You had the authority to prevent irresponsible lending practices that led to the subprime mortgage crisis. You were advised to do so by many others and now our whole economy is paying the price. Do you feel that your ideology pushed you to make decisions that you wish you had not made?"

Greenspan: "...Yes. I've found a flaw. I don't know how significant or permanent it is. But I've been very distressed by that fact..."

Waxman: "You found a flaw in the reality."

Greenspan: "...[A] flaw in the model that I perceived as the critical functioning structure that defines how the world works, so to speak."

Waxman: "In other words, you found that your view of the world, your ideology was not right. It was not working."

Greenspan: "Precisely. That's precisely the reason I was shocked, because I had been going for 40 years or more with very considerable evidence that it was working exceptionally well." (*Greenspan Says...*, 2008)

Under pressure, Greenspan admitted that he adhered to his ideology when faced with contrary views and conflicting evidence. Yet, to the consternation of his critics, Greenspan's "shock" and "distress" were caused by the discovery of an apparent "flaw" in his model of reality, not by his ethical failure; he did not accept responsibility for his role in promoting this model when it diverged from readily available facts, nor was it evident that he was finally willing to alter his fundamental worldview. As Heffernan (2011, 63) writes, "he held fast to his big idea. It wasn't wrong, it was just flawed" (see also Haverston, 2010; Crutsinger and Gordon, 2008).

Not just ideologists: Bounded awareness

Few people are as dogmatically committed to single worldview as Camping or Greenspan. However, the devolution of mental models into obstacles that prevent challenging, conflicting, or novel information from coming to view is not limited to ideologues. To a less extreme degree, this devolution is an ever-present risk that arises from the "bounded awareness" that characterizes human perception. Gino, Moore, and Bazerman (2009) define bounded awareness as a "systematic pattern of cognition that prevents people from noticing or focusing on useful, observable, and relevant data," a parallel, though arguably more methodical, conception of Senge (1990) and Werhane's (1999) analyses of mental models. Gino *et al.* explain that we, as humans, are bound by these patterns to make implicit choices about whether we attend to certain information in our environment and ignore other information. Because these choices are based on omissions, they necessarily embody errors (Bazerman and Chugh, 2005), which we illustrated in Chapter 2.

Certainly, when we intentionally identify and focus on mental models as significant impediments to ethical decision-making, they lose their power to serve as obstacles to fact gathering. However, we are not always aware of the existence or embedded strength of the models, nor are we always attentive to the limits of our attention and awareness when our decision-making skills are most challenged. The most powerful illustrations of this conclusion are often found in the most simple of examples, such as the moonwalking bear or the movie perception tests (Simons, 2010; Veenendaal, 2008; Levin and Simons, 1997). Based on a research stream exploring inattentional blindness that began in 1992 by Mack and Rock (1998) and on experiments carried out by Simons and Chabris (1999), the advertising company Altogether Digital created a massive awareness campaign for the City of London. The campaign involved a one-minute video of eight basketball players passing two balls; four of the players were wearing white shirts and four were wearing black shirts. The voiceover asked viewers to count the number of passes made by the team in white. On first viewing, practically no one notices a man dressed in a brown bear costume moon-walking directly through the middle of the game. We have had countless personal experiences using this particular video and the experience is replicated consistently. When directed to perform a task (counting passes), humans naturally have a tendency to seek success on that task. If something begins to distract us, we do not surrender to the distraction; instead we steel ourselves against it, focusing ever more strongly on the job at hand.

If the "distraction" happens to be, for instance, the possibility of unethical conduct, unfortunately, we may suffer from a focusing failure where the data included in our circle of vision or awareness is simply insufficient to make an effective – or ethical – decision. A recent study of inattentional blindness (Chabris *et al.*, 2011) replicated the conditions of a real-world case in which a police officer was charged with perjury for claiming that he failed to see a brutal assault taking place within his line of vision as he ran by the assault in pursuit of a suspect. Not only did the study's results show that inattentional blindness provided a possible explanation for the officer's failure, but the experimenters also demonstrated that manipulating attentional load affected subjects' perception. In one test variation, subjects were divided into two groups. All subjects were asked to run after a confederate for a fixed distance, but one group was asked to perform a complex counting task that required much attention while in pursuit while the other group was not. Half of the low-attentional load group failed to notice a staged three-person fight taking place just a few feet off of their route as they ran. In the high-attentional load group, the failure rate increased to 72 percent. When our attentional load is high, the limitations on our awareness are intensified. The test subjects, and perhaps the police officer in the case that motivated the research, failed to stop a brutal assault that took place right before their eyes because, quite simply, they were too busy to see it.

Of course, bounded awareness often enables concentrated focus (often a valued quality), in addition to inattentional blindness and focusing failures. It is neither possible nor desirable to focus equal attention on every object within our perceptual field. Selective attention allows us to adjudicate between relevant and irrelevant information, a process that often occurs below the register of conscious awareness. Returning to the basketball study, it is important to note that, if the viewer intentionally focuses on the bear – in other words, watches the sequence a second time and maintains a keen eye for the distraction – of course, the moon-walking bear is clearly visible. However, almost all of these returning viewers fail to focus during repeat screenings on the number of passes made by the team in white. Accordingly, while the returning viewer is appropriately aware of any new element that crosses her or his line of vision, this viewer often is unable to maintain sufficiently detailed focus to continue to "get the job done," as directed by the voiceover, or even to remember the number of passes from prior screenings.

However, the positive effects of bounded awareness – the selective attention that allows us to "get the job done" – can devolve into distorted perceptions when we do not acknowledge and account for the trade-offs that concentrated focus demands from our cognition. Chugh and Bazerman (2007) warn that the consequences of focusing failures can be severe. They offer the examples of an airplane pilot who might pay too much attention to controls and miss another plane in the air as a result, or the driver who is distracted from challenges in traffic by a ringing cell phone. Focusing failures can be exacerbated by mental models that tell us that we can multi-task, or that we have adapted to new technology; but instead we see that this same technology has created a business pace that, while both breathtaking and awe inspiring, also has left in its wake anxiety, apprehension and fear (Suri *et al.*, 2003, 516; Wilfong, 2006; Karavidas *et al.*, 2005; Matanda *et al.*, 2004). The bounded character of human awareness makes focus possible; but, when we are unwilling or unable to acknowledge that we gain focusing depth at the cost of perceptual breadth, we invite focusing failures. We believe we are seeing the "whole picture" when we are not and, as a result, we may fail to see or seek out crucial information.

Bounded awareness, bounded ethicality

Bounded awareness, when it results in inattentional blindness and focusing failures, can lower employee productivity and cause errors; it can also undermine ethical awareness. The first point may seem intuitive, but cognitive bias studies are uncovering new arenas in which the limits of human attention are responsible for performance problems in business. In the securities markets, for example, researchers have demonstrated that certain market abnormalities – underreactions to significant earnings reports, for example – can be explained by the "investor distraction hypothesis." When investors are distracted by extraneous information on a high news day (Hirshleifer *et al.*, 2009), or by the thoughts of weekend plans on Fridays (Dellavigna and Pollet, 2009), they are slower to notice and react to critical reports. When we consider that even the day of the week can have a measurable impact on the likelihood of focusing failures, it should come as little surprise that more extreme situational factors like fatigue, sleep deprivation and information overload sharply impair our cognitive capacities. However, these factors do not only make us more likely to overlook or misjudge the significance of salient information; they also discourage us from thinking about ethics altogether. Bazerman and Moore (2008) term this phenomenon "bounded ethicality." Just as are not aware of the unconscious processes that prevent us from seeing the moonwalking bear in the basketball game, or a crime taking place when we are distracted by a high-attentional task, we may also be unaware of having violated our own standards of ethical behavior; we may make bad decisions without realizing that we have done so.

In practice, bounded awareness and bounded ethicality are often deeply intertwined. For example, working excessive hours not only undermines the "bottom line" by damaging employee productivity; overwork and fatigue are also responsible for a broad range of unethical outcomes in the workplace, including employee health problems, impaired judgments that affect public safety, and spillover effects of employee exhaustion on non-employees (Dembe, 2009). This spillover effect can be seen in the harm to patients that has been attributed to overworked medical interns. A study by the Harvard Work Hours, Health and Safety Group compared the error incident rate of interns working on a traditional schedule, in which every third shift is a twenty-four-hour "on call" shift, with the error rate of interns following a less-intensive schedule. The overworked interns were found to have committed 35.9 percent more serious medical errors than their less-fatigued colleagues (Landrigan *et al.*, 2004).

In Chapter 2, we examined several operative mindsets that contributed to poor judgment exercised by key decision-makers at NASA, resulting in the *Challenger* disaster. An additional contributing factor may have been sleep deprivation and fatigue caused by overwork. Indeed, according to a committee of scientists examining the effects of sleep-related issues on public safety, fatigue problems were significantly involved in *Challenger*, Chernobyl and Three Mile Island disasters (Mitler *et al.*, 1988). What is interesting in the *Columbia* disaster was not merely sleep deprivation, but that those engineers and managers had forgotten the history of the *Challenger* and how their "need to launch" and neglect of signs of fatigue among their team members led to that explosion. Mental models that valorize long work hours as a proxy for productivity ignore more than 100 years of research linking fatigue to decreased employee output (Spurgeon *et al.*, 1997) and unethical working conditions (Dembe, 2009). Corporate cultures that encourage such mental models make their companies vulnerable to moral failures, as well as higher error rates and focusing failures.

Might it be true that when our cognitive capacities are pushed to their limits by overwork, sensory overload, cognitive dissonance or fatigue, the first ability we lose is our capacity for ethical decision-making (Heffernan, 2011)? Milgram (1970) proposes that the relatively lower rate of social responsibility amongst city dwellers – their demonstrably higher levels of bystander inaction in crises and lower rates of helpfulness when approached by strangers, for example – could be explained by the concept of "overload." Overload refers to "the inability of a system to process inputs from the environment because there are too many inputs for the system to cope with, or because successive inputs come so fast that input A cannot be processed when input B is presented" (p. 1462). In response to input overloads, city dwellers gradually adopt adaptive strategies – we would say, mental models – that allow them to unconsciously filter out most of their sensory field, most importantly, the strategic norm of non-involvement.

Strategic adaptation to urban non-involvement norms offer an explanation for the thirty-eight New Yorkers who admitted to having seen Catherine Genovese beaten to death in the street, yet failing to intervene – the 1964 case that first motivated researchers to investigate bystander effects (Hudson and Bruckman, 2004). But cognitive overload and the moral disengagement that it encourages might also explain the failure of so many other neighbors and passers-by to notice the brutal crime taking place at all. Just as it is possible that the police officer discussed earlier failed to notice a crime taking place as he focused on pursuing a suspect, these New Yorkers might have been too overloaded to be aware of and, as a result, too overloaded to care about violations of their most deeply held values. In this sense, the first and second steps – and indeed, as we will see, all of the steps – of the ethical-decision making process are highly interdependent. Mental models that distort our perception of the facts – from dogmatic belief in the validity of ideologies at one extreme, to models that tell us that our competency is unaffected by Friday afternoon day-dreaming or multi-tasking, at the other – may blind us to the unethical behavior of ourselves or others, just as mental models that tell us that we need not consider ethics at all are likely to discourage us from seeing unexpected data or seeking out additional information.

V. Conclusion

We began the preceding analysis with the suggestion that a broad, five-step model provides a productive conceptual structure to describe the process of ethical decision-making, and proposed that many ethical failures occur when the various stages of this process are blocked, tainted or distorted by problematic mindsets, or mental models. We then identified an array of mental models that frustrate the first two steps of responsible decision-making by rendering decision-makers blind to the ethical dimension of a choice context, or to potentially relevant data. An important feature of these distorting mindsets is that, although they tend to generate false or overly-narrow interpretations, it is difficult, if not impossible, to imagine that they might be eradicated, once and for all, by even the most responsible and conscientious decision-maker. We cannot categorically deny that, for example, the role of the bystander might be a wise choice in some contexts, or refusing to acknowledge that striving for self-sufficiency, under some conditions, might provide a path toward ethical action.

Recognizing the pressure on decision-makers to perceive reality in such a way as to avoid taking responsibility, and acknowledging that these perceptions are not easily dismissed as false or mistaken, are not means by which to excuse the possibility of a resulting unethical decision. To the contrary, by accepting that human ethicality is vulnerable to external factors, such as sensory overload or the absence of witnesses to our behavior, and internal biases, such as the desire to be seen by oneself and others as moral or self-sufficient, we become more likely to recognize the partiality of the conceptual apparatuses that we construct to frame our perceptions.

In the next chapter, we will turn to the final three steps in the ethical decision-making model – moving beyond awareness of context and toward the critical analysis that encourages action, or to the contrary, decision surrounding inaction, in order to identify mental models that thwart their effective execution. Again, we will find that it is neither possible nor desirable fully to rid ourselves of mental models that, when left below the register of conscious awareness and out of range of critical interrogation, often become impediments to imaginative, critical reflection regarding alternative solutions, the potential impact of decision possibilities on others, and effective ethical action.

However, as we discuss in greater detail in Chapters 6 and 7, where we investigate strategies that address many of the impediments raised here, overcoming the distorting effects of ethical blind spots is not only possible, but necessary if we wish to encourage effective, ethical decisions at the individual and organizational level. Strategies that work to expose the boundaries of our ethical awareness and the limits of our mental models to critical examination do not guarantee the harmony of our choices and actions with our value commitments; however, when we remain blind to the bounded character of human ethical capacities, and presume our interpretative frameworks to be complete pictures of reality, we all but guarantee ethical failure.

5 | Obstacles to ethical decision-making in impact analysis and action

I. Introduction

In this chapter, we explore the mental models that work to distort or frustrate the later steps of the ethical decision-making process outlined in Chapter 4. In that chapter, we examined the impediments to the initial steps of this model: first, becoming aware of a situation that calls for ethical choice, and second, gathering information relevant to the ethical dilemma. We now turn to the latter three stages of the ethical decision-making process, once the decision-maker identifies the ethical challenge: (3) imagining alternative solutions, (4) considering the impact of these solution possibilities on affected stakeholders, and (5) enacting a decision that accords with consciously-held values.

Most of these mental models under discussion in the following chapter, like those examined in Chapter 4, are not consciously chosen; they are forged or further entrenched below the register of individual awareness. As we discussed in Chapter 2, the mental models that frame human perception are social constructions. Many distorting perceptual frameworks, such as gender or racial stereotypes that may prevent ethical consideration of stakeholder implications, have been acquired contingently through socialization and education processes to which we, as individuals, may not have given our conscious consent. Other problematic mental models are constructed in response to features of human cognition that appear to be neurologically hardwired, such as limited attention capacities, fear of ostracism, and a bias toward familiarity. Despite our lack of control over many of the cognitive and situational factors that render us vulnerable to distorting mental models, however, we remain accountable for the interpretive frameworks that we forge in response to them, just as we remain accountable for the decisions that we make (or allow ourselves *not* to make). Our mental models condition, but do not determine, how we perceive the world; they can be revised and altered by practices that interrogate, expand or imaginatively transform habits of mind.

In Chapter 2, we proposed that this creative act of reasoning, when guided by moral concerns, is captured by the concept of moral imagination, "the ability in particular circumstances to discover and evaluate possibilities not merely determined by that circumstance, or limited by its operative mental models, or merely framed by a set of rules or rule-governed concerns" (Werhane, 1999, 93). We argued, for example, that the Ford Pinto design flaws and the *Challenger* disaster might have been avoided if managers and employees had moved beyond the narrow viewpoint provided by the dominant mental models provided by organizational cultures and role perspectives. In the Pinto case, key decision-makers failed to imagine how the Pinto's design flaws might be perceived from the point of view of Pinto owners who tended to prioritize safety concerns. The ensuing managerial judgments were fatally impoverished as a result of this deficit of moral imagination. Analyzing the causes of the *Challenger* disaster, we suggested that the failure of NASA managers and engineers to look beyond their narrow role perspectives produced distortions that marred the risk assessment process. Engineers were told to "take off your engineering hat and put on your manager hat" (*"Report..."*, Presidential Commission, 1986), rather than to interrogate the managerial viewpoint. The designated decision-makers – managers – were neither encouraged nor habituated to engage in an imaginative decision-making process that considered the ethical impact of decision alternatives from other role perspectives, such as from the risk averse mindset of the engineers. As a result, the narrow managerial mindset of the decision-makers was not challenged by alternative views and the launch proceeded. These examples illustrate the need for moral imagination when responding to ethical dilemmas, and suggest that when moral imagination is not engaged, important steps in the ethical decision-making process may be neglected.

When a conflict with ethical dimensions has been perceived, and data pertinent to the situation is at hand, the further steps for responsible decision-making involve creative, critical thinking. Our ability to discern and to assess decision possibilities beyond the limited framework of preconceived rules or immediately available conceptual rubrics is undermined by distorted mental models that prevent us from conceiving of alternatives, looking at problems from the point of view of other parties, and enacting the choices we have forged through ethical reflection. Though moral imagination is a significant requirement in all stages of ethical reflection, the obstacles identified in this chapter pose a particularly high risk of undermining its practice.

II. Obstacles to identifying alternative solutions

As we outlined in detail in the previous chapter, and briefly reviewed earlier, our formulation of an ethical decision-making process consists of intentional stages of analysis leading toward action followed by reflection. In this section, we examine potential obstacles to the third stage of ethical decision-making. After the decision-maker is aware of the ethical issue or dilemma and gathers those facts that are relevant to the decision, she or he has the tools with which to identify the array of viable alternatives by which to consider responding to the challenge. Our perception of whether moral choices are available in a given situation (or what choices we consider) is linked to our mental models. Of course, we undermine our capacity to devise ethical choices when we neglect the first and second stages of the ethical decision-making process at its onset. Mental models that discourage us from considering the ethical issues at stake and from seeking out relevant facts are unlikely to provide us with the resources to look beyond immediate or obvious possibilities in a practice of moral imagination. Yet, even when we recognize the values at stake in a situation (stage one) and we gather pertinent information (stage two), we remain susceptible to mindsets that reassure us that we are already familiar with the possibilities embedded in a new situation or that our choices are fixed in advance. As a consequence, we may be discouraged from embarking on the critical and imaginative process of exploring alternative modes of resolution.

Like many of the obstacles discussed in this and the previous chapter, the impediments to this third step in the ethical decision-making model that are explored next – avoiding the unfamiliar, trust in intuition, adherence to decision rules and deference to peers or authority figures – are common practices that are not unethical *per se*, but risk devolving into ethical impediments. When we bypass the task of identifying possible resolutions to an ethical dilemma or cede this task to others, we are also giving up some portion of responsibility for the decisions that, ultimately, we make ourselves. When this trade-off takes place below the register of conscious awareness, not only may we be blinded to ethically preferable alternatives; we also may fail to see that we are accountable for the consequences of the path we do choose.

Avoiding the unfamiliar

Our discussion of research into the bystander effect in Chapter 4 noted that the human capacity to make independent judgments is highly susceptible to the behavior of those around us. If other witnesses react to a crisis by intervening, we are more likely to act; however, if others do not intervene, we are more likely to stand by. Like the intuitive practices of pattern recognition and emotional tagging, the tendency to orient ourselves in situations of uncertainty by aligning our perception to conform to prevailing views is a cost-saving short cut. Not only do we bypass the need to analyze each situation for ourselves, we check our own reactions against those of the people around us to see if they may be in error. The other-dependence of our ethical decision-making suggests that our discernment of moral choices may be constrained if we simply adopt the interpretation of a dilemma or problem that corresponds to the dominant view of colleagues, neighbors, or peers. Accordingly, if our environment is populated with people who are much like ourselves, this homogeneity can lead to an echo effect. We may believe that we have sought out a fuller picture of the options available to us by looking beyond ourselves when, in actuality, we have further entrenched our ethical blind spots. This decision-making short cut imposes limits on the courses of action that appear viable when we are confronted with a challenge. We have discussed the sense-making nature of human perception, a phenomenon explored by Denzau and North in detail in connection with our response to uncertainty (1994). These mental models allow us to more effectively communicate with others and share learning. However, when flawed, the communicated and shared models then are perpetuated with unremitting consequences. If our decision-making contexts do not expose us to unfamiliar or conflicting perspectives, our own cognitive biases and partial perspectives are mirrored in our surroundings and risk appearing to us as if they were objective and complete.

Contrary to the common saying, psychologists have found that familiarity breeds admiration more often than contempt. An oft-cited review of over 200 studies of the topic confirms that humans display a strong bias toward familiarity and against unfamiliarity (Baumeister and Bushman, 2008; Bornstein, 1989). Litt *et al.* (2011) refer to this phenomenon as the "flight to the familiar." When exposed to pressure, their study reveals, we display a propensity to favor the familiar option over a new one even when this selection will exacerbate the pressure that we are trying to mitigate. Often this preference shapes our choices before we become aware of them. This tendency can be seen in corporate hiring practices in which "the safest bet often wins out, and in most cases that means a candidate with a background and disposition just like the CEO's. Eventually, and often unintentionally, you wind up with a company of clones" (Gill, 2005). Drawing on behavioral psychology research demonstrating that teams of a similar social background come up with less innovative solutions to problems than heterogeneous teams, Gill argues that managers undermine their hiring goals by seeking out "people cut from the same cloth"; though this is a common mental model, "such teams are far less likely to spur growth" (p. 38).

Although a flight to familiarity appears to be a self-preserving cognitive bias in humans, our capacity to modify, resist, or limit the level of discomfort that unfamiliarity provokes is influenced by our mental models, which in turn are subject to personal, historical and cultural factors. In American social life, Cass Sunstein (2009) argues, the transformations in new media and digital technologies that promised to broaden our exposure to diverse and unfamiliar points of view have worked unexpectedly in the opposite direction. As more news sources, websites, blogs and television stations have become available, the American public has displayed a proclivity to "sort themselves into enclaves in which their own views and opinions are constantly reaffirmed" (p. xii). Provided with the technologies to personalize our media to reflect our interests, we have put ourselves in danger of creating a hall of mirrors that reflects our own preferences back to us as an image of social reality. Sunstein's concern is that the establishment of homogeneous enclaves undermines two important requirements of an informed democratic citizenry: (1) the need for exposure to topics, opinions and perspectives that were not selected oneself and, (2) the need for shared experience across heterogeneous groups within society. The impediments to informed, democratic opinion-formation raised by Sunstein further elaborate the obstacles to innovative solutions that are produced when hiring practices create "a company of clones." When exposed only to confirming viewpoints, we stifle our awareness of alternative courses of action that have been rendered invisible within our current constellation of mental models. This blindness to alternative perspectives is a variation of bounded awareness; to the extent that choices we fail to see are more closely aligned with our deeply held values, this blindness is also a variation of bounded ethicality.

Why do we develop a predisposition to prefer the familiar or selective bias, if exposure to conflicting or novel perspectives is often more beneficial to problem solving? The intense discomfort that social exclusion may cause has been explored by social psychologists. One explanatory factor can be seen in experiments that look at social ostracism, which suggest that the desire to "fit in" is a strong motivator of human behavior. Being ostracized – ignored and excluded – is painful and distressing. It severs our sense of belonging and feelings of connection with others; it makes us realize that others do not value us and consequently lowers our own self-esteem; it takes away a sense of control that we think we have in our social interaction with the others; and at perhaps a deeper level, it challenges our sense of who we are as independent decision-makers (Van Beest and Williams, 2006).

When we are subjected to an unwilled breakage in our social connections, this experience threatens our sense of security at a fundamental level. Examining the neurological activity of ostracized players in an online game, researchers found that "social pain is analogous in its neurocognitive function to physical pain, alerting us when we have sustained injury to our social connections, allowing restorative measures to be taken" (Eisenberger *et al.*, 2003). Social exclusion causes more than hurt feelings; the experience of ostracism mimics physical pain in the brain, triggering self-preserving actions to bring us back into alignment with the group. Studies involving peer pressure, discussed in greater detail next, demonstrate that subjects prefer to adopt the answers of confederates, even when clearly incorrect, to being the only one to provide a correct answer (Asch, 1951). With this evidence in mind, it becomes easier to understand the obstacles that whistleblowers, like Robert Wityczak, must overcome when they lack support from their colleagues or managers in connection with internal reporting of observed wrongdoing. Wityczak, a war veteran confined to a wheelchair, testified before a congressional subcommittee about the pressure he faced while working for a defense contractor in the 1970s, prior to the passage of legislation that created heavy penalties for government contractors found guilty of submitting false claims:

In 1976, I was assigned to the purchased labor section of products support and promoted a year later. It was during this time that I continually saw mischarging of tools and fabricated parts used on other projects to the space shuttle. I reported this to the head of purchased labor. I was told by him to just do as I was told. In addition, I and the other 25 to 35 employees in my office were ordered by our supervisors to bill to the space shuttle time we had actually spent working on other projects. I did file false time cards for a while, because I was feeling pressured to keep my job and go along with peer pressure. Yet it really began to bother my conscience. I told my supervisors in late 1977 that I would no longer mischarge my time cards. They reacted angrily, calling me "anti-management," "anti-Rockwell," and a "pain in the ass." Supervisors often had me sign blank time cards, which they filled in later, often incorrectly. (*"Whistleblowers' Stories ... "*, n.d.)

Wityczak reported that he was gradually stripped of responsibility, excluded from meetings, and assigned to demeaning tasks that were physically damaging or impossible to perform from his wheelchair. Eventually, he was fired.

While Wityczak's story of moral courage in the face of intense harassment is inspiring, the other twenty-five to thirty-five employees in his office who were willing to file false time cards in order to avoid ostracism and retaliation provide evidence that the courage to speak out alone under such conditions is rare. Social connectedness and a sense of belonging are valued within interpersonal communities – whether we are referring to the workplace or other social groups. Mental models that rationalize our preference for fitting in, or for filtering our environment such that it excludes different or conflicting views, may protect us from the painful experience of social exclusion. However, the same mindsets devolve into distorted models if they bar our efforts to seek the broadest array of moral choices available in a challenging situation. Seeking out alternative solutions, we may find that we encounter only an echo chamber that reverberates our own biases back to us and strengthens the blind spots that we are attempting to overcome.

Trust in intuition: The limited value of "gut reactions"

As our discussion of fatigue and stress in Chapter 4 indicated, managers who fail to recognize the bounded character of human cognition and moral decision-making risk developing mindsets that are likely to lead to ethical failure, such as the equation of long work hours with productivity. Taking this insight further, it becomes evident that, under conditions of cognitive overload, intuitive response takes the place of mindful awareness. Despite some variation in the operative definitions across and within academic fields, scholars reviewing the literature on intuition across disciplinary boundaries found that most researchers agree that intuitive responses are rapid judgments that take place below the register of consciousness, and involve matching our experiences with "some deeply held category, pattern or feature" – that is, a mental model – that retains an emotional charge (Dane and Pratt, 2007, 37). When we are faced with a decision involving new circumstances or facts, we often examine our brain's store of past experiences to determine whether we previously have confronted similar fact patterns. If we find a match, it is our tendency to reach assumptions based on these prior experiences. In this sense, the flight to the familiar is often an intuitive reaction; without becoming consciously aware that we have done so, we match external stimuli with the negative emotional charge associated with the unrecognized or the positive emotional charge linked with familiarity. In reality, this short cut could save our lives since a fast reaction based on prior knowledge teaches us to avoid a learned danger. For instance, we learn that a red circle on an electric stovetop indicates that it is hot. On the other hand, one can imagine how the same fast reaction could lead to stereotypes or, at the very least, gross generalizations if we similarly apply them to all individuals whom we meet. Without our conscious awareness, the mental models upon which we depend to guide our intuitions shape how – or whether – we perceive the broadest array of viable choices available to us in a decision-making context. Our own unethical behavior may be obscured from view if we remain unaware that we could have acted otherwise, had we taken the time and effort to reflect on alternative courses of action.

If "bounded ethicality is exacerbated by the demands of executive life, which causes an overreliance on intuition rather than on intentional deliberation" (Tenbrunsel *et al.*, 2007; Chugh, 2004), then creating a habit or tendency toward ethical decision-making, rather than its alternative, becomes exceptionally pivotal. In order to create that habit, decision-makers need to build into their processes more time for reflection and intentional deliberation to remove the tendency for an overreliance on intuition. This conclusion is quite the opposite from a natural inclination to trust our individual "gut reactions" with regard to knowing the "right thing to do." To the contrary, one might say that our "gut" needs to get into shape before we should be relying on it in such critical matters. Recently, neurological evidence that the brain is a "pattern-recognition machine" has provided the basis for novel pedagogical strategies aimed at teaching the brain in its non-conscious capacity or, as one reporter colorfully characterized the trend, for practicing "brain calisthenics" (Carey, 2011). Implicit learning approaches are inspired by insights gained through studying highly trained experts who have gained their knowledge through practice, such as chess players, athletes, and computer programmers. Researchers found that these virtuosos were not always able to provide articulate reasons for the choices they made in their area of expertise. Their tacit knowledge was the result of experience gained over time in a purposeful manner, often by gradually increasing the complexity of their practice over time (Werhane *et al.*, 2011a). A problem for ethical decision-making, and particularly for reflecting on available choices, arises when people turn to personal intuition when they are exposed to situations that do not fit the patterns on which they have learned to rely, rather than when they are confronted with situations for which they have been extensively trained (p. 111).

Certainly, intuition may be all we have on which to rely in conditions that afford limited time and little reliable information to work from; the immediacy of non-deliberative reactions may recommend this short-cut, even for non-experts. However, intuitive judgments put us in jeopardy of relying on flawed mental models that restrict or distort how we see resolution choices. A simple example of these flawed models, where a short-cut is an unfortunate replacement for intentional deliberation, occurs when we engage in the defense of prior art, more commonly known by its explanation: "that's the way it's always been done."[1]

---

[1] A common and oft-repeated pedagogical formulation of this concept refers to a cage containing five apes, a banana on a string and a set of stairs that sits immediately below it. The story is based on research (Stephenson, 1967, cited in Galef, 1976) that, when applied to the workplace, is intended to serve as a reminder that one should question the origins of cultural practices. The story proceeds as follows:

Imagine a cage containing five apes. Inside the cage, you hang a banana on a string and place a set of stairs under it. Before long, an ape will go to the stairs and start to climb towards the banana. As soon as he touches the stairs, spray

A more complicated version of this same model exists in the form of pattern recognition caused by misleading memories. Campbell *et al.* (2009) explain that our memories can mislead our current decisions, in particular when we perceive that the present fact pattern is more similar to our prior experience than it really is. Something that seems exceptionally familiar to us makes us believe that we understand it fully when, in reality, we might not have all the information we need in order to reach the most ethical decision. Dane and Pratt (2007, 50) highlight the importance of domain expertise in intuitive managers, pointing out that "an individual who possesses expert intuition in one field or industry may not be as effective in making intuitive decisions in a field or industry that differs substantially from the environment in which the individual's cognitive schemas were developed." Although expert intuition is surely preferable to uninformed snap judgments, it is important to check claims of domain expertise with the insights of research into misleading memories. Campbell *et al.* (2009) offer the example of Brigadier General Broderick who was in charge of Homeland Security Operations in New Orleans during Hurricane Katrina. The Brigadier General opted to go home the night of the onslaught after reporting to the President that the levees were secure. He had, in fact, received multiple reports of breaches; but, he had also received reports from other sources that the levees were holding. Previously, he had been involved in Vietnam during hurricanes that looked "just like this one," and had experienced circumstances where some early reports were later found to be false alarms. The Brigadier General

all of the apes with cold water. After a while, another ape makes an attempt with the same result: all the apes are sprayed with cold water. Turn off the cold water. If, later another ape tries to climb the stairs, the other apes will try to prevent it even though no water sprays them. Now, remove one ape from the cage and replace it with a new one. The new ape sees the banana and wants to climb the stairs. To his horror, all of the other apes attack him. After another attempt and attack, he knows that if he tries to climb the stairs, he will be assaulted. Next, remove another of the original five apes and replace it with a new one. The newcomer goes to the stairs and is attacked. The previous newcomer takes part in the punishment with enthusiasm. Again, replace a third original ape with a new one. The new one makes it to the stairs and is attacked as well. Two of the four apes that beat him have no idea why they were not permitted to climb the stairs, or why they are participating in the beating of the newest ape. After replacing the fourth and fifth original apes, all the apes, which have been sprayed with cold water, have been replaced. Nevertheless, no ape ever again approaches the stairs. Why not? "Because that's the way it's always been done around here."

believed that the lesson learned was to wait for the emerging "ground truth" from a reliable source. Unfortunately, he did not have experience with a hurricane *just like the one that hit New Orleans*, in a city built below sea level.

Dick Fuld, the final CEO and Chairman of Lehman Brothers, had an analogous experience after he saved Lehman in the aftermath of the Long Term Capital Management crisis in the late 1990s. His expertise and sound judgment was needed ten years later, when he brought principles similar to those he utilized during that and the Asian Financial Crisis to bear in an economy that now suffered from a massive housing-driven credit collapse. Fuld's steadfast response might be explained not only by Campbell *et al.*'s (2009) concept of pattern recognition, but also by their concept of emotional tagging, a cognitive process that links emotions to the experiences that are stored in our memories. It is that emotional information – rather than intentional deliberation – that directs us to pay attention to something or not, or what action to take. Applying this concept, one could interpret Fuld's refusal to make certain decisions that would have saved Lehman Brothers from bankruptcy as based on emotional anchors in Lehman rather than the most reflective, wide-ranging analysis of alternatives (Plumb and Wilchins, 2008). Again, as with pattern recognition, emotional tagging is often a decision-making short cut that could teach us to avoid a learned danger or remind us of an emotional attachment to a prior judgment. However, because the tag is most often operative beneath the register of conscious awareness, it is hard to measure and check its influence at the time we are assessing options in a decision-making context.

Although we are capable of honing and training intuitive judgment in particular areas with effort, without this effort we are liable to rely on familiar patterns and affectively charged memories that may mislead us into a misleading or overly constrained perception of problems. Confident that we classified the situation correctly, we do not seek out ethical alternatives that we otherwise might have discovered through imaginative, deliberate reflection in response to the particular fact pattern at hand.

Adherence to decision rules: Cognitive release

Overreliance on intuition is not the only short cut that restricts our capacity conscientiously to formulate alternative means of resolution to ethical problems. Often, decision rules work to reassure us that alternatives to rule choices are not available. For example, assume you are a business manager who needs to terminate a worker in order to reduce costs. Of course, your first thought may be to uncover alternative means by which to cut costs instead of firing someone; however, assume for the moment that reducing the workforce is the only viable possibility. The question now becomes how to determine whom to fire. There are a number of ways to reach this decision; but, it may be easiest and offer the least amount of conflict to follow a decision rule. You might opt to terminate the last person you hired, explaining, "I can't help it; it must be done, last in/first out, I have no choice. . . ." Using a simple decision rule might *appear* to relieve us of personal accountability for the decision since we could argue that we did not "make" the decision – the *rule* required that the decision to be made, even if it may not be the best possible decision.

Similarly, it may be tempting to limit responsibility for coming up with solutions to the satisfaction of minimum decision criteria, otherwise known as "satisficing." We limit our alternatives to those that will suffice, the ones that people can live with, even if they might not be the best. Imagine a committee at work that needs to make a decision. They spend hours arriving at a result and finally reach agreement. At that point it is unlikely that someone will stand up and say, "Whoa, wait a minute, let's spend another couple of hours and figure out a *better* answer!" The very fact that a decision was reached by consensus can convince everyone involved that it must be the most reasonable decision, and obstruct efforts to seek out options that resonate more fully with the value commitments of those involved and affected by the decision.

If we examine the paramount obstructions to ethical decision-making, in due time, we must confront the question of the abandonment or surrender of individual accountability. We engage in this cognitive release when we rely on a decision rule or minimum decision criteria to resolve a conflict because it allows us to point to the rule as the "responsible party," rather than the rule follower (ourselves) as the source of the decision, and therefore the source of the resulting harm to another. To return to our earlier example, the mental models that assure business managers that no other choice is available but to fire the last hired employee release them from the cognitive dissonance that might otherwise be imposed by their actions; yet, the harm to employees is not lessened. Taking responsibility for the decision, rather than casting oneself as passive rule-follower, would likely induce you, as the manager, to seek out alternative solutions that are more strongly aligned with your value commitments. If following this decision rule still appears to be the most ethically responsible choice after careful reflection and consideration of other possibilities, you will be more likely to take responsibility for the consequences of your choice, and enact the policy in a manner that makes every effort to provide the fired employee with resources to move forward. Deflecting accountability by treating decision rules as if they compel our behavior, we allow these rules to occlude moral choices from view, by structuring our choices in advance of decision-making practices.

Deference to peers or authority figures: Cognitive release in obedience and conformity

The cognitive release made possible by ceding the responsibility for decision-making to decision rules is motivated by self-preservation since, within the framework of the mental models we rely on to justify our rule-following, not only does the rule inflict the injury but, logically, responsibility is deferred to the authority behind the rule. In this sense, cognitive release from individual accountability also arises from casting the *source* of the decision rule as responsible, consciously or unconsciously. Again, the effect of this deferral is to constrain the decision-maker's perception of available choices, and to undermine his or her sense of accountability for the eventual decision. Recall Moberg's (2006) explanation of blind spots as defects that can cloud one's judgment or provide insufficient triggers to appropriate action and consider how peer pressure, for instance, may create blind spots that prevent us from realizing that moral choices exist. The same crowd mentality that may encourage groups of teenage girls to share a seemingly innocuous style sense can translate into a less innocuous pressure towards inappropriate group norms such as ostracizing outsiders or pressure towards drug-use (Kobus and Henry, 2010; Dielman, 1987).

Peer pressure also exists in our professional environments, both because we want to "fit in" and to achieve success in our organizations, and because our *actual* thinking is influenced by our peers. We feel as if our disagreement means that we might be wrong. Accordingly, we either modify our mindsets and models to fit our environments, or we listen specifically for the evidence that supports this new way of thinking until our models slowly change on their own. The Asch (1955, 1951) conformity experiments demonstrated this paradigm through what subjects were led to believe was a vision test. When asked a number of questions about the length of three lines, three confederates in the experiment offered incorrect answers. The lone subject participant, questioning her or his (in fact, correct) perception, tended to conform and affirm the misinformed answers provided by the confederates (Asch, 1951). Significantly, in variations in which just one confederate defected and agreed with the subject, the percentage of subject participants who conformed to the majority was significantly reduced. As we discuss in greater detail next, the desire to belong – and the fear of being ostracized and excluded – explains why we tend to be strongly invested in mental models that discourage us from standing out from the crowd.

When conforming participants were debriefed following the Asch experiments, they attributed their conformity to their own qualities or traits, a "general deficiency in themselves, which at all costs they must hide. On this basis they desperately tried to merge with the majority, not realizing the longer-range consequences to themselves. All the yielding subjects underestimated the frequency with which they conformed" (Asch, 1955, 33). For our purposes, what is most striking about the behavior of the Asch subjects is their unconscious shift from identifying the correct answer to conforming to the incorrect answer provided by the confederates. The subjects adjusted their perception of the available answers, reducing the choice structure to include only that answer provided by the others and eliminating the option of selecting the answer that may have initially seemed more plausible.

Though later seeing their behavior as motivated by a self-preserving fear of being exposed to their peers as deficient in some way, Asch's conforming subjects were unaware of this fear during the experiment. While their choice perception was being influenced unconsciously by the answers of the confederates, the subjects consciously believed that they had decided that the conforming answer was the right one on their own accord. Recently, neurologists have studied the alterations of brain activity in volunteers as they underwent a modified form of the Asch experiment (Berns *et al.*, 2005; cf. Heffernan, 2011). They discovered that the areas in the prefrontal cortex associated with conscious decision-making were inactive as subjects adopted the answers provided by their peers, while the regions of the brain responsible for perception were activated. When we conform to the views of others, it turns out that we are quite literally ceding our decision-making practice to others and, at the same time, unconsciously altering our very perception of the situation in order to release ourselves from the cognitive dissonance that might arise were we to admit to our conforming behavior.

III. Obstacles to considering impacted stakeholders

In the following section, we examine mental models that impede the fourth stage of the ethical decision-making process. Having identified an ethical issue, gathered relevant facts and investigated alternative possible resolutions, the ethical decision-maker now considers how these alternatives might impact various stakeholders. It is particularly crucial to examine available options from the vantage point of others since their consequences may have been rendered invisible by the partial outlook of the decision-maker. As we have emphasized, the mental models that condition our experience and perception are inherently partial and incomplete. While it is impossible to achieve a "complete" picture that accounts for *all* of the facts and values relevant to a particular decision-making context for this reason, ethical decision-making processes involve a conscious effort to acknowledge our partiality and biases, and to seek out inputs that enable a wider view. Conversely, failing to consider the potential outcomes of decision options from the point of view of others puts managers and organizations at risk of creating or strengthening ethical blind spots with dire consequences.

Reflecting upon the impact that a potential action may have on an individual or group requires a deliberate effort to imagine what the decision context looks like from the affected party's perspective. We begin by revisiting several mental models discussed earlier in the chapter in relation to other steps in the ethical-decision making process, in order to draw out the dangers that they pose to our ability to seek out and to value the input of others when assessing decision alternatives. We then turn to an examination of confirmation heuristics, stereotyping and dehumanization, three practices that tend to reinforce – rather than challenge and mitigate – the biases and distortions inherent in human perception. When we neglect voices that challenge our preconceptions, rely upon unexamined stereotypes of groups, or engage in discourses that encourage blindness to the humanity of those affected by our decisions, we hinder our ability to take other perspectives into consideration and therefore may not make the most ethical decisions. Though confirmation heuristics, stereotyping assumptions and dehumanizing strategies work to discourage consideration of other vantage points, and therefore may undermine *any or all* of the stages in an ethical decision-making process, we address them within this section because of their particularly virulent effects upon the moral imagination necessary for responsible consideration of affected stakeholders.

Undervaluing the input of others

Many of the problematic mental models identified in this and the preceding chapter in relation to other decision-making stages also discourage ethical consideration of the consequences of our choices upon impacted stakeholders. For example, the presumption of self-sufficiency discussed in Chapter 4 denies the partiality and bias inherent in each of our particular constellations of mental models. As we noted, the presumption that our perspectives, opinions and viewpoints are formed autonomously, unaffected by our peers, colleagues and the cultures to which we belong, can be comforting and even empowering within certain contexts. However, when they are not interrogated, self-sufficiency assumptions may blind us to the many ways in which our cognitions and intuitions are inherently partial and, as well, deeply vulnerable to situational factors. Also in Chapter 4, we identified the human tendency toward high moral self-assessment as an obstacle to ethical decision-making. Though an uncritical belief in one's moral self-worth hold the promise of utilitarian benefits for individual happiness, this mental model is ethically dangerous when it produces a personal ethics blind spot, discouraging consideration of viewpoints that challenge or conflict with this assessment. One of the means by which to protect against these decision risks is to ensure that decision-makers seek input from others in their decision processes. Input – *any* other input – is likely to be a positive factor since individuals collectively can possess and utilize more information than any single person and, through effective filters, we learn to discriminate between useful information and that which does not help us to make better decisions. However, when we rely upon mental models that deny the beneficial effects that others have on our perceptions, or deny that our judgments are vulnerable to bias motivations, we shore up the narrow boundaries of our ethical viewpoints precisely when we should be seeking to enlarge them. In order to broaden our perspectives to include consideration of how our decisions might impact others, we must admit that our individual or personal picture is incomplete and may be in need of revision.

In our examination of obstacles to the first three stages of the ethical decision-making model, we have focused much of our attention on the motivations that often drive us to adopt mental models that distort our perception of our own ethical behavior. However, similar motivations may lead us to a distorted view of the behavior of others as well. Studies of peer pressure and obedience to authority demonstrate that we tend to overlook our own ethical failures if this willful blindness supports our deeply held self-conceptions, or if it preserves our interest in avoiding ostracism. When ceding moral choice, whether to an authority figure, a peer group or a decision rule, we are also likely to develop distorted view of the value of input from parties who challenge our relationship to the entity to whom we have granted decision-making power with or without our conscious awareness. Milgram notes that those subjects who submitted to the authority figure were likely to perceive the learner as "an unpleasant obstacle interfering with the attainment of a satisfying relationship with the experimenter," a framing that undermined the moral relevance of the learner's cries for help (1974, 144–5).

The cognitive release from responsibility enabled by obedience, conformity and blind rule-following does not only make us vulnerable to distorted views of our own behavior, but also creates an investment in devaluing or distorting voices that might recall us to individual accountability. Corporate malfeasance often goes unnoticed or unreported by employees and managers because of pressures to obey, conform or to blindly follow unethical norms within the organization's culture. However, at other times, efforts by whistleblowers to bring ethical violations to light are ignored or silenced by agencies or individuals that are unwilling or unable to recognize the value of their input. Successful whistleblowers, like Cynthia Cooper, and employees who cave to organizational pressures, like Betty Vinson, are crucial to the study of ethical behavior in business settings. In Chapter 3, we discussed the cases of Cooper and Vinson in the context of the pressure to obey superiors; though both women identified unethical accounting practices at WorldCom, Cooper exposed the fraud while

Vinson, despite her misgivings, continued to do as she was told. However, equally instructive are the stories of whistleblowers like Harry Markopolos who failed, not because of a lack of moral courage on their part, but because no one was willing to consider the possible validity of a dissenting voice. Harry Markopolos

... began contacting the SEC at the beginning of the decade to warn that Madoff was a fraud. He sent detailed memos, listing dozens of red flags, laying out a road map of instructions for SEC investigators to follow, even listing contacts and phone numbers of Wall Street experts whom he said would confirm his findings. (Chernoff, 2009)

In testimony before Congress, he accused the SEC of being "captive to the industry it regulates and... afraid of bringing big cases against the largest most powerful firms" (Chernoff, 2009).

Confirmation heuristics

When we seek out only that information that serves to reinforce our preconceptions, while neglecting conflicting information, we engage in a common cognitive bias referred to as a "confirmation heuristic" (Bazerman and Moore, 2008). Confirmation heuristics, like many of the mental models explored in this chapter, are useful cognitive shortcuts that are often necessary to effective human functioning. However, when applied to judgments of others, confirmation heuristics can block access to the points of view of stakeholders who may be impacted by our decisions, or who may provide us with resources with which to more fully consider the consequences of our choices. Bazerman and Moore (2008) propose that the phenomena of over-claiming credit for individual contributions to group work is symptomatic of the bounded character of human ethicality, a concept we discussed in Chapter 4. Reviewing evidence that demonstrates over-claiming across various social arenas – within households, academia and athletics, for example – the authors conclude that "[e]ven honest people believe that they contribute more to an enterprise than they actually do" (p. 124). Assessing our contribution to a group enterprise from our own vantage point, without interrogating our assessment from the imagined or actual perspective of other participants, "even honest people" are prone to a distorted estimation of the value of other people's contributions, to the detriment of productive working relationships.

To illustrate the obstacles to ethical decision-making presented by confirmation biases, recall our hypothetical example of a parent of a child accused of cheating from Chapter 4. While the parent's first impulse may be to deny an accusation that is in conflict with the preferred image of the child's moral character, a different or better-reasoned position might result from considering the situation from the perspective of other stakeholders. A 2010 survey of high school students conducted by a Rutgers Business School professor found that 95 percent admitted to having engaged in "some form of cheating, whether it was on a test, plagiarism or copying homework" (Meyer, 2010). How might this climate affect a teacher's response to perceived cheating, or a student's conception of what does or does not count as academic dishonesty? Reflection on the evidence that cheating is increasingly accepted among students in today's classrooms, and increasingly difficult for educators to detect with the rising use of digital technologies and Internet resource, might lead the parent to a deeper understanding of the behavior of both the accused and accuser. Similarly, the parent might consider the recent scandal in the Atlanta public school system, which revealed "unethical behavior across the board" in a cheating culture in which teachers, principals and superintendents engaged in a massive effort to falsify standardized test scores and potential whistleblowers were intimidated into silence (Vogell, 2011). Imagining the pressures on many stakeholders groups to produce high test scores at any cost in order to secure federal funding might lead the parent to investigate the context of the accusation before coming to a conclusion. Such considerations need not excuse or justify unethical behavior on the part of students or educators, if evidence is discovered to support such charges. To the contrary, the parent of a child accused of cheating within this organizational culture might discover reasons to hold multiple actors accountable. Examining the situation from the perspective of diverse stakeholders could lead the parent to decision possibilities that extend beyond the choice to defend or punish the child, such as seeking to change public policy through local school board participation or altered voting behavior in state or national elections. Yet, if the parent does not move beyond the initial impulse to deny evidence that conflicts with the presumption that one's child is morally unassailable, the deeper ethical dimensions of the situation are likely to be neglected.

Stereotyping short cuts: Memories can be misleading

Confirmation heuristics share much in common with the cognitive practices of pattern recognition and emotional tagging (Campbell *et al.*, 2009) that, as we argued earlier in relation to intuition, often contribute to the production of useful mental models. To recall a simple example from this previous discussion, when we learn that a red circle on an electric stove top indicates that it is hot we are well-served by mental models that frame our perception of objects that resemble the hot stovetop in terms of danger. The quick reaction that is enabled by instinctively avoiding such objects without entering into a time-consuming decision-making process could prevent serious injury. However, if our memories are built upon biased perceptions or faulty data, the patterns that we instinctively depend upon to make sense of our experience may provide us with a distorted view, say, if we avoided all red circles, presuming they were hot. When applied to individuals, the habit of relying upon emotionally-laden patterns constructed on the basis of past experiences have the potential to lead to gross generalizations and stereotypes, particularly if our memories are misleading or erroneous.

In another example, most managers would deny making decisions about potential employees based upon race- or gender-based stereotypes. To engage in such discriminatory practices would not only be injurious to applicants of the disfavored race or gender, it would also lead to negative consequences for a broad array of other stakeholders, such as other members of the disfavored group throughout the larger community who may be discouraged from seeking employment in the firm or field, current employees who would be deprived of the input of these particular colleagues or those from diverse backgrounds or experiences, and shareholders who might see profits decrease due to the limitations to innovation that have been linked to homogeneity in the workplace (and would certainly see profits fall if the discriminatory practice was exposed to the public). Even if a manager held odious beliefs in the validity of biased stereotypes, he or she would be less likely to express them aloud in the contemporary environment of most businesses. Explicitly racist and sexist attitudes are no longer socially acceptable in most business arenas, and race- or gender-based discrimination can be grounds for legal action in the workplace. However, social psychologists have demonstrated that biased stereotypes often influence our cognitions below the level of conscious awareness, even when forming judgments based upon such generalizations violates our explicit, or consciously held, beliefs and opinions.

Greenwald, McGhee and Schwartz (1998, 1473) developed the Implicit Association Test, or IAT, to measure and identify implicit attitudes that "might not readily be detected through explicit self-report measures," such as racial bias. Now used widely across the social sciences, the I.A.T. is a computer-based test that asks respondents to categorize two words or images with an attribute and tracks the amount of time that respondents take in making their choice. The quicker the response time, the more likely it is that the association reflects an implicit attitude rather than a deliberate decision. Greenwald *et al.* found that white college students more quickly associated "pleasant" with "white" than with "black," despite disavowing this association in testing of explicit attitudes. Using the IAT methodology to examine causes of gender equity, Rudman and Heppen (2003, 1359–60) present evidence that "women who possessed implicit romantic fantasies also tended to choose occupations with reduced economic rewards and lower educational requirements. They also showed less interest in high-status occupations (e.g., business management, corporate lawyer)." Studies using the IAT demonstrate that our actions and choices are limited by implicit attitudes about gender and races of which we are not aware, further evidencing the bounded character of our ethicality (Bazerman and Moore, 2008).

Other studies have revealed the discriminatory effects of race and gender stereotypes in real-world employment contexts. Investigating gender disparity in major symphony orchestras, Goldin and Rouse (2000) discovered that inequality declined significantly when orchestras used blind audition methods. When the musician was hidden behind a screen so that his or her identity was unknown by the committee, women were selected in 35 percent of auditions; when blind audition methods were not used, women were chosen only 10 percent of the time. Whether the judges were motivated by implicit or explicit discriminatory attitudes during the non-blind auditions, the distortion effects of gender stereotyping undermined the judges' capacity to select the best candidate for the job. Similarly, a study of racial bias in the labor markets of two major American cities revealed that, despite identical qualifications, callback rates for resume submissions with

African-American names was 50 percent lower than callback rates for submissions with Caucasian names (Bertrand and Mullainathan, 2004). Some managers might have been conscious of their biased decision-making practices; but the evidence presented by IAT studies tells us that it is highly likely that many managers remained unaware of their discriminatory practice.

Ethical decision-making requires the capacity to imagine how our decisions might affect other individuals and groups. If our perception of others is distorted by mental models constructed on the basis of misinformation or misleading memories, as in the case of the implicit use of race- and gender-based stereotypes in hiring practices, this capacity is eroded. Further, such distorted mental models produce their own confirmation heuristics within organizations that tend to privilege homogeneity over diversity. As we have argued, if the cognitive bias that persuades us to prefer the familiar to the unfamiliar is left unchecked within an organization, the result may be the creation of an echo chamber. While decision makers might believe that they have listened to alternative views and considered impacted stakeholders, in actuality they merely have surrounded themselves with like-minded compatriots that confirm, rather than interrogate and challenge, their implicit attitudes.

Dehumanizing strategies

Finally, we disable our capacity to exercise moral imagination in our consideration of others when we minimize or negate the humanity of those individuals or groups that may be impacted by our choices. Stereotyping attitudes, examined above, can produce a dehumanizing effect when they lead us to treat an individual as if he or she is a representative of a group to whom we ascribe particular characteristics without any evidence that the individual indeed shares these attributes. We find this dehumanization through stereotyping when reference to the *individual* no longer exists, such as when someone refers to "those people" or ascribes a character trait to an individual because of her or his membership in a race or gender group.

Euphemistic labeling also works to discourage moral imagination, when euphemisms are deployed in order to shield us from the human consequences of our actions. Of course, we often rely on euphemistic language to soften or obscure difficult features of our shared reality and, in many contexts, choosing to do so may be a deliberate and compassionate decision. When we speak of the dead, we might refer to the "late John Doe," or talk of a loved one who has "passed away." Telling ourselves that we have put an aged or sick pet "to sleep" helps us to cope with the difficulty of making the decision to end its life, even as we take responsibility for making what we believe to be the most moral choice for the animal. However, euphemistic labeling can be deployed as a strategy of moral disengagement (Bandura, 1990), as well as a tool for coming to terms with morally justified decisions. For example, many managers find that it is easier to fire employees by telling themselves that the company is "downsizing" or that employees are being "let go." The former example depersonalizes the decision, while the latter rhetorically figures the employee as the beneficiary of an emancipatory act; in both cases, the euphemisms are designed to allow the manager to feel less accountable for the negative impact of the decision to fire an employee on that individual's life. Where a decision is based on the implementation of an organization's process, the manager can divorce herself or himself from responsibility entirely, claiming that they did not make the decision, the "rule" made the decision. The implications of this dehumanization are significant since the failure to see the employee as a stakeholder may discourage the manager from assisting the employee in finding new work, or providing the best possible severance package.

Moreover, using euphemisms in place of accurate descriptions reduces the dissonance that performing violent or unethical acts can produce in an otherwise moral actor. Imagine that you are a member of the armed forces called upon by a superior to subject a prisoner to waterboarding, a term that is already euphemistic to the extent that it does not immediately suggest the simulation of drowning, which is a more accurate label of a practice that many lawyers identify as torture. Would you find it easier to obey if you were asked to subject the "enemy combatant" to an "enhanced interrogation technique?" Regardless of whether one finds the practice of waterboarding of suspected criminals or terrorists to be morally justified or an immoral and illegal act of torture, such labels obscure the actual act and dehumanize its human subject, with the consequence of distancing the soldier from the behavior that he or she is asked to perform. Other military euphemisms such as "collateral damage" and "friendly fire" also may serve to mitigate the emotional difficulty faced by well-intentioned soldiers who have accidentally caused the death of innocents; but, at the same time, the use of such language risks minimizing awareness (both public and otherwise) of the human costs of warfare.

The Stanford Prison Experiment (Haney *et al.*, 1973; Zimbardo, 2007), also introduced in Chapter 3, reveals the extent of the moral failures enabled by dehumanizing strategies. In the original experiment, student participants were randomly assigned to the role of "Guard" or "Prisoner" and placed into a prison-like setting that allowed them to engage in these assigned roles. Zimbardo and his colleagues identified sixty-one observable interpersonal interactions between the students, fifty-eight of which were "deindividuating" in nature – that is, rather than referring to one another in personalizing, individuating terms, with the use of names, nicknames, or unique references, the subjects overwhelmingly used deindividuating terms, such as prisoner numbers or a generalized "you" (Haney *et al.*, 1973). The Stanford study, like Milgram's obedience experiments before it, has become famous for its demonstration of the apparent ease with which otherwise moral actors can come to commit highly unethical acts under certain conditions. Zimbardo (2007) contends, further, that the abuse of prisoners at Abu Ghraib can be understood in terms of the effects of dehumanizing prisoners.

Most of us are contemptuous of the tactics used by hate groups, terrorist organizations and totalitarian regimes to dehumanize groups in order to rationalize subjecting them to violence, with examples ranging from the Nazi strategy of referring to Jewish peoples as "cockroaches" to the KKK's depiction of African-Americans and other groups as animals. As well, we tend to understand that the use of similar tactics is comprehensible, if not justifiable, when used by members of the military in democratic societies. Dehumanizing tactics may sometimes represent dangerous coping mechanism, as Zimbardo and his colleagues (Haney *et al.*, 1973) discovered, that otherwise ethical actors might turn in order to continue to function in highly stressful conditions in which they are called upon perform acts that may conflict with their moral values.

Pina e Cuha *et al.* (2010) suggest that some corporations operate in a manner that discourages individuation in a manner that parallels the dehumanizing tactics used by totalitarian institutions, such as fostering a strong in-group/out-group distinction, encouraging ideological zeal within the corporate culture, and mythologizing organizational leaders while sowing distrust among organizational peers. In citing this comparison, by no means do we wish to imply equivalence between strategies of depersonalization aimed at fostering a moral disengagement from acts of violence and those deployed in corporate practice for the sake of maximizing organization goals. Rather, the parallels point to the danger that certain mental models within corporate practice might work to desensitize both managers and employees to human consequences of their actions for affected stakeholders. Margaret Heffernen (2011, 134–5) reflects that:

[i]n the thousands of hours of recorded conversations by Enron power traders, what's most striking (after the criminality of the deals they're discussing) is their language: not just the code names of illegal power contracts ("Get Shorty", "Death Star", and "Fat Boy") nor the saturation of language in expletives, but the pervasive derogation of anyone or anything that is *not* Enron, from "little old grandmothers"' to "dumb consultants" to the whole state of California: "Best thing that can happen, fucking earthquake, let that thing float out the Pacific... they're so fucked." There's even a tacit recognition of the company operating as a quasi-cult in repeated references to "drinking the Kool-Aid." The sense of belonging to a superior team was so strong that no one seems to have remembered that the real people who conformed by drinking the Kool-Aid (in the Jonestown massacre) all died.

We have different ethical responses to injustice depending upon whether the victims are "identifiable" or "statistical" (Gino *et al.*, 2009). It is easier to sympathize with an individual who has been wronged than with an abstract category of victims. Werhane *et al.* (2011b) argue that, when stakeholders are represented by numbers – the 14 million mortgage holders that were underwater in 2009, for example – it is difficult to comprehend the actual consequences on individual human lives that such statistics represent. The anonymity of the mortgage holders to financial traders may have been one of the coping mechanisms that allowed traders to bundle and resell mortgages without considering how their behavior might impact individual homeowners and their families, just as the aggressive, violent rhetoric of the Enron traders may have enabled them to quell the cognitive dissonance between their consciously-held values and their unethical actions. If stakeholder groups are depersonalized and dehumanized, decisions that cause them harm can be justified, excused as ethically irrelevant, or the harm itself prevented from coming into view.

Each of the mental models examined in this section of the chapter – confirmation heuristics, stereotypes, and dehumanizing tactics – work to prevent decision-makers from seeking out the input of others, or from imagining the perspective of others, while evaluating decision alternatives. In practice, these mental models may work together, as stereotyping practices effectively dehumanize groups of people, dehumanizing tactics work to create stereotypes, and these dynamics discourage us from valuing the input of voices that challenge our preconceptions.

IV. Obstacles to reaching an ethical decision

Thus far, we have investigated factors that impede preparatory steps in the process of ethical decision-making: becoming aware of the ethical dimensions of a problem; gathering relevant data; identifying viable courses of action; and considering the potential impact of these options from the perspective of other stakeholders. Our model of ethical deliberation calls upon the decision-maker at this stage to compare and weigh alternative courses of action, often guided by insights offered by philosophical theory or other external guidelines; to examine these options from the perspectives provided by other mental models; and to reach a decision that is in accord with his or her values. As we have seen in the preceding analysis, many ethical failures occur because key decision-makers act without having developed a conscious intent or process, or by skipping a vital element of the above structure. But how do we evaluate those who are not ignorant – willfully or otherwise – of the unethical character of their choices?

Depending on the circumstances, some people may make the choice to be unethical and to live with the consequences of that path in order to reap certain benefits or to avoid penalties. Recall Bernie Madoff's admission that, as he engaged in fraud, he knew that what he was doing "was wrong, indeed criminal" (Jones, 2009). Though Madoff's true motives cannot be known with certainty, we can surmise from his statements that he determined that making a good deal of money – and, perhaps at a later point, evading regulators – was a higher priority than acting in accordance with commonly accepted moral principles. It is difficult to say the same of Betty Vinson, the WorldCom employee who was convicted for her role in inflating that company's profits using fraudulent accounting practices. As we saw in Chapter 3, Vinson – like

Madoff – knew that her decisions led to acts that were both wrong and illegal. However, by all accounts, Vinson – unlike Madoff – was deeply troubled by the unethical behavior at WorldCom. She voiced discomfort to her superiors, repeatedly considered resignation, and communicated her unease to her colleagues; meanwhile, however, she continued to participate in the massive fraud, a decision that would eventually result in a felony conviction and prison sentence (Pulliam, 2003).

We now turn to the final stages of the decision-making process to examine the mental models, such as the myth of invisibility, learned helplessness and a lack of courage that present barriers to reaching an ethical conclusion. Why do some good people fail to act ethically, despite having acknowledged to themselves or to others that they are aware that their behavior violates their own moral principles?

The myth of invisibility

Consider a thought experiment: if you had the power of invisibility, what would you do? Would you act ethically? In an oft-cited scene in Book II of Plato's *Republic*, one of Socrates' interlocutors raises this question to illustrate the argument that no man is so virtuous that he would act ethically if in possession of Gyges' ring, a mythic ring that bestows invisibility on its wearer. The thought experiment maintains its relevance today because it presses us to confront a common tendency to rationalize unethical behavior when we believe that our ethical violation will not be detected. In business ethics, the Gyges ring parable is often raised in connection with the idea that "ethics pays" (e.g., Corvino, 2006; Yeo, 1988). If ethical behavior is justified solely by the profit and social rewards of a moral reputation, and the related fear of social or legal penalty, what motivates us to hold to our values behind closed doors? Would not the best situation be one in which we were able to reap the social benefits of moral reputation as well as the private profits of unethical behavior? Such questions have been explored in moral philosophy and applied ethics at least since Plato's articulation of the Gyges ring story, and they are particularly crucial to practicing ethics in business, where the pressures to increase profit margins may be quite high. Though it is beyond the scope of this chapter to provide a comprehensive survey of the broad array of philosophical responses to the ethical dilemmas posed by the Gyges ring parable, the philosophical literature provides an invaluable resource for decision-makers who seek guidance in reaching an ethical decision.[2] We return to the Gyges ring parable in the context of the discussion of remedies presented in Chapter 6.

In business practice, additional external sources of guidance may include corporate ethics guidelines, professional codes of conduct, corporate mission statements or other codifications of organizational values. However, when we believe that no one will find out about our transgression, we are more vulnerable to mental models that discourage rigorous ethical deliberation, particularly if we can avoid facing up to our decisions in the mirror. If our actions will not come into public view, we are less liable to give a self-accounting of our motivations; in such situations, we tend to find it easier to disengage our moral frames.

Chance and Norton (2009) distinguish two variants of this moral evasion: "foregoing" and "forgetting." Far from being limited to amoral characters, these mental models are quite common. Foregoing occurs when one avoids a situation that would require admitting to a questionable decision, even if this avoidance means foregoing benefits as well. Chance and Norton illustrate foregoing behavior by citing an experimental variation of the classic behavioral economics model, the Dictator Game. In the traditional two-player game, one player (the Dictator) is given a sum of money and is asked to decide how to divide it with the other player, who will not be told the identity of the Dictator: Though basic economic theory hypothesizes that the Dictator will fail this Gyges ring test by acting selfishly, keeping the full sum and giving the other player nothing. However, in practice, most players give some amount. This result suggests that we are capable of valuing fairness above self-interest, at least to some degree, even under conditions of anonymity. Yet, Dana *et al.* (2006) found that when the Dictator is given the option of paying a small sum to exit the game without the other player knowing the game has taken place, nearly a third of the players choose this option. The "quiet exit" decision requires that Dictator give up some benefit and leave the other player with nothing, but it allows the Dictator to forego a direct confrontation with his or her ethical choice. Recalling that the Dictator's identity is anonymous, regardless of their choice, the attraction of the quiet exit appears to be that it enables the Dictator to justify the questionable

---

[2] The dominant traditions of ethical theory include deontology, utilitarianism, and virtue ethics. For an informative survey of philosophical ethics see Hartman and DesJardins (2008).

behavior. The sanction that is avoided is not the judgment of the other player, but the self-sanctioning of the Dictator who forgoes the feelings of guilt and regret that are likely to ensue when violating personal ethics. The "forgetting" variant accomplishes a similar lessoning of guilt and regret. Johansson *et al.* (2005) conducted an experiment in which subjects were asked to choose the more attractive of two female faces. They were then asked why they had chosen "this one," with the experimenter indicating the image initially rated as less attractive. The participants did not only fail to notice the change, but provided a rationale for the choice that they had not actually made.

Chance and Norton argue that these results show that "[p]eople appear to forget their original decisions when those decisions were difficult, allowing them to later be happy with options they may have rejected earlier" (2009, 15). Returning to the Gyges ring parable, one explanation is that foregoing or forgetting behavior involves a choice to allow a part of oneself to become, in a sense, invisible. The Dictator's selfish decision is conscious, but subsequently hidden from his or her own view, just as the participant's initial choice of the more attractive image disappears from conscious awareness when it appears to have been "incorrect." If we can reduce the guilt or regret that accompanies questionable decisions, we believe that we can avoid negative consequences for our moral self-assessment. However, the true cost lies with the damage done to our sense of moral judgment and our efficacy by our own evasion strategies such as foregoing and forgetting.

Learned helplessness

When we hear own ethical voice telling us what to do, through what process do we silence it, such that we fail to reach an ethical conclusion? Moral evasion provides an explanation; but it is important to recognize that this muzzling can be a learned condition. If we are penalized repeatedly for speaking up, we learn passivity. Badhwar (2009) suggests that there may be a connection between the obedient subjects in Milgram's study and the phenomena of "learned helplessness" first identified by animal psychologists in the 1960s. Seligman and Maier (1967) placed three groups of dogs in harnesses. The first group was placed in the harness and then released. The dogs in the second group were subjected to a shock, which they could end by pressing a lever. In the third group, the dogs were subjected to a shock that they could not control. The dogs in the first two groups recovered from their experience, but the Group 3 dogs exhibited signs of chronic depression. In a later experiment, all three groups of dogs were placed in a confined space from which they could easily escape by jumping over a low barrier, and then were subjected to shocks. While the first two groups quickly learned to escape, the majority of the Group 3 dogs passively suffered the shocks, leading Seligman and Maier to posit that they had learned that they could not control their environment.

Later experiments on other animals and on humans have produced a general theory of learned helplessness that asserts that "[i]nescapable aversive events presented to animals or to men result in profound interference with later instrumental learning" (Hiroto and Segilman, 1975). The level of passivity in learned helplessness experiments was identical to the level of obedience in the Milgram subjects – 65 percent – indicating to Badhwar (2009) that, while passivity and obedience are natural propensities, they are not immutable characteristics. As we explained previously, and discussed in greater detail in Chapter 3, some of Milgram's subjects quickly resigned themselves to obedience, undergoing an agentic shift. A third of the subjects halted the experiment, demonstrating a capacity to reach an ethical conclusion in the face of host of situational factors that exacerbated what Badhwar deems to be a natural proclivity to ignore, doubt, or undervalue our capacity to control our environment. The remaining subjects learned to be obedient in the course of the experiment, as their protestations – like those of Betty Vinson – were ignored, dismissed or refuted by a figure of authority. In this sense, the Milgram study does not only demonstrate that pressure by authority figures can lead good people to make bad decisions; it also reveals that ethical options may fall by the wayside when people are repeatedly told that their judgments do not matter. Learning through experience that our actions will not affect our environment, we form mental models that present our capacity for moral action as weak and ineffectual. Such distorted mental models impede our ability to reach an ethical conclusion when faced with a challenge.

Lack of courage

People also sometimes make decisions they later regret because they lack the courage to do otherwise. Our discussions of the myth of invisibility, foregoing and forgetting, and learned helplessness indicate the significant temptations to disregard consciously formed ethical judgments. These temptations are intensified when reaching an ethical conclusion that would put the decision-maker at high risk of economic, social or even physical harm. Sherron Watkins was only one of many Enron employees who explained their reluctance to push their concerns by reference to the culture of intimidation and fear that characterized upper management at Enron. Betty Vinson initially spoke up against the illegal fraud taking place at WorldCom but, discouraged by her superiors, afraid for her job and career prospects, and surrounded by peers who acquiesced, she was unable to muster the courage of her convictions over time. Recognizing the pressure on decision-makers is not a means by which to excuse the possibility of a resulting unethical decision. However, since temptation exists, understanding that to which a professional may succumb it is vital.

In order to foster an ethical corporate culture, organizations must reward managers and employees for asking critical questions, seeking information and stakeholder perspectives – particularly when this process of critical inquiry challenges norms and organizational habits. In Chapters 6 and 7, we discuss strategies for overcoming mental models that impede the formation of ethical organizations in greater depth, but we raise an example here to point to an innovative effort to alter the mental model that frames corporate settings as an inappropriate venue for developing the courage of one's convictions. Paul Birch was a frustrated employee of British Airways until his boss encouraged him to write up a description of the job that he would like to be performing for the company. Inspired by the character of the Fool in King Lear, Birch invented the position of the "corporate jester" who would "draw attention to things that are going wrong" and "stir things up" (Sittenfeld, 1998). Then-CEO of British Airways Colin Marshal appointed Birch the official corporate fool of British Airway in 1994, and Birch now travels to companies to teach the benefits of his approach. Heffernan (2011) cites the corporate fool as an example of institutionalizing dissent in order to discourage groupthink and create an environment in which debate is welcome. Birch describes his role at British Airways as a platform to push other employees to speak up as well. "When things go wrong," Birch says, "employees usually have a good idea of how to fix them. You need to create a state in which they've got the courage to do something. You want to build organizations where everyone sees provocation as one of their essential roles" (Heffernan, 2011, 225; Sittenfeld, 1998). Institutionalizing dissent as British Airways did in the role of the corporate fool makes it difficult for troubling cultures of intimidation and fear to form in the workplace.

The role of the corporate fool is to transform mental models that construe ethical action as impossible to those who do not see themselves as highly courageous. If speaking up in a provocative manner and giving voice to a dissenting view is perceived as a commonplace activity that is not penalized by management, employees are less likely to shy away from ethical conclusions at variance with the status quo and more likely to view themselves as moral agents who are capable of affecting their environment through their efficacy as ethical actors. Corporate cultures that do not emphasize accountability within their organizational structures and penalize debate and dissent risk creating an environment in which employees may have the resources to forge ethical decisions, but find the barriers to enacting those decisions too high. Such employees are likely to feel invisible, helpless, and incapable of mustering the courage to speak out when unethical behavior occurs.

Legal responsibility

Law has long recognized both limits and expectations for individual responsibility in business. We consider individuals reckless if they do not know what they *should have* or *could have* known, within reason. We also hold employers responsible for the acts of their workers, thus broadening the scope of "responsibility" far beyond the decisions one makes intentionally, and on an individual level. For instance, codified as a legal defense in the United States under tort law as *respondeat superior* ("let the master answer" in Latin, also known as the Master-Servant Rule, though that term is considered outdated), our society does accept certain circumstances where an employer is liable for the acts of its employees, where they are performed within the course of employment (Thornton, 2010). A critical exception to this rule arose in connection with the Nuremburg War Crimes Tribunal, where the Superior Orders Defense ("I was only following orders") has become practically synonymous with the Tribunal itself. Where an individual is asked by an employer or person in a position of authority to engage in behavior or to make a decision that the individual knows or should have known violates ethical norms, the individual may be held personally liable. The Nuremburg Principles specifically state: "The fact that a person acted pursuant to order of his Government or of a superior does not relieve him from responsibility under international law, provided a moral choice was in fact possible to him" (United Nations, 1950, gender specificity in original).

In addition to the individual responsibility for ethical violations recognized by international law, the United States has developed a strong jurisprudential tradition that recognizes culpability where the individual did not know, but *should* have known, that a violation was taking place. The Modern Penal Code purposefully defines knowledge of a fact in terms of the probability that a fact could be known, rather than the actual possession of knowledge, in order to address the situation of willful blindness (Marcus, 1993). Some version of a willful blindness doctrine has been articulated by all of the federal circuit courts. Recently, the Supreme Court extended the reach of the legal concept of willful blindness to include patent law violations. Arguing for the majority, Justice Alito elaborated the Court's reason for expanding the doctrine:

Many criminal statutes require proof that a defendant acted knowingly or willfully, and courts applying the doctrine of willful blindness hold that defendants cannot escape the reach of these statutes by deliberately shielding themselves from clear evidence of critical facts that are strongly suggested by the circumstances. The traditional rationale for this doctrine is that defendants who behave in this manner are just as culpable as those who have actual knowledge is no longer feasible defense for violation of ethical norms... Given the doctrine's long history and wide acceptance in the Federal Judiciary, there is no reason why the doctrine should not apply in civil lawsuits for induced patent infringement. (*Global-Tech Inc. v. Sebs S.A.*, 2011)

To be sure, the notion of willful blindness is somewhat counterintuitive. It is not difficult to locate the willfulness in the behavior of Bernie Madoff, who admitted that he was aware that his financial schemes were both morally wrong and prohibited by law. In other cases, such as the failed whistleblower from WorldCom, Betty Vinson, or the distraught Milgram subjects who recognized that they were acting in violation of their moral principles but could not bring themselves to resist authority, the deliberate choice to avoid acknowledgment of critical facts – such as the gravity of the harm to others, or the relative ease of refusal to obey – is identifiable, though more difficult to perceive. It is even more challenging to identify willful ignorance when behavior is governed by distorted mental models that prevent decision-makers from recognizing their capacity for ethical responsibility. In some cases, as we saw in the earlier discussion of Asch's conformity tests, decision-makers may not even realize that they have *decided* at all. Yet, as codified in the legal doctrine of willful blindness, we have a legal responsibility to seek out critical facts. Ethically, our responsibility extends beyond ascertaining the facts necessary to determine if we have violated the law; we must ask ourselves if we exercised the moral imagination that is required if our decisions and actions are to express our consciously held values.

V. Conclusion

Although we have conceptualized the ethical decision-making process in terms of a linear and individual model, the need for moral imagination in the implementation of each of its component steps reminds us that this linearity – and isolated perspective – is often not applicable in practice. Examining decision options from the point of view of those who are likely to be impacted by the outcome (stage four) may raise new ethical dimensions (stage one), bring to light previously unexamined data (stage two), or prompt the creation of innovative resolution possibilities (stage three). Likewise, obstacles that stand in the way of selecting an alternative and following through on ethical choice in action (stage five) may prevent the formation of a habit of engaging in ethical decision-making altogether.

Throughout this and earlier chapters, we have proposed that it is possible to perceive our responsibility for behavior guided by flawed mental models, if we call decision makers to account for their decision-making processes. This responsibility may be difficult to perceive when the preparatory steps to ethical decision-making are impeded, as demonstrated in Chapter 4 and in Sections II and III of this chapter, or when the failure to reach an ethical decision is rendered invisible, as we saw in Section IV. However, the preceding analysis demonstrates that we put ourselves in jeopardy of moral failure we do not work to identify and overcome mental models that present impediments to ethical decision-making processes. Failing to attend to the biases and partiality of the mindsets that we generate to make sense of our experiences, we may put our companies and ourselves in danger of legal sanction. In a world characterized by increasing flow of people, goods, ideas and capital across borders, we may also find ourselves responsible for ethical failures with negative consequences for many innocent stakeholders. Chapters 6 and 7 will raise and analyze specific remedies, at the level of theory and of practice, to the dangers posed by of many of the distorting mental models that we have identified.

6 | *Managing ethical obstacles*

I. Introduction

At the outset of Chapter 4, we identified five steps that thorough ethical decision-making requires. The decision-maker needs to: become aware of a present issue, gather relevant facts, identify alternative possible solutions, consider the likely impact of these solutions on stakeholders, and finally, reach a conclusion by comparing and weighing the options, and testing the options' likely consequences from the perspectives of other mental models. Although one is not required to follow these steps in this order, it is clear that satisfying these requirements is a significant challenge. Previous chapters have discussed many of the obstacles that thwart rigorous ethical reflection. This chapter will explore constructive ways of dealing with them.

II. Mental models, blind spots, and the impartial spectator

Although good ethical decision-making requires us carefully to take into account as much relevant information as is available to us, we have good reason to think that we commonly fall well short of this standard – either by overlooking relevant facts completely or by underestimating their significance. The mental models we employ can contribute to this problem. As we have explained, mental models frame our experiences in ways that both aid and hinder our perceptions. They enable us to focus selectively on ethically relevant matters. By their very nature, they provide incomplete perspectives, resulting in bounded awareness and bounded ethicality. Insofar as our mental modeling practices result in unwarranted partiality, or even ethical blindness, the desired reflective process is distorted. This distortion is aggravated by the fact that our mental models can have this distorting effect without our consciously realizing it. Thus, although we cannot do without mental models, they leave us all vulnerable to blindness and, insofar as we are unaware of this, self-deception.

However, this vulnerability to self-deception does not render us helpless. Our mental models may frame our perceptions and our common ways of dealing with the information (and misinformation) we encounter; but, as previous chapters have shown, we can become aware of this. Sometimes our failure to see the ethical limitations and distortions attributable to our mental models is willful. Rather than despair at this, Margaret Heffernan urges us to take hope, for recognizing our limitations is the first step toward assuming greater responsibility:

We make ourselves powerless when we choose not to know. But we give ourselves hope when we insist on looking. The very fact that willful blindness is willed, that it is the product of a rich mix of experience, knowledge, thinking, neurons, and neuroses, is what gives us the capacity to change it. Like Lear, we can learn to see better, not because our brain changes but because we do. As all wisdom does, seeing starts with simple questions: What could I know, should I know, that I don't know? Just what am I missing here? (Heffernan, 2011, 247)

These are the last lines in Heffernan's book, *Willful Blindness*. Her paragraph begins with "we," but her questions shift to the first person, "I." However, these questions could be framed in the plural, as well. What could *we* know, should *we* know, that *we* don't know? Just what are *we* missing here? In fact, I know much less by myself, or even in small groups of others like me, than I could know with others whose perspectives may be very different than mine.

The eighteenth-century Scottish philosopher Adam Smith elaborates the other-dependence of our moral capacities. Well known for his *Wealth of Nations* and commonly regarded as "the father of capitalism," Smith also wrote *The Theory of Moral Sentiments*, in which he provides a detailed account of moral development from our infancy to adulthood. His account begins with the young child's extreme dependency on caregivers and peers for acquiring the sort of "self-command" necessary for moral responsibility. Caregivers try to help their children learn to control their unruly passions, such as anger. Very soon young children begin to learn lessons from other children. They learn the importance of trying to control, not only their anger, but their other passions as well – "to the degree which [their] play-fellows and companions are likely to be pleased with." Thus, says Smith, the child

... enters into the great school of self-command, it studies to be more and more master of itself, and begins to exercise over its own feelings a discipline which the practice of the longest life is very seldom sufficient to bring to complete perfection. (1790, cited in 1984, 145)

In their earliest forms, children's anger and other affective responses to what happens around them are pre-moral rather than moral sentiments. The transformation of such affective states into moral sentiments, says Smith (p. 110), requires interaction with others. Others serve as our "mirror," and as our first critics. Indeed, as discussed in Chapter 4, we cannot be purely self-sufficient. Our sense of ourselves depends on interaction with others and how they regard us. Judged by others, we become concerned with how we seem to them. This concern requires us to imagine seeing ourselves from a perspective that, in fact, we can only infer from what others say and do. And, of course, their access to us is similarly limited. Nevertheless, awareness of our social setting enables us to adopt a vantage point that can lay claim to greater objectivity than introspection alone can. Smith says:

We begin, upon this account, to examine our own passions and conduct, and to consider how these must appear to them, by considering how they would appear to us if in their situation. We suppose ourselves the spectators of our own behaviour, and endeavour to imagine what effect it would, in this light, produce upon us. This is the only looking-glass by which we can, in some measure, with the eyes of other people, scrutinize the propriety of our own conduct. (p. 112)

Although this "mirror" helps us determine what we need to do to win approval of and acceptance by others, Smith says that this is not enough to make us fit for society. We also must desire "what ought to be approved of" (p. 114). This second desire, the desire actually to *be* fully moral, and not merely appear to be moral, can be satisfied only by our striving to become "impartial spectators of our own character and conduct." It is from this vantage point that merited self-approval is to be sought. Smith concludes, "This self-approbation, if not the only, is at least the principal object, about which he can or ought to be anxious. The love of it, is the love of virtue" (p. 117).

Despite recognizing that we are moved, to at least some extent, by a "love of virtue," Smith acknowledges that we also are naturally inclined to favor ourselves, even at the expense of others. Still, there is a way that we can try to put a check on excessive self-regard. This corrective process involves imagining how *others* might assess our self-regard. Smith observes:

Though it may be true, therefore, that every individual, in his own breast, naturally prefers himself to all mankind, yet he dares not look mankind in the face, and avow that he acts according to this principle. He feels that in this preference they can never go along with him, and that how natural soever it may be to him, it must always appear excessive and extravagant to them. (p. 83)

Because we perceive that self-interest is not an acceptable principle to justify our actions to others, imagining how others see us can have a leveling effect. It moves us is in the direction of impartial self-regard and regard for the interests of others. In this way, our imagination can contribute significantly to recognizing our blind spots.

When we reflect upon ourselves as being one among the many, we are more likely to acknowledge that *each* of us has a legitimate claim to not being wronged. Although Smith's focus here is on the individual, what he has in mind is a social process. He concludes:

Society and conversation, therefore, are the most powerful remedies for restoring the mind to its tranquility, if at any time, it has unfortunately lost it; as well as the best preservatives of that equal and happy temper which is so necessary to self-satisfaction and enjoyment. (p. 23)

Sociality and dialogue help us to take up the imaginative role of the impartial spectator that encourages ethical decision-making.

Nevertheless, taking into account what we have said about mental models – that they are all incomplete – the quest for a perspective that matches that of an ideal, fully informed "impartial spectator" is bound to fail. Smith would agree. He never says that we can achieve this end; rather, he holds that we can, and we should, strive to approximate it as best we can. Furthermore, just as our moral beginnings are with others (a "we"), striving for the perspective of an "impartial spectator" is best done *with* others, at least imaginatively. Whatever this perspective might involve, for Smith, it must be shareable with others in the sense that it takes fairly into account the legitimate interests of each of us so that, insofar as we see through these impartial lenses, we can find the outcome reasonable. In this respect, the perspective of an impartial spectator presents itself as much as "ours" as "mine" or "yours."

Unfortunately, "blind spots" and other obstacles to good moral decision-making are "ours" too. Consequently, it is necessary to make them as clearly visible as we can in order to be in a position to subject them to critical scrutiny. Insofar as we succeed in our efforts to adopt the perspective of an impartial spectator, some of our errors become more transparent. However, it is important not to stop there. It is also important to explore possible ways of minimizing the negative impact of these obstacles on decision-making.

III. Moral self-image, the bystander effect, and choice

One of the obstacles to ethical decision-making that needs to be taken into account is our own self-image. Despite the fact that, as Smith notes, we depend on others to serve as our moral mirror, what we see in that mirror typically is somewhat distorted. Even if our character, motives, and ambitions are fully transparent to others, we cannot always count on others to be fully candid with us about what they see. Realistically, of course, we are not fully transparent to others, and they, too, have difficulty getting beyond appearances to see us as we are. Finally, it is unlikely that we see all that is there to be seen in the mirror that others provide us. Mental models that are operative in our self-perception have much to do with our vulnerability to distorted self-image.

One mental model, addressed in Chapter 4, involves the belief that we are basically decent people regardless of how we act. We want others to see us this way, and we want to see ourselves this way. As Smith would put it, we want the moral approval of others. Fear of their disapproval is so painful that we sometimes try to protect ourselves from it by concealment. Open acknowledgment of our moral shortcomings to others is seldom our first course of action. But this concealment is not just from others. We may hide our shortcomings from ourselves, too. Insofar as our self-appraisal results in a negative verdict, we may not want to face this assessment straightforwardly. Though we may actually seek to *deserve* the moral approval of others, this desire to be worthy of positive moral assessment does not mean that we welcome the self-revelation that we fall short of that mark. One way to protect ourselves from negative self-revelation is through self-deception. Unfortunately, Smith astutely observes, this "self-deceit" underlies much of what is morally amiss in our world.

The sobering lesson of the Milgram studies (1974) is the revelation that a disturbingly high percentage of otherwise decent people are nevertheless willing to participate in activities that conflict with their basic moral principles, under some circumstances. Those whose behavior in these studies conflicted with moral principles to which they are otherwise committed may have received a painful lesson. However, the rest of us are invited to take stock of ourselves, too. As our analysis of the behavior of the Teachers in Chapter 3 suggests, the setting of the Milgram studies, that is, the presence of the person of authority in what seems to be an important laboratory experiment, had the ability to undermine the participants' sense of their own moral effectiveness. While insisting that participants had no choice but continue, the Experimenter offered reassurance that, even in the unlikely event that the Learner were harmed, all responsibility would fall on the Experimenter, not the Teacher. But, as we have noted, a few of the Teachers, those who had a strong sense of self and knew they could choose to opt out, were able to disengage from the researcher and from the experiment.

A constructive response to Milgram's findings challenges the notion that we can be relieved of moral responsibility in this way. The mere presence of others does not license us to be bystanders nor relieve us of responsibility, whether or not there is an authority figure in charge. Although under such circumstances many may fail to realize that the choice is still theirs, this *is* a failure – we still can, and ought to, make choices. In this sense, the Milgram study provides an educational opportunity. Although Milgram obtained his results in a deliberately contrived experimental setting, his original aim was to gain a better understanding of human behavior in the world outside of academia, whether in war, business, or everyday circumstances involving hierarchical authority structures.

A salutary effect of individuals reflecting on the Milgram study is that it might well give all of us reason to reassess our moral self-image – in the direction of some deflation, but not all the way to moral despair. Milgram's study reveals our vulnerability to moral passivity in situations that call for resistance. The realization that this vulnerability includes giving into "authority" even when there are no coercive threats can humble us. But it can also embolden us to resist giving in so easily and uncritically. Our capacity to resist authority may be strengthened by the realization that the willingness of others to take responsibility for harms that we cause does not relieve us of account-ability. This realization, in turn, can encourage an exploration of ways in which the moral strengths of individuals can be more effectively exercised.

In the Milgram studies, "Teachers" were least successful resisting the researcher's entreaties to continue when operating alone. As noted in Chapter 3, there is evidence that Teachers found it easier to with-draw from the experimental setting when accompanied by others who encourage resistance. There can be moral strength in numbers. Of course, as studies of the bystander effect show us, the behavior of others can pose moral challenges, as well as provide moral resources. We revisit and expand on our discussion of the challenges posed by the influence of others on our ethical decision-making processes in the next section.

IV. Reflecting with others

Given that so much human activity is jointly undertaken and can be well understood only in these terms, and as well, that we are limited as individuals by the inherent partiality of our mental models, it is impor-tant that the plural be emphasized. Margaret Gilbert (1996) makes use of the notion of *plural subjects* in her writings in political philosophy. This concept can also be productively adapted to the context of busi-ness ethics. Gilbert begins with a seemingly simple question: What does it mean to take a walk with someone? It is not enough for two people to walk at roughly the same pace, at the same time, down the same path, to the same destination. They need to be walking *together* – and in such a way that they can say that it is *our* walk, not just mine and yours. Insofar as we "walk together" in our work, problems in business are often better cast as "ours" rather than just "mine." This attentiveness to plurality can open us to creative possibilities that, as isolated individuals, we may be unlikely to notice, let alone pursue. Thus, we can see that, through sharing ideas with one another, moral imagination can be "ours" rather than just "mine" or "yours."

The benefits of working with others in this way are often illustrated in research teams. A best design of a product may be the result of creative interaction among team members who are trying, together, to come up with a good design. The design ultimately selected might best be described jointly as "theirs," rather than as the product of one individual. However, as studies of group dynamics reveal, reflecting with others may pose ethical obstacles, as well as providing a remedy to many of our vulnerabilities to ethical blindness. Irving Janis' (1982) "groupthink" research provides a powerful illustration of these obstacles, and extends the discussion of the challenges posed by peer pressure and obedience to authority raised in Chapter 4. As we have stressed in earlier chapters, although mental models are applicable to individuals, they are also shared, thus rendering groups of individuals, not just solitary individuals, ignorant of what they need to know in order to make better ethical decisions. Janis' research focuses on groups described as tightly cohesive and whose members are marked by a high degree of solidarity, and loyalty. Ordinarily, these qualities might be thought to be quite desirable. However, Janis found that many such groups become victims of their own "groupthink" – a tendency to strive for agreement at the expense of critical thinking.

Janis discusses historical fiascos that he claims exhibited symptoms of groupthink. For example, he claims, those responsible for U.S. security at Pearl Harbor just prior to the onset of U.S. involvement in the Second World War failed to heed warning signs that the Japanese would attack. A few years later, the Kennedy administration's invasion of the Cuban Bay of Pigs misfired, also, according to Janis, as a result of flawed decision-making due to the distortions of groupthink dynamics. Although Janis focuses primarily on the political arena, he emphasizes that groupthink can be present in groups of all kinds – committees, teams, work units, and so on. The shared mental models that are exhibited in groupthink are difficult to resist – both because of their collective strength and the fact that group members may be unaware of the dynamics of their group.

To minimize the negative effects of groupthink, group leaders can play a fundamental role. A constructive first step would make sure that members of the group are aware of the ways in which group dynamics can come into play as a form of pressure within deliberations. Janis urges leaders to encourage an atmosphere that is conducive to critical thinking, in order to combat the tendency of cohesive groups to suppress dissenting views. Providing adequate time for critical discussion is essential. As well, group leaders should emphasize the responsibility of each member of the group to serve as a critic and to develop listening and communication skills that contribute to reflective discussion. Janis also suggests that the leader might deliberately stay away from a group meeting on occasion, in order to avoid unduly influencing its deliberations. After the Bay of Pigs fiasco, Janis notes, President John F. Kennedy explicitly told members of his cabinet that each was now expected to be a critic of their proceedings; and he sometimes refrained from attending meetings to increase the chances that cabinet members would exercise their own critical judgment.

In the decades following Janis' research, his groupthink hypothesis has received mixed reviews.[1] The very characterization of groupthink symptoms strongly suggests that, where cohesive groups can be found, they can be at risk of flawed decision making. However, in reviewing literature critical of Janis' groupthink hypothesis, Cass R. Sunstein (2009, 88) notes that there is uncertainty about precisely what relationships there are supposed to be between the symptoms Janis describes and the various fiascos he discusses.[2] While acknowledging that Janis' account of groupthink has considerable merit, Sunstein provides an alternative notion, *group polarization*. Basically, this is the idea that groups that exhibit tendencies to polarize in certain directions are particularly susceptible to moving to extremes, especially under the guidance of strong leadership. Sunstein holds that the idea of group polarization provides a simpler, more straightforward basis for prediction than groupthink hypotheses do:

As a statistical regularity, deliberating groups will end up in a more extreme point in line with their predeliberation tendencies. The idea of groupthink is far more complex and unruly, without any simple predictions. [Janis's] generalizations are suggestive and helpful, but they do not offer a clear account of what characteristics of groups will lead to extremism, blunders, or catastrophes. (p. 89)

Sunstein recommends the idea of "checks and balances" as a way of countering the extremes of group polarization. He cites the history of regulatory commissions such as the Federal Communications Commission, the Federal Trade Commission, the Securities and Exchange Commission, and the National Labor Relations Board. Each of these commissions consists of five members, appointed by the president,

[1] For a sympathetic review, see James Esser (1998).
[2] For example, Sunstein (2009, 88) cites the complaint of Sally Riggs Fuller and Ramon J. Aldag (1998, 167) that "support for the posited groupings of groupthink characteristics derives from anecdote, casual observation, and intuitive appeal rather than rigorous research."

and its decisions are by majority vote. The president is not permitted to appoint more than three members from the same political party. This bipartisan representation, says Sunstein (p. 146), "serves to limit unwarrantedly extreme changes in regulatory policy."

The "checks and balances" approach has applications in a broad range of contexts. Sunstein comments:

> In many domains, private and public institutions consist of like-minded people... Well-functioning groups attempt to ensure a diversity of views, if only to protect themselves against blunders and confusion. If teams of doctors want to make accurate diagnoses, they will promote a norm of skepticism, even among younger and less experienced members. (p. 147)

Turning to the corporate setting, Sunstein advocates boards that can represent diverse perspectives and that do not defer to the CEO, but take up the responsibility to challenge one another on critical and controversial issues.

Whether further research will strengthen the case for Janis' group-think hypothesis, Sunstein's notion of group polarization, or some other theory of group behavior, it seems clear that improving ethical decision making in business and the professions must take into account group dynamics, rather than just individual behavior. Further, strong evidence suggests that critical thinking within groups is crucial to ethical decision making. How leaders might be persuaded to assume the sorts of roles recommended by Janis and Sunstein and how group members might become accustomed to the critical responsibilities that go with this are crucial questions. In Chapter 5, we raised the problem of the "flight to the familiar," the human bias that leads to an aversion to the new or unfamiliar. In business settings, the flight to the familiar can lead to hiring practices that produce homogeneity in the workplace, resulting in "a company of clones" (Gill, 2005).

Though such homogeneity might foster group solidarity, the work of Janis and Sunstein suggests that it may also increase the risk of the flawed decision-making processes associated with groupthink and group polarization. Studies have shown that a diversity of personality types and background experiences within a work team tends to generate more innovation in problem-solving and greater information sharing than a fully homogeneous team (Phillips *et al.*, 2004; Donnellon, 1996). This line of research suggests that managers who wish to improve the performance of their work groups should seek out a diversity of perspectives when hiring, to remedy the challenges to ethical decision-making posed by reflecting with others.

V. The "Who is watching?" test

In Chapter 4, we discussed the obstacles to ethical decision-making that may be presented by high levels of organizational complexity and organizational hierarchy. Tiered divisions of authority within highly complex organizations can promote responsibility, if expectations and responsibilities are clearly defined at each level. However, as illustrated by the *Challenger* and *Columbia* disasters, organizational complexity can also increase our vulnerability to ethical blindness, by encouraging a deferral of moral responsibility. William F. May (1988) draws our attention to the ways in which these obstacles to ethical decision-making are exacerbated in contexts that require highly specialized knowledge. Noting our increasing reliance on the expertise of others for our well-being in virtually all walks of life, May draws our attention to a set of serious ethical challenges that result from this dependency. Not only do we depend on the responsible exercise of expertise by others, those who have this expertise typically work in complex institutional settings whose successful operation depends on the collective expertise of those working within them. Furthermore, institutions similarly depend on one another for their success in society. May expresses concern about how those with expertise handle their responsibilities:

Few others – whether lay people or other professionals – know what any given expert is up to. [They] had better be virtuous. Few may be in a position to discredit [them]. The knowledge explosion is also an ignorance explosion; if knowledge is power, then ignorance is powerlessness. Although it is possible to devise structures that limit the opportunities for the abuse of specialized knowledge, ultimately one needs to cultivate virtue in those who wield that relatively inaccessible power. One test of character and virtue is what a person does when no one is watching. A society that rests on expertise needs more people who can pass this test. (p. 408)

What does "passing" this test involve? May emphasizes the importance of certain virtues, such as honesty, fair-mindedness, competence, and trustworthiness. When he talks about a "knowledge explosion," May is not talking about knowledge shared among experts and non-experts alike. Much of this knowledge is highly specialized and not widely shared even within a given work setting. This unequal distribution of knowledge raises the possibility that those who have expertise can take on only the *appearance* of honesty, fair-mindedness, competence, and trustworthiness. The presentation of a virtuous public face at variance with private behavior can be at the expense of those the experts appear to serve, that is, those who are part of the "ignorance explosion" implied by their lack of relevant expertise, which may include colleagues as well as the general public.

The test posed by May might remind us of Plato's story of the Ring of Gyges in *The Republic*, mentioned in Chapter 5. A shepherd found a special ring on a corpse, placed it on his own finger, and wore it to a meeting of other shepherds with their king:

As he was sitting among the others he happened to twist the hoop of the ring towards himself, to the inside of his hand, and as he did they went on talking as if he had gone. He marveled at this and, fingering the ring, he turned the hoop outward again and became visible. Perceiving this he tested whether the ring had this power and so it happened: if he turned the hoop inwards he became invisible, but was visible when he turned it outwards. When he realized this, he at once arranged to become one of the messengers to the king. He went, committed adultery with the king's wife, attacked the king with her help, killed him, and took over the kingdom. (Plato, 1974, 32)

"What an unjust shepherd!", the storyteller imagines his listeners objecting. However, he goes on to assert that even the most just among us would eventually succumb to temptation if we possessed such a ring. The story concludes:

This, some would say, is a great proof that no one is just willingly but under compulsion, so that justice is not one's private good, since wherever either [the unjust or just] thought he could do wrong with impunity he would do so.(Plato, 1974, 32)

It is often alleged that, as we might say, "Everyone has a price." Whether or not this is true is debatable. Even assuming that the adage is true, it does not follow that, in more everyday workplace settings, we are moved primarily by considerations personal gain rather than, say, fairness, honesty, or compassion; most people's "price" might well exceed whatever "offers" are made to them. Still, opportunities for personal gain at the expense of others cannot be denied; and some may have a lower "price" than others. Furthermore, even those who have no desire to gain personally at the expense of others may be subjected to intense pressure from peers or authority figures to engage in ethically questionable behavior or themselves suffer serious consequences (e.g., demotion or job loss).

May's plea for character and virtue is well-placed. It is hoped that, by the time young people enter business and the professions, good character and appropriate virtues will have become firmly enough grounded that the pressures to engage in questionable behavior can be successfully resisted. However, being *prepared* to resist effectively requires being consciously aware of the ethical pitfalls discussed in this book, as well as an ability to detect these challenges in particular situations before it is too late, and having a willingness to resist them. Again, the idea of an impartial spectator, the ability to step back from one's situation, judge its positive and negative aspects, and assess how others might be affected provides a pathway to become consciously aware of obstacles to ethical decision-making, thereby opening up the possibility of effective remedy.

Vital as individual awareness of ethical pitfalls is, this awareness is necessary at the institutional level, as well. Thus, the recommendations of Janis and Sunstein, particularly in regard to the role of leadership and checks and balances within the structure of organizations, are crucial. Lone dissenters may be admired for their convictions and courage, but it is difficult for them to be effective without collegial and institutional support. Thaler and Sunstein (2009) propose that such support might take the form of "nudging," that is, changing situational factors in order to "nudge" us closer to making decisions that we will find morally agreeable. Store and cafeteria displays might be rearranged to guide us toward selection of healthier options, for example. Freedom of choice remains – I can still select cake rather than spinach – but with a nudge or two, I might settle for what is placed in front of me without having to do anything but accept it.

What Sunstein and Thaler conceptualize as changing our default positions with a little external nudging, Bazerman and Tenbrunsel (2011) call correcting our blind spots. The problem of organ donation illustrates the impact that rearranging or modifying the default position within a choice environment can have on overcoming ethical blind spots (Bazerman and Tenbrunsel, 2011; Thaler and Sunstein, 2009).

Asked if we think that it would be good if organs (such as hearts, kidneys, and eyes) were readily available for those in need, most of us would say, yes. Advances in medical technology make it possible to repair bodies, and even save lives, through organ transplantation. However, first, appropriate organs must be available. It would be ethically (and legally) wrong forcibly to take organs from the living. However, kidney donations are sometimes made voluntarily when the donor has two healthy kidneys and there is a good match with an identifiable intended recipient. But, for the most part, organ donations come from the deceased, with their prior consent. In the United States, this consent is facilitated by encouraging people explicitly and formally (e.g., in one's living will) to indicate that, upon death, their organs may be used for such purposes.

Requiring explicit permission to make use of organs of the deceased is the "default position" in the United States (Bazerman and Tenbrunsel, 2011; Thaler and Sunstein, 2009). However, in most European countries, the default position differs; organs of the deceased are regarded as available for use unless otherwise specified. Most would prefer the outcome of the European default position. If someone dies in an accident, the usable organs of the deceased will be made available; if you need an organ, there's 90 percent chance you will get one. But the United States' default position results in only a 45 percent chance of getting an organ.

Something seems clearly askew here. A remedy would be to introduce a change in the default position by designing a choice environment in which consent is presumed to be granted unless it is explicitly revoked. This "imposition" may seem to some like unwarranted interference with individual freedom. However, given the benefits of changing the default position, this limitation might be regarded as a small sacrifice, especially since greater availability of organs is something that would be welcomed by most. Furthermore, individual freedom is not eliminated; after all that is required is an act of saying "no." We might even say, as Bazerman and Tenbrunsel (2011) do, that such policy changes help us to overcome our "want selves," which bias us toward choices that contradict the preferences of our "should selves." When construed as a way of constructing policies or arranging environments in order to bias choice-makers toward their own ethical commitments, such "nudging" looks less like an external imposition and more like an external resource that provides support to the project of overcoming ethical blind spots.

Still, Thaler and Sunstein (2009) acknowledge that nudging can be quite controversial. There might be issues about the directions in which we are nudged, as well as concerns about "biasing" our choices, even if, in principle, we have retained our freedom of choice. After all, the naïve participants in the Milgram experiments were "nudged" by the experimenter, the person appearing to be in authority, and by the institutional setting of the university, with untoward outcomes. Thus, making an effort to engage the perspective of an impartial spectator, stepping back, recognizing and evaluating the direction and implications of the "nudge" is essential.

VI. The limits of moral hypocrisy or willful blindness

The eighteenth-century philosopher David Hume's hypothetical "sensible knave" extends our worries about Plato's Ring of Gyges. After presenting what he takes to be a quite satisfactory account of the major features of morality, Hume offers a serious challenge to the entire moral enterprise in the Conclusion of his *Enquiry Concerning the Principles of Morals* (1777, cited in 1975, 282). He asks what we should say about a sensible knave, a person who appreciates the advantages rules of justice provide for society and himself, but thinks that he could make further personal gain by making himself an exception to the rules. Such a knave, Hume suggests, "may think that an act of iniquity or infidelity will make a considerable addition to his fortune, without causing any considerable breach in the social union and confederacy."

For this ploy to work, the knave must resort to deception in trying to persuade others that he is fully supportive of justice. So, it seems that the knave is prepared to act in ways that are ethically problematic in two fundamental respects. First, there are the wrongful acts themselves (acts of *iniquity*). Second, they are performed deceptively and, hence, involve *dishonesty*. Regarding dishonesty, Hume (p. 283) attributes the following thinking to the sensible knave:

That *honesty is the best policy*, may be a good general rule, but is liable to many exceptions; and he, it may perhaps be thought, conducts himself with most wisdom, who observes the general rule, and takes advantage of all the exceptions.

Bernie Madoff provides an illustration of this sort of knavery. Madoff made himself and his operations exempt from the expected transparency of market exchanges, even with his so-called friends, later admitting that he remained aware that his actions violated moral and legal norms.

However, one need not be a thoroughgoing sensible knave to appreciate the force of Hume's challenge. Anyone might occasionally have such knavish thoughts. But, says Hume, our sentiments reject the sensible knave's "wisdom," not as irrational, but as abhorrent. For the ordinary person, says Hume:

If his heart rebel not against such pernicious maxims, baseness, he has indeed lost a considerable motive to virtue... But in all ingenuous natures, the antipathy to treachery and roguery is too strong to be counter-balanced by any views of profit or pecuniary advantage. Inward peace of mind, consciousness of integrity, a satisfactory review of our own conduct; these are circumstances very requisite to happiness, and will be cherished and cultivated by every honest man, who feels the importance of them. (p. 283)

Knaves, says Hume, seem willing to trade their integrity for "worthless toys and gewgaws." Hume is convinced that, explicitly confronted with the challenge of the sensible knave, we will protest knavery in others – and, insofar as we recognize it, in ourselves.

It is to be hoped that those who have knavish inclinations will either not act on them or not be successful in their efforts. However, *sensible* knaves can be expected to be clever. Public protest against sensible knavery makes good sense, particularly to those who wish to privately violate the norms against which they protest. It is important to be trusted, to appear to be honest and reliable. Sensible knaves depend on others being seriously committed to these values, and they depend on others seeing them in this way, too. But this commits the sensible knave only to *appearing* to be honest and reliable. This is the knave's *public* face. *Privately*, however, he can retain his opportunistic attitude.

Batson *et al.* (2006) label this phenomenon *moral hypocrisy*. This moral hypocrisy places pragmatic (economic) value on carefully crafted duplicity in the business realm. What matters is reputation, regardless of the underlying reality. In relation to today's business world, Batson *et al.* write:

[T]o be thought moral without actually being so is of as much value as actually being so. Indeed, it is of even more value. As long as others trust me to be fair and honest when I am not, they will deal with me with their guard down, and I can easily take advantage of them – time after time. (p. 322)

To test whether this attitude is alive and well, Batson *et al.* devised a research program that presents participants with an easily understood circumstance in which they have the opportunity to choose between favoring their own self-interest at the expense of acting contrary to what they regard as fair. Undergraduates were instructed to assign themselves and another participant to tasks, with one of the tasks rewarding correct responses with a raffle ticket for a $30 prize and the other not offering any reward. Even when agreeing from the outset that flipping a coin would be the fairest way of making assignments, only about half of the participants chose this method when a coin was made available to them. Most of those who chose not to flip a coin assigned the raffle ticket task to themselves. Significantly more than half of those who chose to flip the coin (and were then left alone to do so) ended up assigning themselves the raffle ticket task – suggesting that, most likely, some manipulated the results in their favor.

Citing the results of their own research and that of others, Batson *et al.* conclude that moral hypocrisy in business is commonplace and perhaps even on the rise. In fact, they claim that what might ordinarily be seen as only a pragmatic virtue (something that works) may be seen by many as morally acceptable, if not commendable:

Not only does there seem to be widespread recognition that moral hypocrisy is pragmatically effective but also increasing recognition that the businessperson not so motivated is morally deficient. Such a person is unable to make the hard decisions that need to be made in the modern business world. He or she lacks sense and savvy. Fettered by needless moral quibbles and constraints, he or she is unable to do what is good for business. (p. 333)

In order to resist this flawed mental model, it is crucial to understand the situational factors that increase our vulnerability to it. While holding that moral hypocrisy in the business world is not "all-important or omnipresent," Batson *et al.* do identify a set of conditions that they believe especially invites such hypocrisy. First, an individual faces making a decision about how some resources are to be distributed among two or more individuals. Second, the decision-maker has a clear preference for a particular distribution, typically one that provides him or

her with more of the valued resources than other possible distribu-
tions would. Third, the decision-maker recognizes that opting for his
or her favored distribution would violate one or more moral principles
(such as being fair or honest, not stealing, not cheating, or the like).
Fourth, although the decision-maker acknowledges that these moral
principles are "oughts," in this circumstance moral awareness is not
enough to overcome the desire to opt for the preferred distribution.
Fifth, the decision-maker still wants to be seen by others as moral
and, therefore, will not openly and blatantly violate the relevant moral
principles.

Given that these five conditions are met, the likelihood of moral
hypocrisy coming into play is increased until, finally, the situation
"provides enough ambiguity or 'wiggle room' to enable the individual to act in a way that appears to be in line with the relevant moral
principles yet assures the preferred distribution" (Batson *et al.*, 2006,
329). Batson *et al.* (p. 331) conclude that this last condition is commonly met due to features of the modern business world that, as they
put it, "create an ideal environment for suspended thought, the form
of self-deception that seems to underlie the most pernicious forms of
moral hypocrisy." For example, business decisions are often "fractured," with decision-making shared among different divisions of the
workplace, making it easy to ignore the implications of one's own part
in decision-making. Even top-level executives tend to make fractured
decisions, based on seeing the proverbial forest rather than the trees.
The business "forests" are sales charts, market share reports, and the
like, rather than "trees" such as safety features in gas tank designs. In
addition, because product development, assessment, production, and
sales are typically handled in different departments, "*selective exposure to morally relevant information is possible, and likely*" (p. 332,
emphasis in original).

We need not presume that moral hypocrisy in the business arena
necessarily carries over into other areas of life. However, Batson *et al.*
assert that there seems to be some sort of "business exemption on
morality." Perhaps, they say, this may be "an unintended legacy of
Adam Smith's ... famous notion of the Invisible Hand – that in business the public good is best served by relentless pursuit of self-interest
and that moral restraint only gets in the way" (p. 330). However, on
this matter it should be objected that this interpretation of Smith's promotion of self-interest is worse than an "unintended legacy." It stands

in direct contradiction with what Smith explicitly says regarding the role of self-interest in the pursuit of the public good.

Famous for saying that the butcher, baker, and brewer should attend to their own business self-interest rather than trying directly to promote the public good, Smith says nothing that should give comfort to Hume's sensible knave. He holds that aiming at personal gain by providing goods and services to others is quite compatible with striving to be fully trustworthy in that capacity. But the sensible knave's readiness to make himself the exception to the rule is inconsistent with being seriously committed to justice, the cornerstone of Smith's view of morality in both *The Theory of Moral Sentiments* and *The Wealth of Nations*. For Smith, our sense of justice serves to constrain the excessive pursuit of personal gain. There is no reason to assume that Smith means to exempt the butcher, baker, and brewer from these constraints. The following passage from *The Theory of Moral Sentiments* could just as well have been included in *The Wealth of Nations:*

In the race for wealth, and honours, and preferments, [a person] may run as hard as he can, and strain every nerve and every muscle, in order to outstrip all his competitors. But if he should justle, or throw down any of them, the indulgence of the spectators is entirely at an end. It is a violation of fair play, which they cannot admit of. (1790, cited in 1984, 83)

Adam Smith was Hume's contemporary and friend, and he was fully familiar with Hume's writings in moral philosophy. Although as unsympathetic to the ambitions of the sensible knave as Hume, Smith was quite sensitive to our human shortcomings – particularly our reliance on self-deception, which he refers to as "this fatal weakness of mankind" that is "the source of half of the disorders of human life" (pp. 158–9). In fact, much of Smith's *Theory of Moral Sentiments* is a depiction of what contributes to this self-deception and what is required of us if we are to resist its more corrosive effects. A key aspect of self-deception, as we discussed earlier, involves an overestimation of how ethical we are, a problem that arises because we all wish to see ourselves as at least ethically decent individuals. Satisfying this desire for a high moral self-assessment requires us to bury from view some of our more unseemly attitudes and desires. Although Smith credits even the most knavish of us with having some sympathy for the suffering of others, he claims that peeling back the coverings of our self-deception would reveal selves that would meet our strong moral disapproval.

Wanting to appear to ourselves to merit moral approval, we are highly motivated to accept the protection that self-deception provides.

Unfortunately, as the research presented in previous chapters indicates, we leave much to be desired in our efforts to match our behavior with the ethical standards we want to live up to. Our failure in satisfying this want is, to a large extent, facilitated by various forms of "ethical blindness." This blindness should not be confused with a conscious intent to act unethically. Contrary to Smith's fears, if we could peel back the coverings of our self-deception, we would not necessarily be *morally disgusted* with what we would see. We would not see ourselves as filled with knavish ambitions (which is not to say that we would not find any knavish tendencies at all). But most likely, we would be *morally disappointed*, for we would realize that, despite our conscious concern to see ourselves as competent, decent people, we are commonly unaware of our complicity in things that are ethically problematic. This disappointment need not be discouraging; in fact, it is revelatory of our aspirations to act in a manner that comports with our values, and can serve as an impetus to resist moral hypocrisy.

VII. Moral education

Moral education in our schools, colleges and organizations is a significant factor in promoting the kind of sound decision-making that can help overcome obstacles such as moral hypocrisy. Education in ethics may be key to addressing worries that ethical decision-making is risky or difficult. Rest (1994), for example, postulates moral awareness, moral judgment, moral intention, and moral action as the key components. Attending to all four of these components is quite challenging. However, Bazerman and Tenbrunsel (2011, 29) are skeptical about what they call "traditional approaches to ethics," including Rest's. They contend that so much of our ethical life is controlled by factors of which we are not consciously aware, and therefore, such approaches are of little use. These approaches, say Bazerman and Tenbrunsel, "assume that people recognize an ethical dilemma for what it is and respond to it intentionally."

However, rather than interpret Rest's model as a normative ideal, Bazerman and Tenbrunsel take it to be offering a descriptive account of how individuals actually do make moral decisions. Since Rest regards his account to be a critique of theoretical paradigms that place a nearly exclusive emphasis on moral reasoning in moral development and moral education, this reading seems quite wide of the mark. For Rest, developing programs to assist us in recognizing the ethical dimensions of situations is critical, as it is one of his central points that this recognition is difficult and requires hard work. Regarding moral reasoning, Rest thinks this, too, is central to good moral decision-making; but, again, he does not assume that, without effort, we are particularly good at practicing such reasoning. What is needed, according to Rest, is careful framing of what is important morally in any given situation; appropriate employment of moral reasoning in framing one's intentions; qualities of character that motivate attempting to carry out these intentions; and, finally, effective execution of these intentions in action.

Rest's "four component" approach to moral education is quite consistent with the approach to teaching ethics in higher education recommended more than thirty years ago by a distinguished group of ethics teachers from across the curriculum that met at the Hastings Center over a three-year period. The culmination of their work in 1980 was the publication of a series of monographs about the goals of teaching ethics in a wide range of areas, such as business, engineering, journalism, law, medicine, philosophy, and the social sciences. The Hastings Center also published a major book, *Ethics Teaching in Higher Education* (Callahan and Bok, 1980). Despite the vast differences among the academic disciplines represented in these publications, each one advanced the same five basic aims and goals, tailored to the different areas of the curriculum. The consensus was that efforts should be made to:

- Stimulate our moral imagination
- Recognize moral issues as early as possible
- Analyze key moral concepts and principles and their application in appropriate contexts
- Stimulate our sense of responsibility
- Identify ways we can deal effectively with moral ambiguity and disagreement

Each of these goals is relevant to good decision-making, as characterized at the outset of this chapter and in previous chapters. The exercise of moral imagination involves stepping back from the immediacy of a situation, examining operative mental models that might limit one's understanding of the moral dimensions of the situation, imagining different possible choices, and evaluating their likely consequences before decisions are actually made. Practicing moral imagination can result in a clearer, more complete grasp of the important issues at stake. In turn, this imaginative practice can suggest constructive ways of dealing with these issues that also take into account new problems likely to arise from whatever is decided now. There is not always be time to go through all these steps in a particular situation. However, reflecting in this way on past situations and realistic, fictional scenarios can help prepare one for situations that do not allow much time for reflection, by instilling mental models conducive to ethical decision-making that work to counter mental models that blind us to the moral dimension of the situations we encounter.

VIII. Trust in intuition and the role of moral reasoning

One of the most serious obstacles to avoiding moral blindness is trust in one's intuition or relying on a habit or pattern to interpret a new situation. For example, as we saw in Chapter 2, Johnson & Johnson had built up a strong reputation because of the habits accrued through the following of the company's credo, as seen in the quick response to the Tylenol incidents. But the presumption that the credo's values were inherent in the company's actions came to replace careful scrutiny of actual decisions, and in 2008, this presumption led Johnson & Johnson to be unable to recognize quality failure in many of its products, such as baby Tylenol and its hip transplants. Similarly, British Petroleum drilled for oil so many times using the same techniques that they failed to imagine that drilling might be different in the Gulf of Mexico with subcontractors supplying the rigs that went as deep as 10,000 feet. As we noted in Chapter 2, BP not only failed to question its habitual approach when entering into a new drilling endeavor, the company also failed to remember its own questionable safety history.

Exercising moral imagination can play a key role in enabling us to recognize moral issues and in avoiding habitual behavior that makes us vulnerable to moral blindness. Often, however, decisions are made first, without fully anticipating and taking into account serious problems that might result. A case in point is the development of roundabouts as an alternative to standard intersections. Commonplace in Europe, construction of roundabouts is on the increase in the United

States. A problem now being addressed that originally seems to have been largely overlooked is the difficulty roundabouts pose for visually disabled pedestrians who want to cross the road (ITRE, 2012). Intersections with stop signs or traffic lights allow visually disabled pedestrians to use auditory cues to help determine when crossing the street is safe. However, cars coming to a full stop at roundabouts is the exception to the rule. Thanks largely to researchers in the areas that focus on problems facing the visually impaired, highway engineers are now addressing this safety issue – not only in designing new roundabouts, but also in making already constructed roundabouts safer.

Of course, new problems resulting from scientific and technological advancements are not confined to how they might affect those with special disabilities. For example, the introduction of cell phones to the general public has resulted in increased driving risks for users and nonusers alike. As the sophistication of cell phones has increased, so have the dangers they pose to driving safety. The issue of the danger of cell phone use while driving points to the broader problem of driver distraction. Research now indicates that use of such electronic equipment while driving may be as profoundly dangerous as drunk driving (Strayer, Drew, and Crouch, 2006). That the introduction of cell phones could pose a safety hazard was not completely unanticipated. Cell phone pioneer Martin Cooper testified before the Michigan State Highway Commission in the 1960s, long before cell phones were available for public use, that using them while driving would pose safety risks (Richtel, 2009). He recommended putting some sort of lock on cell phones that would make dialing while driving impossible. However, this advice was never heeded, and half a century later we are struggling with ways of handling safety issues that industry spokesman Steve Largent says have vastly exceed early expectations: "This was never something we anticipated . . . The reality of distracted driving has become more apparent to all of us."

In his original testimony, Cooper said that not using a cell phone while driving was a matter of common sense. Perhaps confidence that common sense would prevail convinced lawmakers that putting a lock on the dial would not be necessary. Whether they were thinking that someday more than 90 percent of Americans would have cell phones (with much more versatility and sophistication than Cooper's early model) is another matter.

Permitting the introduction of cell phones without legal restrictions of their use, or safety devices like the one recommended by Martin Cooper, is now more complicated. Since this device (in both its earlier and more advanced forms) has already been introduced to the public without such restrictions in use (except in a few places in the United States), one of the issues is whether consumers should have their "freedom" *taken away*. This example illustrates the importance of the Hastings Center's third goal in teaching ethics: analyzing key ethical concepts and principles (and their legal counterparts).

Undertaking analyses of ethical problems like that of the regulation of cell phone usage for drivers can be expected to reveal some disagreement among those who undertake such explorations, which, in turn, raises questions about how these disagreements might be most constructively addressed (the Hastings Center's fifth goal). If the first four goals are pursued with seriousness, this rigor may make the fifth goal more manageable. A clearer grasp of what the basic issues are sometimes leads to a resolution of disagreements. However, in the end, reasonable people who listen carefully to others sometimes can reasonably disagree with each other. Even in the face of such disagreements, it can be necessary for stakeholders to make decisions together. Here an exploration of possible compromises can be helpful.

Philosopher Martin Benjamin (1990) explores possibilities for compromise when it can be achieved without undermining one's moral integrity. He advocates that we develop what he calls a "democratic temperament" – a willingness to share the power to shape and make decisions with other stakeholders, rather than adopting an attitude of "my way, or no way." Benjamin comments:

As a rule, parties to this process try to see matters from the other's point of view, engage in various forms of give-and-take-discussion, and are prepared, at least in principle, to make concessions for the sake of coming to terms. In so doing they acknowledge each other's viewpoints as having some claim to equal respect and consideration. (p. 5)

Of course, much political discourse falls considerably short of matching this model of working our way through differences. The same is likely true in the more private domain of the boardroom and in communication in general within a business setting. However, as Benjamin suggests, at least *in principle*, rational persuasion, mutual trust, and reasonable concessions are available alternatives for those whose mental models are open to them.

James Rest, the Hastings Center group of educators, and others such as Martin Benjamin are not proposing models of moral education that focus too narrowly on moral *reasoning* and that presume that we have a good grasp of the premises from which that reasoning should proceed. However, *in actual practice*, they could agree, blind spots can interfere with our framing of the challenges at hand. As a result, moral reasoning is short-circuited, as the premises from which we should be reasoning are "missing in action." Still, moral reasoning may be employed in *imagining* what one would do if faced with certain decisions; and it may be employed in looking back at what one has actually decided.

IX. Egocentric bias, the "veil of ignorance," and other moral resources

One of the obstacles to any ethical decision-making process is an undue focus on oneself. Although the role that self-absorbed bias plays when we make decisions may be overstated, it cannot be denied that it does often play a significant role. We also have a tendency to be biased in favor of those who share our alma mater, race, or gender, a preference that we have referred to as the "flight to the familiar." This preference for what is familiar and known can give rise to ethical problems that may go unnoticed. For example, a nephew asks his uncle to put in a special word for him to members of his alma mater's admissions committee. The uncle feels he should support his nephew's endeavor to gain admission. What the uncle fails to consider, however, is that he is, in effect, attempting to give his nephew what others might regard as an unfair advantage over other candidates, applicants who may be equally, if not better, qualified for admission. Here we see the uncle's good intentions for his "near and dear" pushing aside broader considerations of fairness.

This in-group favoritism is not necessarily self-consciously embraced. It can reflect a form of egocentric thinking that focuses on the interests of a few (say, our "near and dear"), not from exclusively self-interested motives, but from motives that exclude others whose interests warrant consideration and respect, as well. The shortcoming of egocentric thinking is its tendency to see things, as we might put

it, from *my* eyes only, rather than those of others as well. For example, in the *Challenger* case, management perceived the launch risks
differently than did engineers, as we have noted. More importantly,
in this context, neither group understood the motives or mindsets
of the other. Indeed, it appears that management thought they were
making the correct decision, but they were operating only from their
management-centric perspective.

The first step in combating the tendency of egocentricism is to recognize its effects. However, although this helps us recognize egocentricism in others, Bazerman and Tenbrunsel (2011, 56) note, research
indicates that it does not seem to help us with our own egocentricism.
Here, they suggest, a mental exercise such as John Rawls's (1971)
hypothetical "veil of ignorance" might help.[3] Rawls invites us to imagine a group of people who, as individuals, are temporarily stripped of
special knowledge of who they are, whether they are male or female,
rich or poor, well-educated or poorly educated, what their national-
ity is, and so on. He then asks the members of this group to select
principles of justice by which they would agree to be governed once
the "veil of ignorance" is lifted – but without foreknowledge of where
they might be positioned in society once this thought experiment is
finished. The power of this thought experiment is that the imaginative
effort it requires works to deprive participants of just the sort of special
knowledge about themselves and their circumstances that might bias
their judgment in their favor.

However, are we always biased toward ourselves? Consider the Trolley Case. Introduced to the philosophical world in the late 1960s by
philosopher Philippa Foot (1978), this fictional exercise in moral imagination challenges some of our everyday presumptions. This scenario
and its variations suggest that a self-interested bias is not necessarily
a feature of our "intuitive" decision-making. Asked if they would be
willing to flip a switch on a runaway trolley that would move the
trolley to a track that would kill one person rather than five, most
say they would. Asked if they would be willing to push a large man
onto the tracks in order to stop the trolley from running over five others, most say no. In both cases, however, five lives can be saved and
only one lost. What accounts for the apparently inconsistent responses

---

[3] For a fuller account of Rawls' "veil of ignorance," see his *A Theory of Justice*
(1971), chapter 3, section 24, "The Veil of Ignorance," pp. 136–41.

from those surveyed? This is a very complicated question. Those who say yes to flipping the switch but no to pushing the man in front of the trolley seem at a loss in making good sense of their shift. But all seem concerned about the loss of innocent lives, not just their own self-interest.

Of course, some may be reluctant to push the man in front of the trolley because they fear that they will be punished for doing so. But some may think that pushing a man in front of the trolley is a case of deliberately taking the life of an innocent person, whereas flipping the switch does not implicate them in such an act. Whether or not it does is a topic that deserves considerable discussion. But we will not venture into this moral (and legal) thicket. For our purposes here, it is sufficient to point out that at least some respondents object to their deliberate killing of someone by pushing them onto the tracks. The objection is to the killing, not to their being subjected to punishment. If it were argued that it is also deliberate killing to flip the switch, what would (should) the response be? Perhaps some would say that they would like to reconsider flipping the switch – that, too, they might say, would be wrong. Of course, letting five die when one has the means for saving them hardly leaves one with clean hands, regardless of the basis of the choice.

It seems plausible to conclude that there is no resolution available in the Trolley Case that should leave one feeling morally comfortable with whatever decision is made. Still, the difficulty of the moral choice does not mean that a quick, "intuitive" decision always reflects a self-serving, or even an egocentric, bias. Further, it is not clear that a slower, more "reflective" decision is better in such cases – cases that, fortunately, hardly ever occur, at least not that starkly. In fact, we might well wonder to what extent our theories about morality and moral decision making should be determined by the "what ifs" of such extreme cases. Not only should we be very careful in generalizing from such cases to everyday moral decision making outside the business domain, we should be careful in generalizing from them to decision making in business (which also seldom confronts one with such dramatic, and obvious, stakes).

What examples like the Trolley Case seem to prompt for us are conflicting moral intuitions, rather than subconscious bias in favor of ourselves versus other values that quickly fade from view. Thus, we need not despair that beneath the level of self-conscious awareness lie only self-seeking concerns. Genuine other-regard and concern for doing what is right are available as moral resources. Often, however, these values are not sufficiently foregrounded in our mental models, and consequently, we are at risk of neglecting factors relevant to making good ethical decisions in complex situations. These values need to be supplemented with careful, self-conscious reflection that can bring these morally relevant factors into focus, as well. For example, Greg Smith (2012), a successful director at Goldman Sachs, resigned from Goldman and wrote a scathing op-ed piece in *The New York Times* excoriating the culture at that firm. According to Smith, when he first came to Goldman Sachs, the priority was, "clients first." But today managers and traders at the firm are only interested in profits, even referring to their clients as "muppets." Smith's dilemma preceding this expose was acute. Should he stay with Goldman and work in a firm whose philosophy he strongly disagreed with or "blow the whistle," thereby incurring the wrath of the company and most likely being blackballed from any other positions in the financial industry. Neither choice was going to have positive outcomes. Moreover, the public can never be certain whether Smith's accusations, which Goldman Sachs denies, have validity. Fortunately, not all complicated ethical problems are genuine dilemmas. Good, hard thinking can result in good answers, or at least some that are clearly better than others, even if no clearly "best" answer emerges from our reflections.

Similar comments can be made about the Milgram experiment. Moral conflict seems apparent throughout the experiences of those playing the role of Teacher. For most Milgram subjects, their unease was not experienced as a simple conflict between their self-centered "want self" and their moral concerns about the plight of the Learner. Rather, they experienced a mix of moral concerns – concerns that focused on commitments made to the researcher, on not undermining the research project and its aims, and on respecting the "authority" of the researcher and the institution sanctioning the research. Again, it seems that, whatever decision the Teacher might have made about whether or not to continue in the project, some level of moral unease would result. The psychologists and psychiatrists, and Milgram himself, all seemed to underestimate the moral complexity of the research setting for those who would volunteer to be Teachers, thereby also vastly underestimating the numbers who would cooperate fully.

Some residual unease no matter what final decisions are made in the various Trolley Case scenarios is to be expected as well. This does not mean that all moral decisions are equally good (or bad) in such cases. Nor does it mean that our "intuitions," or "gut" responses, have nothing to be said for them and should be dismissed as irrelevant. It does mean that, as we discussed in Chapter 5, intuition must be subjected to critical examination if we are to remain alert to the risks of bias. Something *more* than "intuition" is needed in complex cases, though describing all our motives, interests, and actions as egocentric, and likely self-serving, is a misdescription of much more complex motivations. We will never know altogether what the motivations for Greg Smith's op-ed piece were. His reasons may have been, in part, self-interested (e.g., to get in the news), or he may have hated Goldman's leadership. But, given what he knew would be the outcome, his motivations had to be more complicated than those.

This analysis applies equally to corporate behavior. While sometimes described as primarily motivated to achieve firm-centric profitability, this simple conclusion belies a great deal of corporate behavior, which is much more complex. One will recall the case of Merck, which in the late 1970s discovered a cure for river blindness, a disease that struck millions of people in the developing world. Unable to market this drug in these countries due to lack of funding, poor infrastructure for distribution, and a weak healthcare system in most of the countries afflicted by river blindness, Merck decided to give the drug away, and to partner with the World Health Organization to distribute the drug throughout each blighted community (Donaldson, 2000). Why did they do this? Perhaps it was partly for public relations (although Merck made no explicit campaign to advertise what they were doing). But it also was in line with its explicitly stated mission to alleviate disease. In other words, it is likely that there were mixed motives behind Merck's decision – but not merely self-interested ones, since this was a very expensive choice with no guarantee of profitable return.

X. Willful blindness, moral motivation, and compliance sanctions

A thread running throughout much of the research we have discussed thus far, is that, although all of us would like to regard ourselves as ethically fair-minded and decent – in fact, most of us give ourselves passing marks – we are not as ethical as we think we are. There are many psychological factors that contribute to this. One of them is *motivated*, or *willful, blindness*. Willful blindness is characteristic of many conflicts of interest, particularly those that escape the immediate notice of those who have them. The initial worry about conflicts of interest is that they can skew the judgment of those who have them in favor of their own vested interests, thus providing an obstacle to exercising their judgment more dispassionately, from the perspective that Smith identified with the impartial spectator. Open, self-conscious awareness of such conflicts of interest can be difficult to accomplish, as one may also have a vested interest in *not* seeing the conflict. Thus, as we discussed in Chapter 5, one's blindness may be motivated by the desire not to have to acknowledge such complications.

Despite such motivated blindness, many agree with Adam Smith's notion that we want not only to be regarded by others as ethical, but by ourselves, as well. Once we become consciously aware of the heretofore unseen factors that determine our behavior, this can be taken into account in ways that can alter behavior in more ethically appropriate directions. Ignorance will no longer serve as an excuse (as it no longer exists), and our basic desire to behave ethically will now have a better opportunity to try to live up to itself. Moral education can provide us with resources at the individual level that help us to overcome forms of moral blindness that hide personal conflicts of interest from self-scrutiny. However, our ability to succeed ethically as individuals acting alone is limited, particularly when our decision-making takes place within corporate cultures that neglect ethical considerations.

To some extent, the limits of moral education are acknowledged in enforceable laws and regulations, codes of ethics, corporate ethics hotlines, and other visible expressions of ethical concern at the corporate level. The codification of ethical guidelines provides an explicit set of rules to guide decision-making in daily practice, and the threat of penalty for violators incentivizes compliance. However, it should not be assumed that employees are aware of the rules and their possible applications; and even if they are, there is reason to be concerned about how these rules are enforced and what attitudes such enforcement encourages in employees. Most important is the sort of motivation one has for acting in accordance with ethical standards. Intrinsic motivation (doing something because it is right) is preferable to external motivation (for example, doing what is right from fear of being penalized for not doing so).

A common worry is that, backed by the threat of legal sanctions, regulations will be seen as external constraints that have no ethical force. Thus, if a company compares the risk of being caught and having to pay a penalty with the savings that can come from violating a regulation, it could well opt for taking the risk of getting caught and penalized (especially if expected profits would substantially exceed the penalty). The worry, then, is that what should be regarded as an ethical issue is recast as an economic one, with the result of encouraging firms to engage in sensible knavery.

Weaver and Trevino (1999) cite studies that suggest that compliance sanctions actually result in less compliance than corporate programs that combine compliance training with ethics. Why? Without a compliance system in place, most decision-makers cast issues in ethical terms (e.g., "What is the right thing to do?"). However, when a compliance system is in place, participants are more inclined to see themselves as facing a business decision. Here the primary concern shifts to the likelihood of getting caught and the costs this might involve. Thus, a compliance system may lead to ethical fading and a greater likelihood of questionable behavior.

This worry that backing up ethical constraints and aspirations with sanctions against non-compliance may result in only external motivation to do what is ethical is a real one. However, there may be creative ways of minimizing this problem. In the mid-1970s, for example, 3M (Minnesota Mining and Manufacturing) decided that, rather than wait for the latest environmental regulations to force them to make environmental improvements, they would try to get ahead of the regulations and do so in ways, that in the long run, would actually save them money (EPA, 2011). Over the next several decades, 3M's success in combining environmental improvements with cost savings (millions of dollars) has become a "bragging point" for the corporation. It is an environmentally friendly *and* financially successful company (York, 2009).

When social responsibility is pursued alongside profit, moral hypocrisy is a legitimate concern. In relation to environmental efforts, critics have coined the term "greenwashing" to refer to the knavery of an "environmental stance a corporation publicizes without putting its rhetoric into practice; talking the talk without walking the walk"

(Vos, 2009, 674). However, environmentally sound policies need not be simply a public relations gimmick. Corporate leaders and their employees can genuinely believe in the environmental values they are serving, and they can endorse them without moral hypocrisy, in their company mission statements, public relations statements, and in their corporate bottom line. All of this can be done with an eye on present and forthcoming environmental regulations, which can guide them in pursuing environmental ends – and profits.

Incorporating social and environmental responsibility and profit-making directly into a company's bottom line is referred to as *triple-bottom-line thinking*. The fundamental assumption of triple-bottom-line thinking is that companies are responsible for their social and environmental impact, not merely the enhancement of their economic gains, and performance in all three areas can and should be measured to assess a company's success (Hindle, 2009). By promoting account-ability for social and environmental performance, the incorporation of triple-bottom-line thinking into company policy can work to overcome the temptation to moral hypocrisy that worries critics. Many compa-nies have now adopted mission statements that express a commit-ment to triple-bottom-line thinking. Others, such as Unilever, measure these three components quantitatively across the whole organization, and the Global Reporting Initiative has set up a voluntary reporting system with guidelines for triple-bottom-line reporting, although to date few American companies have signed up to do so (Cohen, 2011). Company websites that advertise such a commitment appeal to those who share these broader values, showing that a company can increase reputational value by successfully enacting a triple-bottom-line mis-sion. More importantly, from an ethical perspective, triple-bottom-line thinking can offer an alternative to perceiving environmental regula-tions as the imposition of ideas that are alien to the culture of profit-making companies. Although these regulations can carry with them the threat of enforcement (external motivation), they can also be seen as reasonable and fair standards that those companies committed to morally commendable social and environmental values want to sat-isfy. In this way, environmental regulations could be seen as express-ing internally accepted values in much the same way that laws against theft do.

More and more shareholders are taking the initiative in express-ing commitment to social and environmental values in addition to the standard commitment to economic profits (*"Shareholder Interest..."*, 2012). Whether external regulations that impose penalties are a real threat to the moral motivation of companies and their employees to support the values they represent would seem to depend on how companies promote and enact these values. If profit and fear of penalty are the only, or the primary, motivations driving decisions in a business context, the temptations to moral hypocrisy will be high. However, promoting frameworks that highlight the ethical, as well as the compliance, dimensions of a decision will help ensure that employees are not motivated only by fear of penalty. Further, incorporating ethical considerations into the corporate mission, and devising methods to measure performance in relation to mission goals, will help to ensure that social and environmental goals, for example, are taken seriously by corporate leadership.

XI. Ethics and regulations

A common response to widespread, serious ethical failure is to establish legally enforceable standards and regulations. While we have noted that focus on compliance regiments *alone* is inadequate to the promotion of ethical organizational cultures, there are few, if any, who would claim that we could do without all formal and professional regulation and still expect fair play and transparency in the business world. Ethical failures, whether due to knavery or ethical blindness, can expose the need for greater regulation and oversight that, in turn, can lead to innovations in the promotion of ethics. For example, in the mid 1980s, a multitude of scandals erupted in the U.S. defense industry, resulting in charges of corruption, fraud, and exploitation. These scandals led to the launch of the Defense Industry Initiative (DII), an industry-wide program to promote and ensure ethical business practices (DII, 2012). This initiative detailed guidelines for ethics management for corporations doing work with the Department of Defense and provided a rationale for companies having ethics officers.

Though a relatively new profession, the field has developed rapidly in response to the changing legal environment over the past two decades. In 1991, the U.S. Sentencing Commission established Federal Sentencing Guidelines for Organizations (FSGO), which set standards for organizations (large and small, commercial and non-commercial) to follow in order to obtain a reduction in penalties if the organization (or an employee acting in the name of the organization) should be convicted of a federal offense (USSC, 2010). These guidelines serve as self-regulation incentives for businesses and industry. The requirement for the sentencing reductions revolves around the establishment of a continuous ethics and compliance assessment programs. In response to these initiatives, the Ethics & Compliance Officer Association (ECOA) was founded at the Center for Business Ethics (at Bentley University, Waltham, MA) as a professional association (ECOA, n.d.a). ECOA is not the only association for ethics officers, and one does not have to be a member of an ethics officer organization to advise organizations in the area. The Sarbanes–Oxley Act of 2002 resulted in further additions to the accounting and ethics employment areas (SEC, n.d.). Risk assessment officers were soon added to many corporate ethics staffs. The risk officers monitor how shareholders' investments might be affected by the company's decisions. The Dodd–Frank Wall Street Reform and Consumer Protection Act of 2010 is the most recently ratified regulatory act. It not only encourages ethical behavior in all organizations, but a portion of the act has provisions that offer greater protection for whistleblowers.

Since the establishment of the FSGO standards, the prevalence of ethics and compliance programs has increased (ERC, 2012, 48). As a result, many organizations have hired ethics officers to oversee these burgeoning programs. Some companies, in an effort to raise awareness among employees and provide support for ethical behavior, have established special divisions for ethics and compliance training. This individual or office is also responsible for disseminating ethics or compliance information to employees (ECOA, n.d.b). The office is generally charged with uncovering or preventing unethical and illegal actions. In some cases ethics officers report to the Chief Executive Officer (CEO) and are responsible for evaluating the ethical implications of the company's contracts and other undertakings. This individual also suggests to the CEO ethical policies and procedures relating to ethics that should be implemented within the organization.

As it is a relatively new professional field, there is some debate regarding the best practices for ethics and compliance officers. Michael Hoffman (2010), one of the founders of the ECOA, has argued that, to avoid conflicts of interest with management and to be able to create a program that will fully apply to all personnel in an organization, the chief ethics and compliance officer should report directly to the board. This proposal, however, has not received much traction in corporate boardrooms. In response to such concerns about conflicts of interest, some organizations employ an "ethics advisor," rather than an officer, who is often aligned with the human resources division of an organization. This strategy is designed to facilitate an open door policy to report concerns and problems (Krell, 2010). Although ethics advisors are characterized as serving as aides for employees seeking to protect the firm by alerting it to wrongdoing that might well harm the company, speaking with an ethics advisor can still be seen by some as disloyalty to another employee or the organization.

Nevertheless, Krell (2010) urges that one of the major corporate goals of an organization should be genuinely to improve corporate ethics. He recommends that, in addition to having ethics officers and ethics advisors, companies should adopt codes of ethics and conduct quarterly performance reviews that include ethics audits. An ethics audit consists of "a systematic evaluation of an organization's ethics program and performance to determine whether it is effective" (Ferrell *et al.*, 2012, 243). Ferrell *et al.* suggest a general, seven-step framework to guide organizations seeking to evaluate their ethics programs: (1) secure the commitment of top management; (2) establish a team or committee to perform the audit; (3) define the scope of the audit by identifying key risk areas for the company; (4) review the mission, values, goals, and policies of the firm; (5) identify the measurement tools that will be used to assess progress, and collect the relevant information needed to utilize them; and (6) have an independent party – such as ethics auditing consultant or nonprofit group specializing in audits – verify the results of the audit. The seventh step involves communicating the audit results to the organization's board, upper management, and if feasible, to external stakeholders (p. 267).

Regular ethics audits can stop problems before they have a chance to grow, and provide transparency to the organization's stakeholders. However, as Krell (2010) notes, the converse is true as well. Avoiding ethics audits can be dangerous, because when unethical conduct is allowed, it will negatively affect the shareholders and stakeholders, which include suppliers, customers and the overall community. Young and Hasler (2010) maintain that the benefits of strengthening the role of ethical and reputational capital, and the risks of failing to do so, have not been adequately emphasized within corporations. Someday ethics audits and ethics codes may be seen to be essential in building capital. But until management understands that poor ethics makes for poor profits, businesses will continue to slight the place of an ethics core within their organizations.

Policies and procedures followed in conformity with the expectations of an ethics audit have the potential to reinforce mental models that can become habitual, ingrained, and applied in ways that support both good business and good ethics. To increase the chance of success of programs such as ethics audits, Werhane (2008) recommends a systems approach in the internal formation of ethics policies. This approach requires concentration on the network of relationships and patterns of interaction, rather than on individual components of particular relationships. Recalling the imaginative practice of the impartial spectator, enacting a systems approach involves spelling out the networks of relationships from different perspectives. A systems approach may be more appropriate for ethical problems among stakeholders of multinational organizations, where values from countries and corporations often clash. But the systems approach can also work well within an organization, whether local or global, as it recommends internal and external understanding of each division and stakeholder in an organization in need of ethical repair. When combined with the engagement of moral imagination, systems thinking can improve values grounded in change within a network of relationships. It can provide:

- An evaluative perspective that asks "What values are at stake for which stakeholders?" And "Which take priority, or should take priority"
- A proactive approach both within the system and in initiating structural change
- Careful reflection about whether and what organizations or individuals within the system might be capable of and willing to risk in carrying out changes (Werhane, 2008, 466)

By creating detailed rules for ethical behavior that take multiple perspectives into account, and by performing audits regularly to evaluate the effectiveness of these rules and the officers and programs that support them, a culture can be created in which ethical practices and corporate and industry rules are respected.

XII. Overcoming blind spots with moral imagination

As we mentioned previously, Bazerman and Tenbrunsel (2011) propose that ethical blind spots can be conceptualized in terms of a gap between the individual's "want" and "should" selves. If we hope to reduce this gap, it is important to recognize our vulnerability to our own unconscious biases, which operate within this gap in our awareness. Recognizing the source of such vulnerabilities to bias has been the task of the preceding chapters, and as we have argued in this chapter, an impartial spectator approach is crucial. The perspective of the impartial spectator is not produced from a position outside of our mental models – such a position does not exist, as it would be a "view from nowhere." As we have explained, the impartial spectator's viewpoint is produced by practice of considering alternative viewpoints to those that immediately come to mind. In terms of Bazerman and Tenbrunsel's "want" and "should" selves, one way to envision closing the gap between them would consist of imagining, in advance, how each "self" might view a choice situation. The very act of imagining opens up the possibility of increased impartiality, that is, a point of view that is not limited to one perspective or the other, but is capable of assessing both. When trying to predict our behavior, we need to try to think about our likely motivations at the time of decision. This can help bring the "want" self out of hiding during the planning stage for action; as well, we should try to bring the more abstract, principled thinking commonly employed in the prediction stage into the decision-making time. Active engagement with both our "want" and "should" selves can help us to prepare "for the hidden psychological forces that crop up before, during, and after we confront ethical dilemmas" (Bazerman and Tenbrunsel, 2011, 154). In other words, before making a decision, we should engage our moral imagination to predict what our self-interested "wants" might be, to reflect on our ethical value commitments, and most importantly, to attempt an impartial assessment of potential points of conflict between our wants and our "shoulds," or value commitments. Practicing moral imagination involves the effort to try to think beyond the range of options available within the mental models that are currently framing our experience, and pushes us to move beyond simply asking whether or not to behave unethically within a given choice context.

The following case of a critical response of a real-life engineer to the hypothetical choices presented by an ethics training video illustrates the productivity of moral imagination. The video *Gilbane Gold* is a popular case study used to dramatize the ethical dilemma of whistle-blowing in the context of a crisis, offering a fictional portrayal of a situation in which a young environmental engineer is trying to decide whether or not to blow the whistle on his company for covering up its failure to comply with local environmental regulations (Pritchard and Holtzapple, 1997). The engineer brings the crisis to his manager's attention: the company is dumping waste that is marginally more toxic than city law allows, but due to plans to increase production, the problem will drastically increase. The company could be brought into compliance by simply releasing more water with the toxic waste being emitted, thus maintaining the legally required proportion of toxic waster per volume of water. However, because the toxic waste (lead and arsenic) would still settle in larger amounts downstream, this purported solution would not really resolve the pollution problem; the regulation itself was flawed from the standpoint of protecting the environment. The engineer wants his company to act ethically, rather than settle for mere compliance, but the company's refusal leads him to blow the whistle.

Because the film situates the choice within a crisis, the engineer's limited choices are understandable. However, as a film that aims to provide ethics training, it is problematic that the issue of how the crisis came into being in the first place is not adequately addressed. Nowhere in the story is the engineer, or anyone else, shown trying to take action that might have prevented the crisis at earlier stages, though the fictional engineer is depicted as having had more than a year to work on the problem within the company. In short, *Gilbane Gold* offers no depiction of moral imagination at work. The fictional engineer is confronted with a choice that is defined for him by the crisis at hand: become complicit in the environmental threat being posed by the company; or blow the whistle, lose his job, and risk exposing the company to a scandal that could be fatal, causing hundreds of others to lose their jobs, as well. By the time this choice situation arises, the only viable options are tragic.

After showing *Gilbane Gold* to an audience of engineers attending a week-long workshop, one of the authors of this book was told that an environmental engineer should have been able to solve the problem in a way that would reduce the emission of toxic waste and keep costs under control. A member of the audience, Texas A&M engineer Mark Holtzapple, said that he would return to the workshop the next day with some concrete suggestions. He did so, outlining several possible ways of reducing the company's outflow of toxic waste. Each was projected to be significantly less costly to the company than the only "solution" suggested in the video (increasing the volume of water released with the increased volume of toxic waste, thus satisfying the required water/waste ratio). Holtzapple's solutions kept a steady eye on both the threat of pollution and the cost of making improvements. By exercising his imagination in this way, he was able to offer two additional options to having to choose between blowing the whistle or aggravating the environmental problem by going along with a solution that would cause harm and was, at best, only marginally legal.

Holtzapple was responding to a fictional example that presented more than an engineering problem to be resolved. The company represented in the film also presented the environmental engineers watching the film with an institutional setting in which communication among key managers was poor, planning ahead seemed marginal at best, and the predominant managerial attitude seemed to set profit margins and formal legal compliance above ethical responsibility to protect the environment. If we assume that managers with this profit-driven and compliance-only attitude would have considered Holtzapple's alternative solutions, they could have resolved the question of what should be done.

However, *Gilbane Gold* does teach the lesson – despite doing so inadvertently – that some situations do not so clearly lend themselves to "win-win" resolutions, even for individuals like Holtzapple who are willing and able to exercise moral imagination. Although one might come to a reasonably confident conclusion about what the right choice is, the question "Should I behave unethically or not?" may loom large unless one has some assurance that he or she will not *suffer* from behaving ethically (e.g., by being demoted or even losing one's job).

Acknowledging the limits of the individual employee's power to ensure that managers will be receptive to ethical concerns brings to light the importance of the organizational setting in determining how one's actions are likely to be received. Though it is not always feasible

to exit an employment situation, due to financial and other considerations, employees and managers would be well-served by assessing
the ethical culture of their workplace organization. Paying attention to
what is *not* said in organizations can be a useful way of determining
what informal values are at play. For example, if discussions focus
primarily on costs rather than safety, this may signal that safety is
undervalued and efforts to raise safety concerns may not be heard. It is
important to notice how unethical behavior is described – or disguised.
One needs to be alert to what Bazerman and Tenbrunsel call "sink-
holes": uncertainty, time pressure, short-term horizons, and isolation.
They conclude: "Once an organization has identified its 'ethics sink-
holes,' it needs to promote ethical values within these areas" (2011,
pp. 164–5). Notice the emphasis on what the *organization* should do.
An organization that does not take pains to avoid making significant
choices under these four conditions, which characterize a crisis situation like that depicted in *Gilbane Gold*, is likely to find itself in
"lose-lose" situations. This is a call for ethical leadership in the organization – by those in the top positions.

Greg Smith, the former director of Goldman Sachs whom we mentioned in the Introduction, echoes this call for ethical leadership in a
set of recommendations to that company:

I hope this is a wake-up call to the board of directors. Make the client the
focal point of your business again. Without clients you will not make money.
In fact, you will not exist. Weed out the morally bankrupt people, no matter
how much money they make for the firm. And get the culture right again, so
people want to work here for the right reasons. People who care only about
making money will not sustain this firm – or the trust of its clients – for very
much longer. (2012)

Individuals in lower-level positions can be expected to respond to ethical leadership. But, left on their own as individuals, they often copy
the behavior of their managers. They might reasonably fear that they
will be ineffective at making changes and that they will risk their jobs
if they become outspoken critics in their organizations. Such leadership at Goldman, however, if Smith's description of that corporate
culture were even partly correct, would require a radical revision of
the prevailing operative mindsets. According to a recent *New York
Times* article, Goldman is trying to "put on a friendly public face"
with a number of television interviews including a speech by the CEO

Lloyd Blankfein to a gay, bisexual and transgender conference (De la Merced, 2012, B1). Whether changing its public image will seep into the organizational culture is at least not impossible.

XIII. Conclusion

Earlier in this chapter we mentioned William F. May's concern that the "knowledge explosion" is an "ignorance explosion." We depend on expertise (increased knowledge), but it is not widely shared among those most affected by that expertise (those who receive the services – directly or indirectly), nor even widely within companies who employ those with expertise, but within separate "silos." Furthermore, many organizations are so complex that a vast amount of our ignorance is attributable to that fact itself. However, although some of the ignorance that comes with expertise, division of work, and sheer complexity is unavoidable, much of it is *willful*. Becoming critically aware of this willfulness is a first step toward remedying the ethical problems associated with this kind of ignorance.

Heffernan (2011) suggests that we may exaggerate corporate leadership's resistance to critical questions raised by those within their organizations who are accountable to them. For example, reflecting on the disastrous 2010 oil spill in the Gulf of Mexico, former BP chief executive John Browne comments, "I wish someone had challenged me and been brave enough to say: "We need to ask more disagreeable questions" (Browne, 2010, 211; quoted in Heffernan 2011, 227). However, without inviting such challenges, those in positions of leadership can expect most either to strive to please their leaders by trying to determine what they want or to use their present position as a steppingstone to advance their personal ambitions. In either case, the sort of moral imagination that engages critical thinking can be expected to be in short supply. As we have seen, this is the message of Irving Janis' research as well.

That we have strong tendencies to be compliant, obedient, conformists in situations that are structured along hierarchical authority lines is supported, not only by the research of Stanley Milgram, but also by the famous Stanford Prison Experiment, conducted by psychologist Philip Zimbardo in the 1970s, as we read in Chapter 3. Zimbardo's most recent project is to develop a "hero curriculum" for fifth graders. Designed to combat the fear of conflict and to help students not to be bystanders, his program emphasizes focusing on "we" rather than simply "me." Zimbardo's Heroic Imagination Project has the aim of helping children become adults who will see beyond their otherwise narrow perspectives and be "ordinary heroes." In a 2009 interview, Zimbardo said of the project:

> The goal is to change people's patterns of understanding, altering their thinking from "me" to "we." We do think that anyone can be a hero, but it's about compassion, altruism, empathy, and moral courage to empower people to take positive action during crucial moments in their lives. (Heffernan, 2011, 232)

Although current research may support the notion that all of us are somewhat disabled morally by blind spots, it is not enough to gain an understanding of this. It is also necessary to explore, as we have in this chapter, ways in which we might deal effectively with them. Finally, it is necessary for us to *want* to make better decisions from an ethical point of view. Sensible knaves can be expected to make different use of this understanding. David Hume and Adam Smith were convinced that most of us, including leaders, are not sensible knaves and would not knowingly opt for their way of life even if they thought they had something like the Ring of Gyges. Current research does not suggest that they were mistaken.

Standing in the way of effectively dealing with our blind spots are what Dennis Moberg identifies as systematic errors in "person perception" that threaten to undermine moral agency in organizations (Moberg, 2006). As we saw in Chapter 4, Moberg focuses on two patterns, or "frames," of perception. The first concentrates on moral qualities (e.g., being honest, generous, altruistic, or kind). The second concentrates on competence (e.g., being capable, smart, efficient, creative, or strong). Ethics blind spots render our perception of moral qualities incomplete, or even quite distorted. This can occur at both personal and interpersonal levels.

At the personal level, Moberg notes that self-perception tends to be more concerned about personal competence than moral self-assessment. We have a tendency to regard ourselves as basically moral persons in the workplace. However, our concerns about competency can come at the expense of not attending enough to moral matters. As Moberg puts it, "the personal ethics blind spot exists when persons are so keen on developing a competent self that they overlook the substance and expression of their moral selves" (p. 418). This blind spot may be a function of how managers tend to assess their subordinates, which, Moberg says, tends to be more in terms of criteria of competence than moral qualities.

At the interpersonal level, Moberg claims that, although the perception of organizational peers and superiors often focuses more on concerns about morality than competence, the overriding focus is on negative rather than positive traits. So, there is an interpersonal blind spot that results in overlooking the positive and exaggerating the negative. For whatever reasons, positive elements of character tend to be less salient than negative ones. As a result, employees are not likely to be morally inspired by those around them in their organization. Instead, they are more likely to find fault with their co-workers. But, Moberg concludes, "When subordinates see their coworkers behaving unethically and report it upward, they are greeted by bosses that are resistant to framing it in moral terms and therefore indifferent to the need for corrective action" (p. 421). The message to subordinates is that ethics is not a priority in their organization, and this is reinforced by the absence of overt ethics leadership by those at the top of the organization.

Moberg's turns to the notion of "reframing" as a possible remedy for this set of problems. Reframing, he says, is a common therapeutic tool of psychologists and counselors and a key to self-improvement. Applied to employee self-improvement, this requires three new frames: First, a frame is needed that answers the question "Why be moral?" in terms of intrinsic motivation (rather than the threat of punishment or the promise of reward). Second, a frame that features role models is needed. If role models from within the organization are not readily available, well-known models from outside the organization such as Mother Teresa or Gandhi are available, or less well-known exemplaries can be identified. Finally, a frame that welcomes support from peers and subordinates who show an appreciation for moral qualities in the organization can help (p. 422).

At the managerial level, Moberg urges, moral improvement is both needed and possible. First, special efforts need to be made by those in positions of leadership to communicate moral standards publicly and in ways that that indicate how these standards are reflected in their decision-making. Second, managers need to make special efforts to recognize morally desirable employee behavior. Third, they need to make special efforts to be informed about the moral behavior (and misbehavior) of those accountable to them. Finally, they need to deal effectively with violators. The importance of such efforts, and the challenges to their being successful, will be explored in detail in Chapter 7.

7 | Problematic mental models: Some applications

I. Introduction

This chapter will present a series of examples that illustrate the narrowing, compromising, and blinding effects of mental models and how they might be revisited and revised. Understanding how distorting mental models can be altered should be a matter of first importance for individuals as well as vital for organizational leadership. As we have noted in our analysis of the Milgram studies (1974), those in leadership roles can, by virtue of their perceived authority, move decent individuals to do things that we would expect them to find ethically unacceptable and refuse to do. The combination of this tendency to defer to authority with our mental models' ability to block or distort our recognition of ethical issues can make ethical decision making precarious. However, as we have seen in Chapter 3, changes in discourse can help empower individuals to move beyond the "silo mentality" that often limits the availability of alternative perspectives to those defined by organizational roles. The key factors in decision-making involve self-conscious reasoning and imaginative reflection that starts from, but also critically challenges, the immediate framing of a given choice-making context.

In reviewing Milgram's experiment, we may wonder how we would fare under similar circumstances. Most of us hope that our stance would be to immediately tell the researcher, "No, I won't give this individual an electric shock. This would be wrong!" Transcripts of the experiment and follow-up debriefings of the participants indicate that most did experience serious moral conflict as they administered what they took to be shocks. Apparently what enabled them to come to terms with what they would otherwise regard ethically unacceptable was the researcher's assurance that he, not they, would assume responsibility for any harm that might (improbably) occur. Milgram (1974, 133) called this deferral of responsibility an "agentic shift," which occurs when the decision-maker "no longer views himself as acting out of his own purposes but rather comes to see himself as an agent for executing the wishes of another person."

When faced with a corporate, professional or organizational opportunity to say "no" to an inappropriate request or expectation, what will be our operative mental model or the operative mental model of our organization? Will we cede our sense of responsibility, as many obedient Milgram subjects did? Or will we recognize the request or expectation as problematic, demonstrate commitment to our individual choices and values, and then take a firm stance as needed, as modeled by the disobedient subjects in Milgram's study? Will we inform an appropriate authority within our organization? Will we notify the Securities and Exchange Commission or the police if we witnessed an immoral or criminal act in the work place? Most of us do not expect to find ourselves witnessing a crime, moral problem or even questionable situation that would call for such actions. But, as we have learned from previous chapters, our workplace mindsets tend to dwell primarily on the most immediately transparent instances of wrongdoing.

We have characterized mental models as ways of representing, or cognitively framing, our experiences by selectively attending to stimuli in our social environment. These frameworks operate as "lenses" that set up parameters through which our experiences are filtered and organized. Applying this to organizational and business arenas, Dennis Moberg (2006) draws an analogy between business blind spots and blind spots encountered by a driver in a vehicle. The previous chapters remind us that our mental models can be revised and altered by practices that reinforce moral imagination. If regular attention is given to the deficit area, better moral understanding (or more defensive driving) could become a standard practice. Members of an organization may find that within a bounded mental model one can ignore or omit information that is important in the decision-making process. Managers are further challenged when they are blind to inconvenient or negative information. Awareness of expected role behaviors and their limits can help an organizational participant to take into account such information. With a new focus, members can broaden their perspective and consider a wider range of harms and benefits. Organizations, like individuals, need continually to determine whether ethical problems exist, and whether they indicate an isolated incident or repeated behavior, a time pressured decision, a decision with a short-term horizon, or otherwise appear symptomatic of ethical blindness. In any case, once an organization has identified ethical problems, ethical remedies need immediately to be put in action. In Chapter 6, we examined several remedies that may assist in the reframing of decision-making contexts, and stressed the need to gather information from a variety of sources to assist in the formation of ethically preferable outcomes.

This chapter examines current and historical cases and practices that characterize how organizational decision-making can be rife with ethical problems. Sometimes mental models become deeply embedded and reinforced within a social structure, and flawed habits can become choices. This embedded structure is part of an analysis of the Penn State football scandal of 2011, this chapter's first illustration. The next example, the 2008 meltdown of Wall Street, is obviously much broader in scope than college football. In exploring various investment cases, we bring to light flawed mental models that have severe financial, legal and ethical complications. The decline of ethical decision making within investment banking and other professional lending fields is a continuing problem for individuals and investors across the globe. Goldman Sachs is used as a focus because, historically, it has been cited as one of the most respected investment banks globally. We examine the Dodd–Frank Act as well as other governmental regulations that impose restrictions in many facets of the investment area, and we also question whether revised mental models have been put in place that could remedy serious risks and harms to investors.

When organizations are resistant to efforts to identify and remedy ethical problems, employees may be faced with difficult challenges. The exposure of inappropriate or illicit corporate activities by employees ties corporate morality to an individual's principles through "blowing the whistle" on improper activities. Historically, individuals both within and outside of organizations have exposed unethical and illegal behaviors in a variety of ways, including through use of the media, government oversight programs, or compliance groups. We examine a variety of uses of whistleblowing and consider whether loyalty to the company is ethically more important than safety to a consuming public. The conclusion of the chapter presents an exemplary case of how organizational "best practices" can become habituated. As a model, the Belmont Report of 1978 provides an ethical framework designed to protect participants in behavioral and medical research. Congress has not passed the Report into law, but nonetheless, it is strictly followed by the scientific community through institutional review boards, granting agencies, and various other bodies. Through good habits and practices researchers have generated a respect for the guidelines in the Report. The success of the Report suggests that principled guidelines, drawn from industry-specific experience, can positively affect the culture and behavior of any organization.

II. The Penn State football problem

To illustrate the seriousness of ethical failures that can arise at the organizational level, consider the case of Pennsylvania State University's football program. Football is a big business at Pennsylvania State University. In the fiscal year ending June 30, 2011, the program generated $72.7 million in gross revenues and $53.2 million in profit as reported to the U.S. Department of Education. This can be compared with the Chrysler Corporation, which cleared about $50 million in 2011. Penn State had an Aa1 credit rating (Chappatta and Chang, 2011).

In November of 2011, it was revealed that Jerry Sandusky, former defensive coach of the university's highly touted football team, was alleged to have sexually molested at least eight boys who were as young as ten years old. In 2002, graduate assistant Mike McQueary reported to legendary football coach Joe Paterno that he had witnessed Jerry Sandusky sexually molesting a young boy in a Penn State shower. Paterno, a longtime friend of Sandusky, said he then reported this incident to Penn State's athletic director Tim Curley (Berube, 2011, S1). Curley and university vice president Gary Schultz met with McQueary ten days later, but apparently this is where the matter stopped, as no record was found of either campus or city police being informed of the allegations. Nor, apparently, did Paterno discuss the matter with Sandusky. Nine years later, after a long-term grand jury investigation, the episode came to light and Sandusky was arrested and indicted (Chappell, 2012).

The failure of the university to involve the police promptly and decisively resulted in the dismissal of Joe Paterno, who at age eighty-four was college football's most successful coach (with 409 wins) and who was revered around the country for the academic and athletic integrity of his program. But the dismissals did not stop there. Also removed from office were Curley and University President Graham B. Spanier (Chappell, 2012). Complaints about the firing of Paterno from students and other supporters continued for months, suggesting that many were unable or unwilling to acknowledge that this popular figure had committed a serious ethical violation. The seriousness of the offense was reinforced on March 14, 2012, when the Penn State Board of Trustees released a public statement on the university website, once again defending its firing of Paterno. "The Board determined that his decision to do his minimum legal duty and not to do more to follow up constituted a failure of leadership by Coach Paterno," the report said (*"Report . . . "*, 2012).

In light of Paterno's reputation for demanding integrity from his athletic organization, and the damage to this reputation that he might have predicted as the likely result of going beyond "his minimum legal duty" to expose Sandusky's crimes, it is possible that Paterno was motivated to neglect his ethical responsibility. This is not to accuse Paterno of deciding to sacrifice the safety of young children for the sake of his personal or professional reputations; while we may never have access to Paterno's motivations, there is no evidence to suggest that he was fully aware of the threat that Sandusky posed to children. This lack of awareness is precisely the danger of ethical blind spots. Under the sway of willful or motivated blindness to evidence that challenged this self-assessment, the Penn State coach could attempt to justify his own behavior, which fulfilled only the minimum requirements of law, while holding others to a higher standard of integrity. As we discussed in Chapters 4 and 6, research indicates that most of us believe we are ethical; even convicted felons find a "self-morality" (Baumeister 1998; Allison *et al.*, 1989). Penn State's athletic department construed athletic successes and resulting fame in a manner that strengthened this self-perception, while remaining blind to evidence that clearly contradicted it. Ignorance may underlie poor choices; yet that ignorance can rise to the level of ethical failure when it is motivated by a desire to sustain a moral self-assessment.

In organizational "inside cases" like this, Seyla Benhabib recommends we consider the role of the "other" (1990, 359). Often key individuals or even organizational components are invisible because they are not primary stakeholders within the organization. Benhabib notes that when we do not see the "other" as another individual human being, problems of discrimination and injustice can easily arise (2004, 6, 8). The boys alleged to have been molested by Sandusky fall into this category. The Penn State University administration's attention seemed to focus primarily on constituents within the university community. The boys were not boosters, students, or alumni. They were boys from low-income circumstances and were part of a youth program endorsed, but not run, by the university. The boys were not part of the Penn State community and, therefore, did not register significantly within the administration's and athletic department's operative mental models.

Benhabib warns that, when there is a unified "us" (here, the Penn State "family"), there is also "an other" who is at risk of damage because of neglect or lack of concern. For Benhabib, failure to recognize the others around us as individual human beings jeopardizes our own human and democratic rights, as well as those of the immediate victims (2004, 36, 37, 39). The immorality and criminality of the sexual molestation of children is evident to nearly everyone. This is not a minor offense, and its victims are relatively powerless; they depend on adults for protection. What were the ethical and legal perceptions of Joe Paterno, his athletic director Tim Curley, or the Penn State Academic Vice President Gary Schultz? If Sandusky's actions were acknowledged as criminal, why was nothing further done? Their failure to respond appropriately suggests that their mental models were characterized by willful blindness. The athletic department believed their organization was well steeped in ethics, but did not appear open to revising this belief in the wake of new information.

In January of 2012, Joe Paterno expressed regret to a *Washington Post* reporter at not having done more when he was first told of the shower room incident by Mike McQueary:

I didn't know exactly how to handle it and I was afraid to do something that might jeopardize what the university procedure was. So I backed away and turned it over to some other people, people I thought would have a little more expertise than I did. It didn't work out that way[.]" (Jenkins, 2012)

Paterno did not know why he failed to follow up more aggressively, but in hindsight, he said, "I wish I had done more."

People are involved in a variety of overlapping social, professional, and religious roles. Each of these roles makes demands (Werhane, 2005, 39). In the case of Paterno, perhaps the demands of his overlapping roles clashed with his common-sense morality. The pressures to be a preeminent, competitive, and profitable coach may have kept him from understanding what one should do in such a situation. However, the need for action is well captured in Pennsylvania State Police Commissioner Frank Noonan's statement: "Somebody has to question... the moral requirements for a human being that knows of sexual things that are taking place with a child." He added, "I think you have the moral responsibility, whether you're a football coach or a university president or the guy sweeping the building. I think you have a moral responsibility to call us" (Soshnick and Novy-Williams, 2011).

Throughout the years of its highly profitable program, Penn State's athletic program succeeded in protecting its reputation as a place of integrity, avoiding stories of unsportsmanlike athletes or the recruitment of "rent-a-players," who come to a university only for short-term preparation for the "pros." The football program prided itself in the graduation rate of its players. When McQueary came to Paterno in 2002, the university was nearing the end of a $1.4 billion fundraising campaign, and it had recently expanded the football stadium to become the nation's second largest. In six years it would open a $55 million basketball arena (Soshnick and Novy-Williams, 2011). In 2011, with the abuse scandal in the public eye, school officials found themselves accused of covering up the criminal and heinous activities of one of their own. The win/loss record, the outstanding recruiting, the full stands, the television contracts, and the merchandise sales seemingly were more important than aggressively investigating evidence of ongoing criminal behavior that, by law, should have been reported to the police.

There was another problem that had been brewing at Penn State for about eight years: documented accounts that athletes were protected from being punished through the university's student judicial division. On November 22, 2011, *The Wall Street Journal* reported that over a two-year period of time Coach Paterno, President Spanier and others repeatedly argued with Dr Vicky Triponey, Vice President for Student Affairs, the official charged with adjudicating student violations of school regulations (Albergotti, 2011). In principle, this oversight responsibility extends to university athletes, as well as the general student population. However, Dr Triponey's internal emails from 2005 to 2007 complained that Coach Paterno believed she should have "no interest (or business) holding our football players accountable to our community standards... And I think he was saying we should treat football players different from other students in this regard" (p. 1). Dr Triponey, as chief disciplinary officer for the university, wrote an e-mail to President Spanier, stating: "I would respectfully ask that you please do something to stop this atrocious behavior before this team and an entire generation of Penn State students leave here believing this is appropriate and acceptable behavior within a civil university community" (p. 1). Paterno and other members of the Penn State coaching staff demonstrated the patterns that occur with "bounded awareness." Recall from Chapter 5 that bounded awareness is a "systematic pattern of cognition that prevents people from noticing or focusing on useful, observable, and relevant data" (Gino *et al.*, 2009, 248). The football administrators made implicit choices to attend to some information and ignore other details.

Understandably, Dr Triponey's mindset was characterized by a focus upon adherence to a set of policies and procedures established for all students, faculty and employees of the University. Her job was to fairly enforce student judiciary policies. However, she was not allowed to question student athletes and they were not held to the same regulations as other students and employees. Dr Triponey reasonably expected the same ethical and legal rules would apply to all. The capacity for fundraising, particularly in athletics, may have been partially responsible. Warren Zola, an administrator from Boston College, comments, "The revenue opportunities are so substantial that the pressure placed upon the athletic department and coach, specifically, make it ever more difficult to pursue a school's mission" (Soshnick and Novy-Williams, 2011).

Dr Triponey's final Penn State problem occurred in 2007 when police charged six Penn State football players after they broke into a campus apartment and beat up several students, one of them severely. Later that year, following a "tense meeting" with Paterno over the case because of "philosophical differences," Triponey left the university (Albergotti, 2011, 1). "There were numerous meetings and discussions about specific and pending student discipline cases that involved football players," Triponey said, which included "demands" to adjust the judicial process for football players. The end result was that football players were treated "more favorably than other students accused of violating the community standards as defined by the student code of conduct" (p. 1). Penn State administrators exhibited willful blindness and bounded ethicality in their failure to acknowledge the need to punish athletes for violation of university rules.

In the wake of the Sandusky scandal, Penn State appointed Dr Rodney Erickson as interim president. Dr Erikson suggested that the prevailing Penn State culture promoted football at the expense of focusing on academics, research, and scholarship. He announced that Penn State would build a great research facility and a center for abused children (Johnson and Whiteside, 2011). Can Penn State move away from the mental models that distracted them from the University's mission? Change is difficult, but in these critical circumstances a renewed commitment to a more appropriate balance of university values may result. For this to happen, new organizational mental models are needed to mediate and shape the responses to ethical challenge.

As noted earlier, the most serious problem in practical ethics, or at least in business ethics, is not that we frame experiences; it is not that these mental models are incomplete and likely biased in favor of local values. The larger problem is that most of us, either individually or as groups, do not realize that we are framing issues too narrowly, disregarding data, ignoring counterevidence, or not adequately taking into account other points of view (Werhane, 2007, 404).

III. Unraveling of Wall Street

The September 2008 Wall Street crash was due to toxic mortgages and irregular trading by banks, particularly investment banks. By the end of October of 2008 the United States was in the most severe recession it had faced since 1930. The immediate effects were the firing and laying off of hundreds of thousands of workers. Graduates from most colleges and universities struggled to find jobs, and to pay back their student loans. Auto sales plunged more than 40 percent, and scores of Americans began paying cash for purchases rather than making unnecessary expenditures on credit cards. The stock market fell and kept falling. Many Americans on the verge of retirement watched as their portfolios shrunk by half. For a short time, the use of derivatives was slowed. When President Bush signed the Troubled Asset Relief Program (TARP) into law in 2008, capital was at the lowest point of the financial crisis. More than 650 banks received injections of public capital from TARP.

In the following section, we examine several major figures, institutions, and historical trends in finance and financial regulation that bear at least partial responsibility for the collapse, and identify troubling mental models that resulted in impeded or distorted ethical decision-making by individuals, and within organizational cultures.

Bernanke, Greenspan, and Paulson

In early fall of 2008, the United States financial market faced one of its worst disasters in history. Many of the fiscal problems originated from sub-prime mortgages and their entanglements with investment banks and opaque financial instruments known as derivatives (McLean, 2010). Bankers and instrument creators were not the only individuals at fault. Many savvy and non-savvy investors listened to "so-called experts" who told them how to make large profits in the booming housing and investment markets, while ignoring the effects of the actions on impacted stakeholders (Bazerman and Moore, 2008). Most likely because of high profits, high commissions, and high hopes, there was a strong undervaluing of experts who warned against these investments (Lewis 2010, 198). Many traditional bankers voiced strong concern when individuals purchased homes with little or no documentation or income. Few listened to the banker's concerns (p. 211). Packaging these subprime mortgages into bond tranches, many investment executives participated in the unethical, reckless and sometimes fraudulent behavior taking place within the market. Contributing to this troubled ethical culture in the finance industry was the improper rating of these bonds. A disturbingly flawed ethical culture also permeated many governmental offices. Three economic leaders in high governmental positions – Ben Bernanke, Alan Greenspan, and Henry Paulson – had particular areas of blindness in the market crash. Each experienced a narrowing of mental models that harmed the economy.

Ben Bernanke, the Federal Reserve chair, acknowledged that he noticed market problems between banks and subprime mortgages in 2007, but admitted later that he did not give the matter the careful attention it required. By the end of the crisis, he described the collapsed situation as a failure of all parties "to appreciate that our sophisticated, hypermodern, highly hedged, derivatives-based financial system – how ultimately fragile it really was" (Lowenstein, 2012, 55). Bernanke's admitted blindness to the impending collapse was a result of not closely analyzing how mortgage-backed securities had come to make up a sizable portion of the assets of the biggest banks.

"Risk was concentrated in key financial intermediaries. It led to panics and runs. That's what made it all so bad" (Lowenstein, 2012). Rising prices in residential real estate was the first clue that Bernanke misdiagnosed. Bernanke said he determined the residential prices were rising because money from China and other countries was rolling into the U.S. mortgage market. His decision to do nothing exhibits bounded ethicality. Bernanke's mental model of the market concentrated on the large investment participants such as banks, brokerage firms, and hedge funds, and hence he failed to consider the many impacted shareholders, in particular new small home owners and local banks, all of whom would be harmed in a market collapse. Bernanke's 2007 mindset did not include thinking about the problems in the financial markets caused by the subprime mortgages. As the crisis of 2008 got closer, Bernanke said he continued following his academic hero, Milton Friedman, believing the market would right itself before a depression. It did not correct itself and a market collapse of unprecedented proportions became Bernanke's responsibility to disentangle (Lowenstein, 2012, 57).

The market crash was probably inevitable, in part because of policies during the term of Bernanke's predecessor, Alan Greenspan. As we noted in Chapter 4, in his 2008 testimony before the House Committee of Oversight and Government Reform, Greenspan himself admitted to flaws in his thinking. As the devastating market forces unfolded, Greenspan was ill-prepared, acknowledging that "[t]hose of us who have looked to the self-interest of lending institutions to protect shareholder's equity, myself included, are in a state of shocked disbelief" (Andrews, 2008). As chair of the Federal Reserve from 1987 to 2006, Greenspan oversaw a long financial and economic market boom. Willful and motivated blindness was exacerbated when Greenspan failed to analyze his economic theories and philosophies in relation to a developing disaster. He kept interest rates low while ignoring the growing bubble in housing prices and risky financial transactions filling the market. He also failed to note the unsafe and fraudulently growing real estate market.

Critics, including many economists and members of the U.S. Congress, believed that Greenspan contributed significantly to the financial crisis by ignoring problems in the banking and mortgage industries. Representative Henry Waxman, Chair of the Oversight Committee demanded an answer from Greenspan in 2008:

You had the authority to prevent irresponsible lending practices that led to the subprime mortgage crisis. You were advised to do so by many others. Do you feel that your ideology pushed you to make decisions that you wish you had not made? (Andrews, 2008)

Greenspan reluctantly acknowledged, "Yes, I've found a flaw. I don't know how significant or permanent it is. But I've been very distressed by that fact" (Andrews, 2008).

Henry Paulson became Treasury Secretary in 2006 after leading Goldman Sachs as CEO for twelve years. When Paulson accepted the Treasury position, it was amid criticism of conflicts of interest. Paulson left Goldman Sachs with a net worth of $700 million and a large pension. He "was one of the first Wall Street leaders to recognize how drastically investment banks could enhance their profitability by betting with their own capital instead of acting as intermediaries" (Eley, 2008). Inattention to the dangers of investment banking leveraging was often cited as a reason for the 2008 market crash. The obstacles in Paulson's mental models might have developed because of his overestimation of investment banking as a tool for financial well-being and reform, which bounded his awareness. As details of the collapse unfolded, it appeared that organizational complexity as well as the hierarchy within the mortgage and banking communities often interfered with Paulson's ability to reframe his thinking, and individuals and organizations under Paulson's control, too, thus remained blind to ethical and financial problems.

William K. Black, a professor of law, says of Paulson,

He's brought on people who have the same life experiences and ideologies as he does. These people were trained by Paulson, evaluated by Paulson so their mind-set is not just shaped in generalized group think – it's specific Paulson group think. (Creswell and White, 2008)

Paulson brought in trusted others for counsel as the collapse was occurring and received an "ethics waiver" to talk directly with Goldman Sachs for twenty-four hours prior to the TARP bailout.

From a perspective of bounded awareness, members of Paulson's team negotiated in a variety of arenas regarding who would survive the financial crisis, who would be partnered with stronger banks, who would face foreclosure, and what would be done with the staggering problems facing American International Group (AIG), the insurer of many of the subprime loans, and many of these banks (Creswell and

White, 2008). Some of the leaders involved in the bailout provided examples of individuals who framed their experiences to fit only within their own worldview. That the largest of the investment banks and American International Group needed to survive was imperative in their decision-making.

So how did the bailout play out? Bear Stearns's clients were rescued by JP Morgan Chase and the Federal Reserve, Merrill Lynch was acquired by Bank of America, and Citibank and American International Group (AIG) could not survive without a bailout from the federal government in the form of TARP (Sorkin, 2008). Among the major financial entities utilizing the first dispersal of TARP funding were: Fannie Mae, Freddy Mac, AIG, Bank of America, JPMorgan Chase, Wells Fargo, Goldman Sachs and, Morgan Stanley (Karnitschnig *et al.*, 2008). Lehman Brothers was the one bank that was not given a lifeline.

The special case of Lehman Brothers

As noted in Chapters 3 and 4, complex and hierarchical structures can lead the most powerful members of organizations to develop mental models in which they see themselves as mere bystanders, free from accountability for the behavior of their employees. This may have been the case at Lehman Brothers in 2007 and 2008, as a disaster within this disaster was brewing for their clients, employees, and thousands of investors who would be harmed by their failure. Lehman had leveraged its borrowing of funds to a 31:1 ratio ($1 for Lehman and $31 elsewhere), leaving open the possibility of multi-billion dollar losses (Barr, 2011). Much of Lehman's leveraged investing was in housing-related assets. The investment bank had been in a financial downturn for months prior to the complete collapse. The firm had tried to find partners in Korea and England to help stabilize its base. But executives in these countries would not partner with the firm, and Lehman Brothers was forced to file for bankruptcy on September 15, 2008.

For months leading up to the bankruptcy, decision-making at Lehman bore marks of being governed by "confirmation heuristics." A confirmation heuristic is a cognitive shortcut that can block access to understanding a full spectrum of stakeholders' views. When utilizing this shortcut, individuals seek out only the details that reinforce their point of view, thereby neglecting conflicting information (Bazerman and Moore, 2008). As we saw in Chapter 5, confirmation heuristics contribute to ethics obstacles when their use impedes decision-makers from examining resources with which to more fully consider the consequences of their choices. There had been opportunities for Lehman to sell its position in mortgage trenches, but the company was stuck in a mindset that ignored data that did not conform to its preferred perspective; consequently, it did not react quickly enough to remain solvent.

In May 2008, Matthew Lee, then a senior vice president overseeing Lehman's global balance sheets, sent a letter to senior management detailing several problems with the firm's accounting. The letter identified serious irregularities in Lehman Brother's appraisals of assets. Lee specified that the asset appraisals were unrealistic (*"Lehman Brothers'..."* Saphi, 2010). The letter was addressed to Martin Kelly, Lehman's controller, Gerard Reilly, head of capital markets product control, Erin Callan, chief financial officer, and Christopher J. O'Meara, chief risk officer (*"The Letter..."*, 2010). A copy was also sent to Mr Lee's lawyer, Erwin J. Shustak. A few days later Matthew Lee was pulled out of a meeting and immediately fired. It was two months later when Lehman Brothers was forced to file bankruptcy, the largest in U.S. History (Corkery, 2010).

The leadership at Lehman Brothers refused to recognize the disastrous financial system of the firm before it was too late. Flawed mental models or blind spots on the part of Lehman's leadership caused global harm to employees, investors, consumers and others when the overall bankruptcy occurred. According to Moberg (2000) and Bazerman and Tenbrunsel (2011), most of us have a tendency to predict what we will do on the basis of what we think we should do. However, when it comes time to act, we have a tendency to do what we want to do, thus allowing self-interest and our impulses of the moment to take over. This blind spot allows ethical factors that may have been prominent in our predictive mode to fade out of sight. When ethical considerations were allowed to fade out of sight, the corporation followed suit (Bazerman and Tenbrunsel, 2011, 2006).

Flawed mental models and the 2008 Collapse

Mental models are "the mechanisms whereby humans are able to generate descriptions of system purpose and form, explanations of system functioning and observed system states, and predictions of future

system states" (Rouse and Morris, 1986, 351). How did the dominant mental models in the finance world devolve into ethical obstacles? In the 1990s, members of the American investment community
were insisting on deregulation that would allow for greater profits.
Champions of deregulation included another Goldman Sachs CEO,
Robert Rubin, who was President Bill Clinton's Secretary of the Treasury. The mental models behind the push for deregulation vary. Some
of the mindsets relied upon to interpret banking and investment systems prior to 1999 were based on experiences learned from the Great
Depression. With early twentieth-century regulatory mind sets now
seen as an impediment to investing, as well as to large commissions
and bonuses, new schemas were formed that justified greater leveraging
as beneficial to the economy, particularly Wall Street. At the outset, no
one was expecting ethical decision-making problems to result from the
move to revoke the Glass–Steagall Act of 1933, the act that regulated
much of the banking industry (Freed, 2012). Indeed, it appears that little thought was given to ethics prior to reducing regulatory oversight.
When the Glass–Steagall Act was in place, investment banks could
only leverage their own money for investments (Sanati, 2009). With
the revocation of Glass–Steagall, investment banks were now cleared
to participate in high leveraging of funds, rather than working from
the funds of the banks' owners. Instead of banks serving as a utility for
customers, they became financial institutions working for "agents" of
the owners. The financial institutions' owners were not at risk for loss;
the risk was relegated to distant "others," in most cases without their
knowledge. Also, many of these new investments were complex derivatives (Welby, 1997, 86). From these two factors, increased leveraging
and complex derivatives, organizations created structured investment
vehicles, such as Collateralized Debt Obligations (CDOs), and began
selling them to unsuspecting investors (Sorkin, 2008).

These conditions and instruments were created, at least in part,
because investors were demanding greater yields on their investments.
This chain of events resulted in lower market values for homes plus
mortgages with balloon or other adjustable measures that raised interest rates. In turn, these interest rates and lowered values led to delin-
quencies and defaults by homeowners (Sorkin, 2008). When values in
residential real estate plummeted as a consequence, the financial structures, instruments and the institutions – primarily financial – that held
their mortgages were also negatively affected (Labaton, 2008). The

operative mindsets within the investment banking industry encouraged executives and their sales staffs to ignore the mortgage defaults that were happening in record numbers, and to continue to sell bond instruments based on the sub-prime mortgages. From a self-interested perspective, the financiers assumed they would prosper because of an insurance instrument that would keep the investors from losing on mortgages they did not own (Sorkin, 2008). Most of this insurance was provided by American International Group (AIG), who at one time controlled 85 percent of all insurance on the subprime mortgage bonds.

Many of these moral failures can be traced to narrow or blinded mental models. These moral failures are caused by an inability to question managerial decisions and commands from a moral point of view. Little moral imagination was employed when analyzing a portfolio or making a decision to sell a home to yet another unqualified client. Moral imagination may have encouraged a stronger evaluation of financial instruments before proceeding. It also appears that a limited set of operative mental models were in place: models based on sales and profit but not on prudence. Related to this "profit over prudence" model were the risks being taken by investment banks. These banks are not subject to the same regulations applied to depository banks. Investment banks are allowed to leverage owners' assets with debt. The mental models within the elite banking system distorted ethical and financial decision-making. A broad picture was no longer available to these bankers; rather, the framework for decision-making had become a limited perspective that blocked ethical considerations from view, resulting in catastrophic financial losses for millions of Americans in both the real estate and stock markets.

A paucity of moral responsibility

John C. Bogle, the founder of Vanguard Group, asserts that a lack of ethics throughout Wall Street was responsible for the 2008 bailout. He does not excuse any one firm from responsibility. In a 2009 *Wall Street Journal* editorial, Bogle laments the unchecked market forces, particularly in the fields of investment banking, banking, and finance that almost destroyed the global economy. He calls for the firms to make long-term investments in lieu of short-term gains, and to create an overall culture of ethics in all practices. Instead of being publicly traded or privately owned, money managers now hold 75 percent of all shares of public companies. Bogle and others believe these money managers fostered the global crisis by engaging in dangerous speculation in a variety of ways. Some institutions created tranches of bonds within a sub-prime mortgage industry that was destined to fail. But superficial ratings and weak controls from financial firms also enabled these investments to skyrocket and then plummet (Lewis, 2010, 211). To many analysts, regulations that were passed in the wake of the financial crisis of 2008 seem inadequate to the task of limiting risk-taking within the institutions that threatened the overall stability of the global economic system. In the investment banking sector and other corporate settings, it may be that managers refused to change organizational mindsets. At some point these managers may have accepted these mindsets as providing full and complete pictures of their industry. As we have argued throughout the previous chapter, this kind of ideological thinking results in the failure to engage in proactive sense making with regard to new regulatory forces, public changes in economic needs, and unforeseen pressures from the media. Re-evaluating organizational behavior should be part of a learning experience, yet it is often a rationalization for continuing to operate under the same mental models.

Blankfein and Goldman Sachs

As *The New York Times* notes, "Goldman Sachs has arguably been the most successful firm on Wall Street for decades, with some of the world's biggest private equity and hedge funds and investment bankers and traders who practically minted money" (*"Goldman . . . "*, 2012). Given the corporation's status and the profits it gained from engaging in high-risk behavior, it was unlikely that Goldman Sachs CEO Lloyd Blankfein would willingly accept any blame for the financial failures taking place throughout the country and the world.

Blankfein was called before the U.S. Congress in February of 2009 to explain Goldman Sachs' part in the 2008 financial collapse and continuing decline. In his testimony, Blankfein thanked Congress for generously loaning Goldman Sachs funds during the financial crisis of 2008 (US House, 2009). He emphasized that he understood how Americans might be skeptical of the investment banking industry and its part in a global market collapse. However, Blankfein deflected blame, arguing that rating agencies and regulators failed to "sound the alarm that there was too much lending and too much leverage in the system – that credit had become too cheap" (p. 2). He also noted that Goldman Sachs did not need the bailout funds and repaid them; yet, he failed to mention that the bailout funds provided to AIG went first to pay their $12 billion debt to Goldman Sachs, before stabilizing other parts of the company (Lewis, 2010, 260; Sorkin, 2008).

The perspective that Blankfein presented to Congress, to the investment banking industry, and to consumers was that Goldman Sachs was too big to fail, and too moral to be blamed for any illegal or unethical conduct. He attributed much of the financial collapse to confusion regarding complex derivatives that lacked transparency (US House, 2009, 3). In his testimony, Blankfein explained that his firm's risk management processes "did not and could not provide absolute clarity" on the day to day transactions within the sub-prime mortgage market, but emphasized his firm had little exposure in the derivative market. This claim also turned out to be false (Lewis, 2010, 263). Further, Blankfein stressed that maintaining his firm's reputation is paramount at all times. His final statement to the Senate panel investigating the financial crisis asserted, "We didn't have a massive short against the housing market and we certainly did not bet against our clients." This statement, as well, may be proven false.

The "myth of invisibility" seems to be one of Blankfein's obstacles to ethical decision-making. Like the wearer of Plato's Ring of Gyges that we discussed in Chapters 5 and 6, Blankfein seemed to think that if the real actions of Goldman Sachs were invisible to the rest of the world, the ethical character of the company remained untainted. Believing in this invisibility of Goldman's real actions, Blankfein testified that government regulations would be a solution to the massive financial meltdown, and he affirmed that Goldman Sachs would support regulations (Creswell and White, 2008, B1). Perhaps unsurprisingly, Goldman Sachs and many other investment banks and firms would later oppose the bulk of the directives that would come to form the Fraud Enforcement and Recovery Act of 2009 and the Dodd–Frank Wall Street Reform and Consumer Protection Act of 2010 ("*Goldman Sachs Spent...*", 2011).

One year after Blankfein's testimony, Bethany McLean wrote the following after interviewing him for *Vanity Fair*:

In what one person describes as "hand-to-hand combat" in the dark alleys of D.C., Goldman and the other big dealers are seeking exemptions to some proposed new requirements that would help shine a big spotlight on derivatives trading – thereby hoping to keep the market murky. 'Every time we go into a member of Congress's office, they already have a Goldman Sachs white paper on this,' marvels another person who is active in Washington. The dealers, including Goldman, argue that they are trying to preserve their clients' profits, not their own. (McLean, 2010)

On June 2, 2011, Goldman Sachs was subpoenaed by the Manhattan District Attorney's office over its activities leading up to the financial crisis (Sorkin and Craig, 2011). This subpoena suggests that several government agencies may be running parallel investigations. It is limited to ground covered in an April 2011 Senate report that showed Goldman Sachs had steered investors toward mortgage securities it knew would likely fail. The report found that Goldman Sachs marketed four sets of complex mortgage securities to banks and other investors, but failed to disclose that the securities were very risky. Further, the firm secretly bet against the investors' positions and deceived them about its own positions. The panel's report found these behaviors were part of an effort to shift risk from Goldman Sachs' own balance sheets to those of investors. While unsettling, neither the report nor the subpoena have yet resulted in convictions of fraud against the giant investment bank.

A skewed "moral self-image" may also be a factor in the decision making at Goldman Sachs. Publicly, at least, Blankfein has made efforts to justify his behavior, suggesting that Goldman Sachs' actions are good for the company's clients and good for the country. When this mental model is operative, only actions that strengthen a positive moral self-assessment are acknowledged, while evidence that might serve to disprove this evaluation is ignored or undervalued. Consciously, the executives may claim to hold certain values dear. However, they may have developed blind spots that prevent them from considering fully their practices. Concluding his 2009 testimony, Blankfein stated that, overall, he was grateful for the government bailout of 2008, but he insisted that his firm has always displayed integrity in its actions.

The Goldman Sachs example reminds us "[n]o organization can properly be understood apart from its wider social and cultural context" (Scott, 1995, cited in 2001, 151). Further, it illustrates Chapter 2's observation that, like individuals, the Goldman Sachs organization was created and affected by its social and political contexts. Organizations like Goldman Sachs are filled with individual and group decision makers. Some of these decision makers have flexible mindsets and can change the corporate culture to one that demonstrates responsibility to the remaining 99 percent of the economic population (Stiglitz, 2011). However, we find little evidence of such moral imagination within Blankfein's testimony or Goldman Sachs' actions. Expecting such ethical understanding and action from individuals who are not in executive positions is unrealistic when the top executive officers are not setting standards themselves. Compounding the problem, Goldman Sachs has had a privileged position on Wall Street and within the George W. Bush and Barak Obama administrations. The firm's relationship to the Treasury Department is so strong that "other bankers and competitors have given the star-studded firm a new nickname: Government Sachs," as Creswell and White (2008) reported in *The New York Times*. The *Times* reporters described the workings of this relationship:

This summer [2008], when Treasury Secretary Henry M. Paulson, Jr. sought help navigating the Wall Street meltdown, he turned to his old firm, Goldman Sachs, snagging a handful of former bankers and other experts in corporate restructurings. In September, after the government bailed out the American International Group, the faltering insurance giant, for $85 billion, Mr Paulson helped select a director from Goldman's own board to lead A.I.G. And earlier this month, when Mr Paulson needed someone to oversee the government's proposed $700 billion bailout fund, he again recruited someone with a Goldman pedigree, giving the post to a 35-year-old former investment banker who, before coming to the Treasury Department, had little background in housing finance. (Creswell and White, 2008)

Although the administrations of Bush and Obama deny favoritism, problems of familiarity and homogeneity are evident in the government hiring of so many Goldman employees. Ethical obstacles of familiarity and homogeneity harm the decision-making process, as most individuals display a tendency to support the familiar choice rather than try something new. As we discuss in Chapter 5, Litt *et al.* (2011) call this phenomenon as the "flight to the familiar" (p. 526). This preference for familiarity may shape a variety of choices within an organization, from hiring to promotion to awarding contracts, without registering as a conscious decision.

As an aside, Blankfein was so captivated by the spiritual nature of his corporation's moral self-image that he defended large executive bonuses with a comment that caught the headline in the UK's *Sunday Times*:

He said modern banking performed a vital function and described himself as just a banker "doing God's work." "We're very important. We help companies to grow by helping them to raise capital. Companies that grow create wealth. This, in turn, allows people to have jobs that create more growth and more wealth. We have a social purpose."[1] (Arlidge, 2009)

Organizations such as Goldman Sachs and circumstances such as the market crash of 2008 may intensify motivated self-deception. Moberg (2006) explains that in organizational settings, we are likely to partition our practice of moral frames and competency frames. In doing so, we adopt a positive moral self-appraisal, hence utilizing competency criteria when evaluating our own behavior. Recall from Chapter 4 that Moberg refers to this tendency as a "personal ethics blind spot." Personal ethics blind spots are reinforced by mental models that deem moral frames as "private," and consequently, as unsuitable for organizational judgments. The resulting power of organizational competency frames can lead executives such as Blankfein, as well as other employees, to fail to generate moral frames when challenged with situations that call for both ethically responsible and competent decisions. Even if only partially accurate, Greg Smith's exposé of Goldman in 2012, discussed in Chapter 6, illustrates that self-deception.

Throughout this book we have emphasized the importance of being aware that often we are dependent upon particular mental models in troubling ways. Once we understand the limits of a model's scope, this understanding requires that we continually seek diverse viewpoints, alternate frameworks, and theoretical constructs that challenge this dependence. We understand that all mental models are incomplete; those models that devolve into impediments to ethical deliberation do so when our reliance upon them encourages us to lose sight of this

---

[1] A year after this pronouncement, JP Morgan's CEO Jamie Dimon was giving a presentation at an industry event. He was struggling with his laptop when Blankfein joked from the audience, "I'm feeling better about my competitive position" (Levin, 2010). Dimon responded, "Just doing God's work up here, Lloyd."

partiality. It appears that an ethical blind spot exists in the relationship between the giant investment banking firm and the U.S. Government.

Interestingly, as the 2008 financial crisis unfolded, Federal Reserve Chair Bernanke did more than just acknowledge his failure to grasp the causes and seriousness of the crisis. With his moral and economic vision expanded, he made some unpopular decisions to interfere with the financial system. Abandoning his idol, Milton Friedman, and remembering his own graduate studies of the Great Depression of the 1930s, Bernanke worked to leverage the financial instruments of the Federal Reserve System. Continuing until the publication of this book, he has worked tirelessly to try to repair the economy with infusions of Federal Reserve funds into the economy and the institution of very low interest rates. Today some commentators argue that this new focused decision-making and financial input by the Fed are responsible for the improvement in the economy (Lowenstein, 2012). Whether or not such actions will be to the long-term benefit of the economy remains to be seen as the United States works its way out of the 2008 recession. For our purposes, what is important is that Bernanke was able to evaluate and revise his own economic mindset in light of the economic crisis. That this revision is possible, that mindsets are not static and unchanging, is exemplified by Bernanke's new vision of the direction of the Federal Reserve.

Judge Jed Rakoff

To date few individuals and corporations have been tried for a part in the overall Wall Street scheme that caused trillion dollar losses and threatened global economic stability (Ferguson, 2010, Part 5; Lowenstein, 2010, 280). In 2009, however, Judge Jed Rakoff, of the U.S. District Court in Manhattan, rejected a $33 million settlement between the SEC and Citigroup on the grounds that he could not approve an agreement that did not require Citigroup to admit any wrongdoing. The judge scorned the SEC's ruling that described the criminal act as "negligence" instead of intentional fraud. Asking two fundamental questions, Rakoff shifted interpretation of the situation from an ethics-impeding mental model to a responsible, reasonable, and ethical decision-making model: (1) "Why should the court impose a judgment in a case in which the SEC alleges a serious securities fraud but the defendant neither admits nor denies wrongdoing?" and

(2) "How can a securities fraud of this nature and magnitude be the result simply of negligence?" (Wyatt, 2011). Rakoff explicitly framed his questions and subsequent decisions as interventions aimed at pressuring corporations into public admissions of responsibility, which could compel them to revise the mindsets shared by both the SEC and investment banks.

In November of 2011, Judge Rakoff once again rejected a settlement between Citigroup Inc. and federal regulators, this time for $285 million (Wyatt, 2011). Rakoff affirmed that he would continue to prevent corporations from settling without admitting they have done anything wrong (Van Voris, 2011). The bank was accused of misleading investors in collateralized debt obligations. Rakoff asked Brad Karp, a lawyer for Citigroup, if the bank acknowledged the veracity of the SEC charges. "We do not admit the allegations," Karp said, to laughter in the standing-room-only courtroom, "but if it's any consolation, we don't deny them." Karp may have laughed about the alleged crime, but Rakoff saw the situation as fraud. The bank bet against its own product and its own customers and then lied to investors. Customers lost $700 million in the transaction while Citigroup made $160 million in profits. Rakoff disputed the bank's framework that portrayed the harm to customers as an accidental loss. The bank and the SEC have processed mental models that create obstacles to the ethical decision-making process. In doing so the bank has failed to acknowledge that a situation has moral as well as legal dimensions. They also failed to fruitfully attend to alternative solutions, examine data and recognize probable consequences crucial to forging future ethical responses. In his courageous rulings, Judge Rakoff has pushed for this acknowledgment.

Rakoff asserts that he opposes settlement policies that do not require acknowledgment of guilt because they are "hallowed by history, but not by reason" (Wyatt, 2011). There is substantial potential for abuse in such a settlement policy because "it asks the court to employ its power and assert its authority when it does not know the facts." This practice can undermine the constitutional separation of powers, Rakoff states, "by asking the judiciary to rubber-stamp the executive branch's interpretation of the law." The mental models of financial reform still stand in need of revision; however, Rakoff stands apart from some other jurists by forcing the important discussions necessary in the process of admission of guilt. Perhaps novel precedents, such as

those set by Rakoff, can foster better mental models for the SEC and
investment banks with similar attitudes and problems.

IV. Whistleblowing

Whistleblowing defined

How does the public at large learn of an ethical problem? How do
individuals expose ethical problems in the workplace if those in leadership refuse to listen to their concerns? In many cases, details of
unethical activities come forward because an employee, investor, or
other interested party will "blow the whistle." Norman Bowie defines
whistleblowing as, "[t]he act by an employee of informing the public of
the immoral or illegal behavior of an employer or supervisor," (1982,
140). Bowie argues that loyalty to the employer is a *prima facie* duty
of an employee when that employee is considering exposing a questionable corporate practice to the public. "Whistleblowing violates a
prima facie duty of loyalty to one's employer. There is a duty of loyalty
that normally prohibits one from reporting his employer or company"
(p. 143). Bowie writes:

A whistleblower is an employee or officer of an institution, profit or non-
profit, private or public, who believes that either he/she has been ordered
to perform some act or he/she has obtained knowledge that the institution
is engaged in activities which (1) are believed to cause unnecessary harm
to third parties (2) are in violation of human rights or (3) run counter to
the defined purpose of the inspection and who inform the public of this
fact." (Bowie, 1982, 142–3)

Loyalty to one's employer is an important value. However, this does
not mean that whistleblowing is never morally justified, or even
required. Bowie explains, "[o]ne should be loyal; but the object of
one's loyalty should be morally appropriate" (1982, 14). The virtue of
loyalty does not necessitate that an employee accept blindly an occupational assignment. "To be loyal to an employer does not require
that the employee should do what the employer says come what may.
Regrettably, however, it is just this kind of blind loyalty some employers demand," Bowie observes (p. 14).

Sissela Bok notes that whistleblowers often find themselves in the
difficult situation of have to choose between conforming and "sticking

their necks out" (1980, 4). Whistleblowing in sports is done by referees, who have the authority and power to call fouls, impose penalties, suspend play, and declare that the game is over. In contrast, "the whistleblower [in business] hopes to stop the game; but since he is neither referee nor coach, and since he blows the whistle on his own team, his act is seen as a violation of loyalty." Like Bowie, Bok affirms that whistleblowing is sometimes justified, but it must be defended against the charge of unjustified disloyalty.

However, according to Ronald Duska (2007), whistleblowing, whether justified or not, is not an act of disloyalty. While releasing organizational information to the public should describe wrongful harm, there is no need to worry about whether this is an act of disloyalty. Duska proposes that an organization should not be an object of loyalty for its employees:

Business as an instrument is just that, and hence amoral. To *treat* corporations as people whether by treating them as objects of loyalty or thinking they are moral agents because they haw [sic] responsibility is misguided. Ultimately, the commercialization of everything – the buying of loyalty for example gets the tail wagging the dog. (p. 145)

Within this conception of business, loyalty toward a company bestows on it a status it does not deserve; therefore, blowing the whistle under warranted circumstances is the right thing to do. Duska asserts that rules are very different for businesses competing with other businesses than in sporting competitions. While most sporting events have a referee who enforces uniform rules for all competitors, most often business competition in business does not require the uniform rules or governance. Further, the stakes are higher than with sports competition because everyone can be affected by business. "People cannot choose to participate in business. It permeates everyone's life," writes Duska (p. 145).

Decisions to blow the whistle: Case examples

When should individuals release details of unethical behavior by their employer? Noreen Harrington was a long-term employee in the mutual fund industry. After numerous in-house complaints about improper transactions went unheeded, she resigned from Stern Asset Management (Chatzky, 2004). She did not intend to tell authorities about the improper transactions until a year after she left the company. Harrington's sister asked for advice about her ailing 401(k). Essentially she had lost a lot of money and was not sure that she would be able to retire. Noreen Harrington's mental model changed when she saw her sister's pained face. She recounts:

> All of a sudden, I thought about this from a different vantage point. I saw one face – my sister's face – and then I saw the faces of everyone whose only asset was a 401(k). At that point I felt the need to try to make the regulators look into [these] abuses. (p. 156)

Harrington's ethical framework changed from one of company loyalty to one of consumer loyalty, allowing her to see that many individuals who were just like her sister were currently being harmed, and that many more could be harmed unless legal action was imposed. Harrington called the office of New York State Attorney General Eliot Spitzer, who was on a crusade to clean up the mutual fund industry (p. 156).

The decision to blow the whistle is often one wrought with contradictions. Most employees have expectations of professional and ethical behavior within the rubric of the organization that employs them. Attaining employment is often a difficult and political process, and most employees do not want to threaten compensation, benefits and continued employment by complaining about problems. However, when severe harms are occurring and the organization resists remedy, as in Harrington's case, whistleblowing may be the only viable choice available to ethical decision-makers.

There are many well-known whistleblowing cases in government and business operations. Karen Silkwood was killed under mysterious circumstances after investigating and reporting claims of contamination, malfeasance and other injurious behaviors at the Kerr-McGee plant (Los Alamos, 1995). Silkwood's job included making plutonium pellets for nuclear reactor fuel rods. Prior to her death in 1974, she testified before the Atomic Energy Commission regarding personal contamination, unauthorized practices and harassment at the plant. Her estate was paid $1.4 million by Kerr-McGee after her suspicious death. Silkwood faced the most severe of unethical and criminal retaliation – her life was taken and can never be reclaimed. Her case reveals the depth of criminality and lack of morality that can occur when an employee gets in the way of particular individuals within a business or organization that is making large amounts of money and wants to continue, no matter what.

In a classic case of "defying obedience to authority," a whistleblower was punished by the highest voice in the country, the President of the United States. In 1965, Ernest Fitzgerald was an engineer and manager employed by the U.S. Air Force as Deputy for Management Systems at the Pentagon. In 1968 and 1969 he testified before Congress about $2.3 billion in concealed cost overruns in the Lockheed C-5A transport plane (Wimsatt, 2005). This malfeasance could have gone unnoticed or unreported because other employees and managers submitted to the pressure to conform or blindly follow unethical norms. For his insistence on ethics and testimony before Congress, Fitzgerald was fired by order of President Richard M. Nixon for allegedly revealing classified information: "It was reported that Nixon told aids to 'get rid of that son of a bitch'" (Kempen and Bakaj, 2009, 6). Fitzgerald appealed the order and was reinstated, becoming a driving force for whistleblower protections (Wimsatt, 2005). He was involved in several legal cases that established presidential immunity and defined government employees' rights, and was influential in the passage the Civil Reform Act of 1978, which was the forerunner to the Whistleblower Protection Act of 1989.

Two additional whistleblowing cases – those of Charles Atchison and Christine Casey – exemplify individuals who were able to assess and discern ethical decision possibilities beyond the limited options or framework given by management. Distorted mental models had prevented others from discussing the problems with other parties; however, these individuals said they had to act out of a sense of conscience.

Charles Atchison was employed by Brown and Root as an inspector at a nuclear power plant for Texas Utilities Electric Company. He was concerned about the lack of attention to welds in the nuclear plant construction as well as other issues of shoddy workmanship. After he complained, he was fired and remained unemployed for years. Atchison's story challenges the stereotype of the whistleblower as a snitch, tattletale, and troublemaker. An organizational climate generally discourages whistleblowing by alluding to disloyalty and financial harm if allegedly wrongful practices are exposed. Often both the whistleblower and those involved in the alleged wrongdoing are treated as suspect. Implicit and explicit retaliation often accompany the charges. Whistleblowers may come forward with allegations against others, only to face severe scrutiny and charges of disloyalty. They are commonly pressured to withdraw their charges, ostracized by co-workers, and even threatened with lawsuits. Whistleblowers may be moved into less attractive jobs in their workplace or even, like Atchison, lose their jobs and be "blackballed" in the industry. Because of the negative consequences, analysts find that many whistleblowers would not press allegations against a fellow employee again (Kalichman, 2001).

Making the decision to prevent wrongdoing or harm can be costly to one's professional reputation, risky personally, and even dangerous, particularly if that action is unaided by others. The bystander model is often linked to failure to expose unethical behaviors in the organization. Studies indicate that we are less likely to intervene in a harmful situation if we are surrounded by others who refuse to help or move forward with an ethical decision-making plan (Hudson and Bruckman, 2004; Latané and Nina, 1981; Darley and Latané, 1968). Personal ethics blind spots are notably influenced by others' choices. Darley and Latané (1968) explain that each observer looks for assistance or reaction from others for confirmation before risking assistance or interference.

A lone whistleblower, surrounded by bystanders, Christine Casey was employed by toy giant, Mattel from 1994 to 1999 ("*Christine Casey* . . . ", 2003). It was Casey's job to develop a system to allocate production forecasts among its factories. She was dismayed to find that Mattel's sales forecasts were consistently too high. They were so high that managers routinely kept two sets of figures and would telephone around to find out what they should really tell their factories to produce. Casey believed the situation should be immediately corrected and went to a company director with a proposal to forecast profits more accurately. This move cost her dearly. First, she was treated with hostility by company executives and received her first negative performance review. The next demotion was to a tiny office, where her responsibilities were severely reduced. Mattel's chief financial officer disregarded her concerns, as did the human-resources department. Casey called the Securities and Exchange Commission in September of 1999. She said she had imagined being a hero for making the company better with the help of the SEC. The story does not turn out well for Mattel, Casey, or the SEC. Ultimately, Mattel had to pay $122 million to shareholders who sued it for deliberately inflating sales forecasts.

Casey filed and lost a wrongful-termination suit against Mattel. Her claim was that she was harassed into resigning.

Organizations benefit from creating organizational mindsets and an organizational culture based on transparency, inclusion, and ethical reflection. Rather than act as a bystander waiting for others to "tattle" on a problem, managers should strive to allow employees to come forward with advice and encourage open discourse in areas that require change. Such openness can serve to eliminate the blind spots within the organization that bring about the need for whistleblowing.

Whistleblowing regulation

There may be a bright light for whistleblowers. Whistleblowing protection is now expanded with the passage of both the Sarbanes–Oxley Act of 2002 and the Dodd–Frank Act of 2010. Whistleblowing is encouraged, and even financially rewarded in many instances. As has been noted earlier, ethical issues surrounding whistleblowing within business and finance often center on notions of fair warning and loyalty. Curtis Verschoor (2010) defines internal whistleblowing as involving someone within a firm alleging wrongdoing to an authority within that firm. In ideal ethical cases, the individual should only report on events where facts can be established, where there is a real possibility of significant harm, where the employee can follow a chain of command in reporting the wrongdoing, and where it can be understood that reporting of the wrongdoing could result in important changes for the firm (p. 62). Verschoor supports the Dodd–Frank Act and suggests that whistleblowing may be a more attractive option in today's organizations because of the market collapse of 2008. For many firms, the collapse uncovered accounting and other irregularities within their organizations that decreased public trust in their integrity.

In today's marketplace, there is a greater chance an employee will either refuse to perform an illegal action or will blow the whistle on a current infraction. However, Vershoor predicts, we can expect even more fraudulent financial reporting in today's market:

More than half of the respondents to a webcast poll conducted by Deloitte think more financial statement fraud will be uncovered in 2010 and 2011 compared with the past, and 45 percent believe fraud is getting harder to detect because of changes in the risk environment. (Verschoor, 2010)

The Dodd–Frank Act allows employees to report the fraud before it is uncovered in an audit. Additionally, under Dodd–Frank provisions, employees who are whistleblowers can be awarded a percentage of the funds that are deemed fraudulent, under certain conditions (Roberts, 2011). For example, awards can range from 10–30 percent of the amount of monetary sanctions in cases over $1 million.

A snag in the Dodd–Frank whistleblowing law is the hefty compensation. In order to receive compensation, employees may be motivated to release sensitive information to outside regulators or other entities before notifying the organization of the problem. This leaves the possibility that whistleblowing may be undertaken in the expectation of financial gain rather than improving the organization (Roberts, 2011). In these cases an executive or officer does not have the opportunity to address an area's wrongdoing and correct it for the organization. A mental model based on exploitation of the new law does not support a firm's efforts to strengthen its internal business practices or its moral models of integrity, honesty and ethical reflection within the organization. The new whistleblowing incentives could reduce the ability to correct problems within the organization's overall culture. Additionally, the need for monetary rewards reveals a morally distorted mental model at the level of corporate culture (Werhane and Moriarty, 2009). If a reward is needed to react morally to an immoral situation, the entire situation becomes suspect (Verschoor, 2010).

V. Best practices and shared values

As this chapter has observed, some corporate managers and employees feel obliged and committed to act in conformity with corporate pressures and policies even when they are questionable or unethical. We have pointed out that the rationalization for these behaviors may be as simple as, "The boss says she will take responsibility for my unethical act that she ordered," or "I just want to go along with the other employees. I don't want to let others know that I think their behavior and hence my behavior is bad." Obedience may be a virtue in many instances, but there are more important ethical decision tools in the world of business than mere obedience. For example, courage is a virtue that is practiced by the thinkers and leaders in the next section of this chapter. These individuals have the courage to test new programs, spend extra money, and require long-term, non-traditional programs in the name of business ethics. We first draw attention to the importance of shared values between business and community in making profits for everyone concerned. The next spotlight will be on the educational and communication practices of an "off Wall Street" securities firm.

Defining shared value

Creating social and financial benefits for a business and the community in which it participates is the substance of theories by Michael Porter and Mark Kramer (2011). Porter and Kramer propose that companies must do more than think about profits; firms "must take the lead in bringing business and society back together" (p. 63). The solution, they propose, "lies in the principle of shared value, which involves creating economic value in a way that also creates value for society by addressing its needs and challenges" (p. 64). Society and business have been pitted against each other for many years, but the two can develop shared values designed to show appreciation for societal needs, bases of productivity, and collaboration across profit and non-profit boundaries (p. 64). For example, in farming, Porter and Kramer do not recommended donations or inflated prices to the farmer:

A shared value perspective, instead, focuses on improving growing techniques and strengthening the local cluster of supporting suppliers and other institutions in order to increase the farmer's efficiency, yields, product quality, and sustainability. This leads to a bigger pie of revenue and profits that benefits both farmers and the companies that buy from them. (p. 65)

Research shows that too many companies have lost sight of the most basic question: "Is our product good for our customers?" As an example, food companies have traditionally based profits on high levels of consumption. Porter and Kramer challenge these companies to focus products on health and nutrition improvement (p. 67). They credit Wells Fargo with seeking to meet the challenge of the shared value perspective by developing products and tools to assist customers with budgeting, managing credit and paying down debt. They also focus on General Electric's Ecomagination products, which are financially successful, yet also have an impact in stabilizing the environment (p. 68).

The shared value approach advocated by Porter and Kramer is highly critical of any economic theory that gives primacy to creating value for shareholders. It is a dated notion to focus on short-term performance pressures from shareholders, as this model may entice consumers to purchase more and more of inferior products. To continue making profits when following that model, companies may find it necessary to restructure and move off shore to produce at lower costs. This move harms the community that loses the business, and places the business in a location where societal needs are even more pressing. This framework brings little true innovation, slows organic growth, and offers no clear competitive advantage (p. 65). Taking a shared value approach requires that companies reconceive products and markets; redefine productivity in a value chain; and build supportive industry clusters at company locations. Porter and Kramer predict that the net effect will reset the boundaries of capitalism by better connecting a company's successes with societal improvement (p. 67). There are many ways to serve new needs, gain efficiency, create differentiation, and expand markets, while serving the public good.

Companies that do move to developing countries should build shared value with these new communities. In Kenya, Vodafone's M-PESA mobile banking service provided low-priced cell phones with capabilities of mobile banking services (Porter and Kramer, 2011, 66). This shared value helped the poor save money, and also gave small farmers the ability to market their crops. Within three years Vodafone signed up 10 million customers, representing 11 percent of the country's GDP. In India, Thomson Reuters developed a monthly service that provides weather and crop-pricing information and agricultural advice. An estimated 2 million farmers use the service and research indicates that 60 percent have increased their income.

Porter and Kramer (2011, 69) present a formula for creating shared value. First, a company should identify all the societal needs, benefits and harms that are, or could be, within the reach of the firm's product. Next, it is important to acknowledge that opportunities are constantly changing as technology evolves, economies develop, and societal priorities shift. The redesign of products and distribution methods can assist in sharing values between the company and community. The rewards can be big for businesses, as ongoing exploration of societal needs should lead companies to discover new opportunities for differentiation and repositioning in traditional markets. Companies could also discover potential in markets previously overlooked (p. 70).

*Shared value in independent securities regulation: The
Financial Industry Regulatory Authority (FINRA)*

The shared value approach suggests that ethics concerns and profit
concerns need not be understood to be pulling in opposite directions.
Indeed, by prioritizing ethics within the organization, companies may
find new ways to create value for shareholders and community stakeholders alike. For instance, organizations should proudly detail how
they have instituted tough, long-term ethics and compliance training. Through ethics and compliance training, an organization has
the opportunity to build strong mental models for current and future
employees. Creating an ethical culture within the company is crucial to
fostering the innovative approach to creating shared value that Porter
and Kramer describe.

In light of Sarbanes–Oxley and Dodd–Frank, most large corporations today have compliance officers and compliance training. But
fewer companies step back and think about what they should do, all
things considered, that is, fewer have ethics officers and ethics programs that are distinct from compliance. As we learned in Chapter 6,
compliance programs without ethics programs tend to be less successful at compliance then when these two exist in a company. In our last
chapter we also learned that ethical compliance is required by agencies within the federal government as well as by public and private
businesses. As an example of private regulation, the Financial Industry
Regulatory Authority (FINRA) is the largest independent regulator for
all securities firms doing business in the United States. FINRA over-
sees nearly 4,460 brokerage firms, about 160,485 branch offices and
approximately 629,520 registered securities representatives to make
sure they are operating fairly and honestly (FINRA, n.d.). It was established more than seventy years ago as an independent regulator to
protect investors in America's financial system. It is estimated that 53
million American investing households are affected by FINRA's work.
This independent organization plays a role in registering and educat-
ing all brokers, examining securities firms, writing the rules they must
follow and enforcing those rules and federal securities laws. According to Chairman and CEO Richard G. Ketchum, FINRA also mon-
itors trading in the U.S. stock markets and administers the largest
securities-related dispute resolution forum in the world. The organization identifies high-risk firms, brokers, activities, and products.

When rules are broken, FINRA disciplines agencies where investors have been harmed. In 2011, with the assistance of whistleblowing and fraud detection divisions, the organization banned 329 individuals and suspended 475 brokers from association with FINRA-regulated firms. It also levied fines totaling more than $63 million and ordered more than $19 million in restitution to harmed investors. Many, but not all, brokerage organizations establish their mutual fund management practices according to the ethical guidelines, rules, and regulations established by FINRA.

Raymond James, a Florida based firm, exemplifies ethical self-compliance in the finance and securities areas. Raymond James, following FINRA guidelines, requires all registered employees, including those involved in the trading, dealing, or selling of securities, to participate in annual continuing education (Hollister, 2012). To complete this training, these employees are required to complete a number of educational classes in securities industry policies, ethics, law, and financial reform. Going beyond FINRA requirements, Raymond James has established national and regional conferences for their agents as part of a systems model aimed at fostering the practices the company would like to see exhibited in each individual sales office throughout the country. It is the firm's position that employees whose education is kept current in securities industry policies, ethics and law are more effective in their jobs, are more likely to competently advise financial clients, manage ethical operations in their individual offices and, in general, contribute to smoother day-to-day operations in each office and within the corporation.

Transparency is an important ethical guideline for the corporation (Hollister, 2012). Detailed explanations are produced for all investors or interested parties in a variety of areas. These include areas such as fees and compensation, types of clients and disciplinary actions. Transparency allows ethics to be maintained at the forefront of all business practices, and provides a bulwark against ethical fading and short-term decision making that might cause problems. The ethical violations of one investment advisor have the potential to do significant reputational damage to the firm as a whole. A mental model of responsible behavior and respect for others in the industry is also part of the training program offered by Raymond James.

Tash Elwin, the new president of Raymond James, predicts that the firm's growth will occur in both quality and quantity (De la Merced,

2012). After acquiring Memphis-based Morgan Keegan unit for $930 million in December of 2011, Elwin reaffirmed the goals that have guided the firm in the past. "Raymond James is not to morph into the biggest firm. Our goal has been to be the premier alternative to Wall Street. I think the most significant challenge is first demonstrating and affirming what's NOT changing" (Konish and McMorris, 2012).

Raymond James has been receiving high marks across the financial corridors for its limited involvement in the financial crisis, and its ability to rebound and attract new employees who were seeking an ethical financial company (De la Merced, 2012). As exemplified by this firm, it is possible to forge mental models in the financial industry that sustain an ethical culture within the organization, thereby opening up the possibility of creating social value together with economic value.

A model for shared values: The Belmont Report

This section concludes with a discussion of the development of the Belmont Report, a historically important enterprise that brought together disparate individuals to address ethical problems in medical and behavioral research. The development and acceptance of the Report, while addressed to those conducting research involving human participants, can serve as a model for other industries to adopt.

Impetus for the Belmont Commission came from several disturbing research projects that had come to public attention. The most notorious of these projects is the Tuskegee syphilis study, a research project conducted between 1932 and 1972, sponsored by the U.S. Public Health Service (CDC, 2011). The study, conducted in Tuskegee, Alabama, involved about 400 impoverished African-American sharecroppers who had syphilis. The research centered on the natural progression of the untreated disease. By 1940 the researchers knew that penicillin was an effective cure for the disease, but they continued with the research without informing the individuals they had syphilis, and that their syphilis could be cured. Physicians, nurses, and government workers were among those involved with the Tuskegee syphilis experiment.

Behavioral scientists were also concerned about the experiments of Stanley Milgram discussed in previous chapters of this book. The experiment was deceptive even though teachers were debriefed after the experiment and told they had not delivered actual shocks. The

problem was the experiment was not about teaching and learning, as
the Teachers were told. Rather, it was designed to study obedience to
authority. The Teachers were tested on their obedience to demands of
a researcher rather than on learning, and many were deeply troubled
by the demands. Milgram's research was even seen as abusive by the
American Psychological Association (Blass, 1999).

In February of 1974, the Secretary of Health, Education and Wel-
fare brought together some of the best minds in the country to study
medical and behavioral research under the title of the Belmont Commission (NIH, 1979). The Secretary charged the Belmont Commission
with recommending ethical guidelines for research in the medical and
behavioral research fields. The Commission's work resulted in the Belmont Report. It is still in use today by all Institutional Research Boards
in this country, and is overseen by the Secretary of Health Resources
and Services Administration. The individuals who were part of the Belmont Commission had diverse backgrounds and interests. They came
from a variety of religions or no religion, and from professions and
disciplines that often have opposing views. Of the eleven commissioners, five were scientists (including physicians) and the other six were
theologians, attorneys, and other non-scientists. All were individuals
of scholarly prominence. Somehow, this group of individuals needed
to develop appropriate mental models for conducting research in the
important area of biomedical ethics, and share their findings with the
national scientific community. When the commissioners were named,
many expressed dismay, stating that these eleven individuals would
not be capable of coming to any type of consensus. It was believed
that the five scientists would likely vote together, perhaps bringing one
or two members from the "non-scientific" group to their point of view.
However, according to Stephan Toulmin (1981), a staff member for
the Commission, the vote was never a division between the scientists
and the non-scientists:

In almost every case, they came close to agreement, even about quite detailed
recommendations – at least for so long as their discussions proceeded taxo-
nomically, taking one difficult class of cases at a time comparing it in detail
with clearer and easier classes of cases. (p. 31)

It is notable that the Belmont Commission was forming a new social
construction of reality – a framing of interactions between these individuals, the data of a variety of poorly conducted experiments, and

differing and incomplete mental models of the commission members from the fields of medical and behavioral research. Toulmin went on to explain that even when the commission's decisions weren't unanimous, they did not mimic the "Tower of Babel": "The Commissioners were never in any doubt what it was they were not quite unanimous about" (1981, 32). The group's mandate was to set aside their differences for the greater good of their project and determine on a case by case basis what practices would be acceptable and unacceptable for human subjects research (Jonsen and Toulmin, 1988). Initially, this posed a difficult challenge. The ethical principles underlying their conclusions about cases were quite different. Toulmin explains that the Catholics appealed to Catholic principles, and the humanists appealed to humanist principles. "They could agree what they were agreeing about, but apparently they could not agree why they agreed about it" (Toulmin, 1981, 32). But by staying focused on the importance of the goal, the commission members worked together to complete their shared task.

The Commission was to identify the basic ethical principles that should underlie the conduct of biomedical and behavioral research involving human subjects. They were also to develop guidelines that should be followed to assure this research was conducted in accordance with those principles at any institution doing biomedical or behavioral research. The Belmont Report is the result of four days of exhaustive and rigorous deliberation to summarize the basic ethical principles identified by the Commission. These discussions were followed by two years of monthly commission deliberations. Their groundbreaking report found three basic principles were necessary in medical and behavioral research: respect for persons, beneficence, and justice (Toulmin, 1981, 32).

In 1981, the U.S. Department of Health and Human Services (DHHS) and the U.S. Food and Drug Administration (FDA) issued regulations based on the Belmont Report. A decade later, the core DHHS regulations were formally adopted by more than a dozen other departments and agencies that fund or conduct research involving human subjects. The DHHS regulatory schema became known as the "Common Rule." Both the Common Rule and the FDA regulations provide protections for human subjects in research. Congress did not adopt the recommendations of Belmont Report as formal legal requirements. Yet the Belmont Report values are still flourishing in research practices across this country and the globe. The Report is recognized as the United States' ethical contribution to protecting human subjects internationally (NIH, 1979).

Our mental models are constructed and reconstructed as time and circumstances change. An ethical framework is constructed within those mental models to help us recognize and promote ethical practice in research. The Belmont Report does not impose a detailed ethical system. It gives guidelines that are helpful for regulating human behavior within the scientific and medical communities. These guidelines are needed so that members of these communities may live together with each other, and with broader stakeholder groups, harmoniously and ethically. The Belmont Report ethical system differs from a stringent legal system. The ethics posed in the report take the form of basic and less formal statements of principles and suggestions for implementation. This is important because authority in ethics resides in a shared system of rules understood and accepted by everyone in general. The Belmont Report represents the best of ethical common sense. It is expected that those attempting to follow its guidelines will be able to make good use of it in addressing ethical issues in research involving human participants (NIH, 1979).

Many involved with the Belmont report are convinced that the goals of ethical human research depend on an objective third party – the Institutional Review Board – to ensure that that the research being done by the university, laboratory, organization, or other agency will protect the well-being and respect the moral standing of participants in research. IRBs are required to morally evaluate human subject research designs, and to follow the rules and guidelines outlined by their institutions.

The Belmont Report serves as a reminder that there are important synergies for the next generation of ethical leaders based on the alignment of modified or adjusted mental models. This entails an application of moral imagination through collaborative input and critique, rather than "me too" obedience. By advocating basic moral guidelines and enforcing their practice though institutional review boards, the Belmont Report sets out a model for other organizations and industries, a voluntary set of principles and enforcement mechanisms that might, through peer evaluations and pressures, be worthwhile for other industries. In Chapter 6, we mentioned the Defense Industry initiative, which is just such a model, as is FINRA. These sorts of agencies raise to organizational consciousness and behavior the importance of very basic ethical principles.

VI. Conclusion

The purpose of this chapter has been to provide concrete examples of individual and organizational mental models in action. As was noted, all of our experiences and reflections are conditioned by mental models, but these mental models are socially constructed and thus not immutable. Nevertheless, when embedded in a social structure and reinforced, they are often not questioned, and thus become determinate of our behavior. This was evident in the analysis of the Penn State Football scandal that erupted at the end of Joe Paterno's illustrious career. Allegedly, former Defensive Coach Jerry Sandusky had molested at least eight boys. At least one incident was reported to Paterno. Yet in nine years, he did nothing further to resolve the situation. Additionally, no one else at Penn State was willing to try to rectify the situation. It had to be settled outside of the university.

The 2008 meltdown of Wall Street is a difficult story for the American people as well as for individuals and investors across the globe (Ferguson, 2010). In this chapter we described a continual decline in leadership and in the ethical culture within the arenas of investment banking and mortgage lending. A focus was an examination of Goldman Sachs, generally cited as the most respected investment bank on Wall Street.

It appears that many of the practices that brought about the Wall Street crash of 2008 are still in place, even though the Dodd–Frank Act established new regulations for investment banks and rating agencies. Portions of the financial sector seem to lack the courage to change their mental models in light of growing evidence regarding the harm that their actions have caused to others. One reason it is difficult to change the mindsets operative within the American financial culture is the fear of loss of reputation and loss of significant funds, even in the wake of charges that "gambling" with other's funds in the subprime mortgage catastrophe led to financial and reputational losses for the industry. Judge Jed Rakoff insists that these investment banks admit guilt while being fined for their unethical, immoral and illegal actions. It remains to be seen how effective he will be in this endeavor.

The chapter then moved to an in-depth coverage of whistleblowing. From philosophical and historical depictions of harms to individuals within organizations, we learned that individuals seeking justice will often find ways to let individuals in power assist in overturning the corrupt practices. Whistleblowing was linked to the Penn State problem, and from various philosophers we found that loyalty is often considered the primary value rather than other moral principles in some organizations.

In the last sections of the chapter we analyzed three areas in which federal regulations are not in place, yet industry rules and guidelines are being forged to keep ethical practices moving forward. The first example was with the Financial Industry Regulatory Authority. It is the largest independent regulator for all securities firms doing business in the United States. Second, a challenge was issued for business to create shared values with society. Through innovation and a better understanding the values and needs of a community, we proposed that innovation and capital growth can occur in positive ways. The Belmont Report provided a third example. The Report demonstrates the facility and courage of a group of individuals to continually seek out information, alternate viewpoints, and theoretical frameworks that challenge the problems found in medical and behavioral research. The diverse eleven members of the commission were able to pull together rules that are ethically important in medical and behavioral research. Though the Report was not enacted as law, it has been strictly adhered to by the scientific community, including public and private granting agencies and institutional review boards. Through good habits and practices researchers have generated a respect for the guidelines in the report, as well as the desire to prevent ethical failures from occurring within their institutions in the future. This sort of model should inspire other organizations and industries, hopefully with similar positive results.

Even with the best of intentions, we understand that our mental models facilitate particular modes of experience and can organize an individual or organization's perception of a situation in ways that make some thought and practices possible, while negating others. These practical examples help us understand that sometimes we only have a partial vision of a moral problem. When we truly challenge our framing of a situation, we are better positioned to understand there are many others who are affected by our practices. While we organize and order our world through mental models, we do not often do so with the luxury of analytical hindsight. To the contrary, if we doubt whether our actions might have been different from those individuals discussed in this chapter, we are simply asking whether we order the world in a manner so terribly distinct from others – and have thereby confirmed our thesis surrounding the manufacture of bounded constructs from incomplete data.

8 | Conclusion

In 1999, Bayer CropScience, a division of Bayer Corporation, acquired a company in India, Proagro Seed Company, which produced hybrid cotton seeds. Bayer had been operating in India in various capacities since 1896, mostly in chemical manufacturing. This would be a new venture for Bayer CropScience. Unlike chemical manufacture, usually located in a few factories, hybrid seed production is spread out through thousands of small farms throughout India. Getting to those farms and creating bonds with the Indian farmers was to be a new challenge. Moreover, Bayer soon discovered that children harvested much of the cotton. In areas where cotton is grown in India, Some estimates put the number of cotton child workers in India as high as half a million (Hawksley, 2012). Although child labor has been a common tradition throughout India for centuries, Bayer prohibits child labor as a matter of corporate policy. According to Bayer,

We follow a clear "zero tolerance to child labor" policy in our business operations worldwide. We do not tolerate child labor in our supply chain either, where we take action against known cases of violations. Our efforts to fight against child labor are consistent with the International Labor Organization's core labor standards and the United Nations Global Compact principles. (Bayer, 2012)

Should Bayer pull out of the Proagro acquisition, and give up a lucrative hybrid cotton seed project, or should it instead simply ban child labor in those fields, a ban that would, among other consequences, defy local customs and significantly affect the incomes of farmers, the families of these children (Subramanian *et al.*, 2010a)?

The challenge facing Bayer CropScience proved very difficult to resolve. There was a great deal of pressure on Bayer from the media and investors to resolve the child labor problem or pull out of India. But Michael Schneider, the manager of Corporate Social Responsibility at Bayer CropScience, saw a broader set of options:

I had dealt with complex issues before and understood that a huge challenge like child labor needed dedication and focused attention. In a country like India [W]estern company ethics could not simply be put to work without major efforts. Though our company including our India unit [was] trying its best to respond to the situation, there was a good chance to fail with all negative consequences to our reputation and brand . . . The area was vast and the challenge was how to effectively monitor thousands of such farms on a regular basis. Even more important [was how would] it be possible to win the hearts and minds of farmers who saw no wrong in using children for labor. (Subramanian, 2010a, 12; see also Lawrence and Beamish, 2013, 326)

We began this book by suggesting that it is a book about hope, and it is. There are viable remedies to the set of thorny issues faced by Bayer CropScience, and to many other ethical dilemmas in commerce. But, as the various examples in this book illustrate, when we are preoccupied with – or blinded by – a limited set of mental models, or when we presume that situations such as Bayer's in India are either/or choices, we miss critical facts and opportunities. As a result, many of these scenarios do not turn out well. What is needed, we have proposed, is a sound decision model, a strong dose of self-awareness, consciousness of our fallibilities, and a well-developed moral imagination. Part of this is a matter of building trust and trustworthiness, just as part of Bayer CropScience's challenge was to develop and earn the trust of the farmers and families working on the farms. Trust matters. It matters because most of us believe that all human beings have basic rights and should be treated with equal dignity as human beings. It also matters because, without trust in an industry, clients and customers invest their money elsewhere, even in their mattresses, or they become skeptical of their financial relationships. Indeed, as Greg Smith argued in his *New York Times* op-ed piece, discussed in the Introduction and in Chapter 6, the free enterprise system cannot work or work well without trust, because no one can be sure that what is being represented to them is truly as it appears.

Faced with the choice of abetting child labor or withdrawing from the hybrid cotton seed agribusiness in India, Bayer Corporation reexamined its operative mindsets. Child labor was abhorrent to the company, and in explicit violation of its mission statement. But the opportunity to have access to a worthwhile hybrid cotton seed was also important, as was the economic plights of families in these rural regions of India. But was this an "either/or" decision? Bayer did not think so. The company rethought its options and decided to take a different route. Bayer CropScience initiated what they call a Child Care program near their cotton fields. First, however, the company had to change prevailing mindsets in the villages providing child labor. This entailed convincing parents and farmers that production would be improved and families would be better off if adults, rather than children, worked in the cotton fields. Bayer CropScience reinforced this conviction by paying the farmers a bonus if they stopped hiring children. The company also arranged with local banks to provide low-interest loans to farmers, who had traditionally been paying high interest rates for the loans often needed to tide them over between each harvest. Next, the firm partnered with the Naandi Foundation, an Indian nongovernment organization committed to improving primary school education. With Naandi, Bayer CropScience invested in local "bridge" schools in the region, which are schools that concentrate on children with no formal education, bringing them up to their grade level so that they can attend local public schools. Only after this diverse set of initiatives had been launched did Bayer CropScience begin to require farmers to sign a pledge affirming that they would not hire child workers.

As a result of the moral imagination exercised by leadership at Bayer CropScience, today there are almost no child laborers in their cotton fields (Bayer CropScience, n.d.; Bayer Group India, n.d.). When asked why the company did all of this, a senior executive replied,

[W]hy should Bayer *not* do this? Here is an issue where we as a company have a professed value of zero tolerance to child labor. We are an agricultural company, and India is one of the largest agricultural markets. It is an opportunity for us to mean what we say and walk the talk. (Subramanian *et al.*, 2010b; quoted in Dhanaraj and Khanna, 2011, 697)

References

Abelson, Reed. 2010. "F.D.A. Official Cites Failures at Multiple J&J Plants." *The New York Times*, October 1.

Aerospace Guide. 2003. "Space Shuttle Columbia Disaster." Accessed July 24, 2011. www.aerospaceguide.net/spaceshuttle/columbia_disaster.html.

Albergotti, Reed. 2011. "Discipline Problem: Paterno Fought Penn State Official Over Punishment of Players." *Wall Street Journal*, November 22.

Alexander, Meredith. 2001. "Thirty Years Later, Stanford Prison Experiment Lives On." *Stanford Report*, August 22. Accessed May 11, 2012. http://news.stanford.edu/news/2001/august22/prison2-822.html.

Allison, Scott T., Messick, David M. and Goethals, George R. 1989. "On Being Better But Not Smarter Than Others: The Muhammad Ali Effect." *Social Cognition* 7 (3): 275–96.

Anderson, John. 2007. "Gang-Related Witness Intimidation." *National Gang Center Bulletin*. Accessed on March 16, 2012. www.nationalgangcenter.gov/Publications.

Andrews, Edmund L. 2008. "Greenspan Concedes Error on Regulation." *The New York Times*, October 23.

Anscombe, G. E. M. 1976. "The Question of Linguistic Idealism." In *Essays on Wittgenstein in Honour of G. H. Yon Wright: Acta Philosophica Fennica*, Vol. 28, edited by Jaakko Hintikka, 181–215. Amsterdam: North Holland Publishing.

Arendt, Hannah. [1951] 1973. *The Origins of Totalitarianism*. New York: Harcourt/Harvest.

Arendt, Hannah. [1963] 2006. *Eichmann in Jerusalem*. New York: Penguin.

Arendt, Hannah. [1969] 1972. "Lying in Politics." In *Crises of the Republic*, 3–47. New York: Harcourt Brace.

Ariely, Dan. 2008. "Are We in Control of Our Own Decisions?" TED: Ideas Worth Spreading. Talks: TED Partner Series, December. Video. Accessed June 5, 2012. www.ted.com/index.php/talks/dan_ariely_asks_are_we_in_control_of_our_own_decisions.html.

Arlidge, John. 2009. "I'm Doing 'God's Work'. Meet Mr Goldman Sachs." *The Sunday Times*, UK, November 8. Accessed May 30, 2012. www. thesundaytimes.co.uk/sto/news/world_news/article189615.ece.

Asch, S. E. 1951. "Effects of Group Pressure upon the Modification and Distortion of Judgments." In *Groups, Leadership, and Men*, edited by H. Guetzkow. Pittsburgh, PA: Carnegie Press.

Asch, S. E. 1955. "Opinions and Social Pressure." *Scientific American* 193 (5): 31–5.

Badhwar, Neera. 2009. "The Milgram Experiments, Learned Helplessness, and Character Traits." *Journal of Ethics* 13: 257–89.

Bajaj, Vikas. 2011. "Luster Dims for a Public Microlender." *New York Times*, May 5. Accessed June 3, 2011. www.nytimes.com/2011/05/11/ business/global/11micro.html.

Banaji, M., Bazerman, M. and Chugh, D. 2003. "How (Un)Ethical Are You?" *Harvard Business Review* 81 (12): 56–64.

Bandura, Albert. 1990. "Mechanisms of Moral Disengagement." In *Origins of Terrorism: Psychologies, Ideologies, Theologies, States of Mind*, edited by W. Reich, 161–91. Cambridge University Press.

Bandura, Albert. 1999. "Moral Disengagement in the Perpetuation of Inhumanities." *Personality and Social Psychology Review* 3 (3): 193–209.

Barr, Colin. 2011. "Europe's Sickly Banks." *CNN Money*, June 20. Accessed May 21, 2012. http://finance.fortune.cnn.com/2011/06/20/europes-sickly-banks/.

Barry, D., Barstow, D., Glater, J. D., Liptak, A. and Steinberg, J. 2003. "Correcting the Record: *Times* Reporter Who Resigned Leaves Long Trail of Deception." *The New York Times*, May 11. Accessed on March 16, 2012. www.nytimes.com/2003/05/11/us/correcting-the-record-times-reporter-who-resigned-leaves-long-trail-of-deception.html?

Bass, Thomas A. 2009. "Derivatives: The Crystal Meth of Finance." *The Huffington Post*, May 5. Accessed on May 30, 2012. www.huffingtonpost.com/thomas-a-bass/derivatives-the-crystalm_b_195221.html.

Batson, Daniel C., Collins, Elizabeth and Powell, Adam A. 2006. "Doing Business After the Fall: The Virtue of Moral Hypocrisy." *Journal of Business Ethics* 66 (4): 321–35.

Baumeister, Roy F. 1998. "The Self." In *Handbook of Social Psychology*, edited by D. T. Gilbert, S. T. Fiske and G. Lindzey, 680–740. New York: McGraw-Hill.

Baumeister, Roy F. and Bushman, Brad J. 2008. *Social Psychology and Human Nature*. Belmont, CA: Thompson Wadsworth.

Bayer. 2012. "Bayer Human Rights Position." Accessed June 1, 2012. www. bayer.com/en/bayer-human-rights-position.aspx.

Bayer CropScience Child Care Program. n.d. "Protecting Children's Rights in Agriculture." Accessed June 1, 2012. www.childcareprogram. bayercropscience.com/.

Bayer Group India. n.d. "Bayer CropScience Intensifies Efforts Against Child Labor in India." Bayer: Science For a Better Life: India. Accessed June 1, 2012. www.bayergroupindia.com/naandi.html.

Bazerman, Max and Tenbrunsel, Ann. 2011. *Blind Spots*. Princeton University Press.

Bazerman, Max and Chugh, Dolly. 2005. "Bounded Awareness: Focusing Problems in Negotiation." In *Frontiers of Social Psychology: Negotiations*, edited by L. Thompson. College Park, MD: Psychology Press.

Bazerman, Max and Chugh, Dolly. 2006. "Decisions without Blinders." *Harvard Business Review* 84 (1): 88–97.

Bazerman, M. H. and Moore, D. A. 2008. *Judgment in Managerial Decision Making*. 7th edn. New York: Wiley.

Beauvois, J.-L., Courbet, D. and Oberléc, D. 2012. "The Prescriptive Power of the Television Host. A Transposition of Milgram's Obedience Paradigm to the Context of TV Game Show." *Revue Européenne de Psychologie Appliquée* (April): 1–9. doi:10.1016/j.erap.2012.02.001.

Benhabib, Seyla. 1990. *The Communicative Ethics Controversy*. Boston: MIT Press.

Benhabib, Seyla. 2004. *The Rights of Others*. Cambridge University Press.

Benjamin, Martin. 1990. *Splitting the Difference*. Lawrence, KS: University Press of Kansas.

Berns, Gregory S., Chappelow, Jonathan, Zink, Caroline F., Pagnoni, Giuseppe, Martin-Skurski, Megan E. and Richards, Jim. 2005. "Neurobiological Correlates of Social Conformity and Independence During Mental Rotation." *Journal of Biological Psychiatry* 58: 245–53.

Bertrand, Marianne and Mullainathan, Sendhil. 2004. "Are Emily and Greg More Employable Than Lakisha and Jamal? A Field Experiment on Labor Market Discrimination." *American Economic Review* 94: 991–1013.

Berube, Michael. 2011. "At Penn State a Bitter Reckoning." *The New York Times*. November 17.

Blakeslee, Sandra. 2012. "Mind Games: Sometimes a White Coat Isn't Just a White Coat." *The New York Times*, April 3.

Blass, Thomas. 1991. "Understanding Behavior in the Milgram Obedience Experiment." *Journal of Personality and Social Psychology* 60: 398–413.

Blass, Thomas. 1999. "The Milgram Paradigm After 35 Years: Some Things We Now Know about Obedience to Authority." *Journal of Applied Social Psychology* 28 (5): 955–78.

Boddy, Clive R. 2010. "Corporate Psychopaths and Organisational Type." *Journal of Public Affairs* 10 (4): 300–12.

Boddy, Clive R. 2011. "The Corporate Psychopaths Theory of the Global Financial Crisis." *Journal of Business Ethics* 102: 255–9. doi:10.1007/s10551-011-0810-4.

Bogle, John C. 2009. "A Crisis of Ethic Proportions." *Wall Street Journal*, April 21.

Bok, Sissela. 1980. "Whistleblowing and Professional Responsibility." *New York University Education Quarterly* 11: 2–7.

Bornstein, R. F. 1989. "Exposure and Affect: Overview and Meta-Analysis of Research, 1968–1987." *Psychological Bulletin* 106: 265–89.

Bowie, Norman E. 1982. *Business Ethics*. Englewood Cliffs, NJ: Prentice Hall.

Brenner, M. 1996. "The Man Who Knew Too Much." *Vanity Fair* (May). Accessed May 1, 2011. www.mariebrenner.com/content/other_writing.asp#themanwhoknewtoomuch.

Brickey, Kathleen. 2003. "From Enron to WorldCom and Beyond: Life and Crime after Sarbanes–Oxley." *Washington Law Quarterly* 8: 357–401. doi:10.2139/ssrn.447100.

Browne, John. 2010. *Beyond Business: An Inspirational Memoir From a Visionary Leader*. London: Weidenfield.

Burger, Jerry. 2009. "Replicating Milgram: Will People Still Obey Today?" *American Psychologist* 64 (1): 1–11.

Callahan, Daniel and Bok, Sissela (eds.). 1980. *Ethics Teaching in Higher Education*. New York: Plenum Press.

Campbell, A., Whitehead, J. and Finklestein, S. 2009. "Why Good Leaders Make Bad Decisions," *Harvard Business Review* (February). Accessed September 12, 2011. http://hbr.org/2009/02/why-good-leaders-make-bad-decisions/ar/1.

Cane, Will. 2011. "Harold Camping 'Flabbergasted': Rapture a No-Show." *San Francisco Chronicle*, May 23. Accessed September 12, 2011. www.sfgate.com/cgi-bin/article.cgi?f=/c/a/2011/05/22/BAKO1JJIK7.DTL.

Carey, Benedict. 2011. "Brain Calisthenics for Abstract Ideas." *The New York Times*, June 7. Accessed on September 12, 2011. www.nytimes.com/2011/06/07/health/07learn.html?pagewanted=all.

Centers for Disease Control and Prevention (CDC). 2011. "U.S. Public Health Service Syphilis Study at Tuskegee: The Tuskegee Timeline." Accessed October 22, 2011. www.cdc.gov/tuskegee/timeline.htm.

Chabris, Christopher F., Weinberger, Adam, Fontaine, Matthew and Simons, Daniel J. 2011. "You Do Not Talk about Fight Club If You Do Not Notice Fight Club: Inattentional Blindness for a Simulated Real-World Assault." *iPerception* 2: 150–3.

Chance, Z. and Norton, M. 2009. "'I Read *Playboy* for the Articles': Justifying and Rationalizing Questionable Preferences." Harvard Business School Working Paper Series 10–018. Accessed on September 12, 2011. http://hbswk.hbs.edu/item/6283.html.

Chandavarkar, Pia. 2011. "Indian Microfinance Industry Mired in Scandal." *Deutsche Welle*, January 14. Accessed September 20, 2011. www.dw.de/dw/article/0,,6405968,00.html.

Chappatta, Brian and Chang, Greg. 2011. "Penn State Debt May be Cut by Moody's on Child Sex-Abuse Scandal." *Bloomburg Businessweek*, November 14. Accessed on September 2, 2012. www.businessweek.com/news/2011-11-14/penn-state-debt-may-be-cut-by-moody-s-on-child-sex-abuse-scandal.html.

Chappell, Bill. 2012. "Penn State Abuse Scandal: A Guide and Timeline." *NPR News: Sports*. January 8. Accessed May 6, 2012. www.npr.org/2011/11/08/142111804/penn-state-abuse-scandal-a-guide-and-timeline.

Chatzky, Jean. 2004. "Meet the Whistle-Blower." *CNN Money*, February 1. Accessed June 1, 2012. http://money.cnn.com/magazines/moneymag/moneymag_archive/2004/02/01/358879/index.htm.

Chernoff, Allan. 2009. "Madoff Whistleblower Blasts SEC." *CNNMoney*, February 4. Accessed August 21, 2011. http://money.cnn.com/2009/02/04/news/newsmakers/madoff_whistleblower/.

"Christine Casey: Whistleblower." *The Economist*, January 16. Accessed June 1, 2012. www.economist.com/node/1534854.

Chugh, D. 2004. "Why Milliseconds Matter: Societal and Managerial Implications of Implicit Social Cognition." *Social Justice Research* 17 (2): 203–22.

Chugh, D. and Bazerman, M. 2007. "Bounded Awareness: What You Fail To See Can Hurt You." *Mind & Society* 6: 1–18.

Clark, Andrew. 2009. "US Safety Authorities Impose Record £53m Fine on BP for Texas City Failings." *The Guardian*, October 30. Accessed September 24, 2011. www.guardian.co.uk/business/2009/oct/30/bp-texas-city-safety-fine?INTCMP=SRCH.

Coffee Jr., John C. 2006. *Gatekeepers: The Professions and Corporate Governance*. New York: Oxford University Press.

Cohan, William. 2012. "Lehman E-Mails Show Wall Street Arrogance Led to the Fall." *Bloomberg News*, May 6. Accessed September 2,

2012. www.bloomberg.com/news/2012-05-06/lehman-e-mails-show-wall-street-arrogance-led-to-the-fall.html.

Cohen, Elaine. 2011. "How GRI Can Bring the Other 90% of Companies to the CSR Table." *GreenBiz.com*, August 2. Accessed June 5, 2012. www.greenbiz.com/blog/2011/08/02/how-gri-can-bring-other-90-companies-csr-table.

Columbia Accident Investigation Board (CAIB). 2003. Report. Accessed September 25, 2011. http://caib.nasa.gov/.

Corkery, Michael. 2010. "The Lehman Whistleblower's Letter." *Wall Street Journal: WSJ Blogs*, March 19. Accessed June 5, 2012. http://blogs.wsj.com/deals/2010/03/19/breaking-news-here-is-the-letter-at-the-center-of-the-lehman-report/.

Corvino, John. 2006. "Reframing 'Morality Pays': Toward a Better Answer to 'Why Be Moral?' in Business." *Journal of Business Ethics* 67 (1): 1–14.

Creswell, Julie and White, Ben. 2008. "The Guys from 'Government Sachs.'" *The New York Times*, October 17.

Crutsinger, Martin and Gordon, Marcy. 2008. "Greenspan Denies Blame For Crisis, Admits 'Flaw'." *USA Today*, October 24. Accessed July 15, 2011. www.usatoday.com/news/topstories/2008-10-24-3784489146_x.htm.

Dana, J., Cain, D. M. and Dawes, R. M. 2006. "What You Don't Know Won't Hurt Me: Costly (But Quiet) Exit in Dictator Games." *Organizational Behavior and Human Decision Processes* 100 (2): 193–201.

Dane, Erik and Pratt, Michael G. 2007. "Exploring Intuition and its Role in Managerial Decision Making." *Academy of Management Review* 32 (1): 33–54.

Darley, J. and Latané, B. 1968. "Bystander Intervention in Emergencies: Diffusion of Responsibility." *Journal of Personality and Social Psychology* 8 (4): 377–83.

Defense Industry Initiative on Business Ethics and Conduct (DII). 2012. "Origins of DII." Accessed April 24, 2012. www.dii.org/about-us/history/.

De la Merced, Michael. 2012. "Once Remote, Goldman Sachs Puts on a Friendly Public Face." *The New York Times*, May 4.

Dellavigna, Stefano and Pollet, Joshua M. 2009. "Investor Inattention and Friday Earnings Announcements." *The Journal of Finance* 64 (2): 709–49.

Dembe, Allard E. 2009. "Ethical Issues Relating to the Health Effects of Long Working Hours." *Journal of Business Ethics* 84: 195–208.

Denzau, A. T. and North, D. C. 1994. "Shared Mental Models." *Kyklos* 47: 3–31.

Department of Justice. 2009. "Madoff Pleads Guilty to Eleven-Count Criminal Information and is Remanded into Custody." Press Release, March 12. Accessed June 18, 2011. www.justice.gov/usao/nys/pressreleases/March09/madoffbernardpleapr.pdf.

Dhanaraj, Charles and Khanna, Tarun. 2011. "Transforming Mental Models on Emerging Markets." *Academy of Management Learning and Education* 10: 684–701.

Dielman T. E., Campanelli, Pamela C., Shope, Jean T. and Butchart, Amy T. 1987. "Susceptibility to Peer Pressure, Self-Esteem, and Health Locus of Control as Correlates of Adolescent Substance Abuse." *Health Education Quarterly* 14: 207–21.

Donaldson, Thomas. 2000. "Adding Corporate Ethics to the Bottom Line." *Financial Times*, Financial Times Mastering Management Series, November 9. Accessed September 7, 2012. https://lgst.wharton.upenn.edu/files/?whdmsaction=public:main.file&fileID=1560.

Donnellon, Anne. 1996. *Team Talk: The Power of Language in Team Dynamics*. Cambridge, MA: The Presidents and Fellows of Harvard College.

Doty, Elizabeth. 2007. "Winning the Devil's Bargain." *strategy + business* 46. Accessed September 16, 2011. www.strategy-business.com/article/07101?pg=all–authors.

Dozier, Janelle Brinker and Miceli, Marcia P. 1985. "Potential Predictors of Whistle-Blowing: A Prosocial Behavior Perspective." *The Academy of Management Review* 10 (4): 823–36.

Duska, Ronald. 2007. *Contemporary Reflections on Business Ethics*. Dordrecht, The Netherlands: Springer.

"Ecomagination is GE." 2008. General Electric: Ecomagination Annual Report. Accessed September 25, 2011. http://ge.ecomagination.com/report.html.

Eisenberger, N. I., Lieberman, M. D. and Williams, K. D. 2003. "Does Rejection Hurt? An fMRI Study of Social Exclusion." *Science* 302: 290–2.

Eley, Tom. 2008. "Who is Henry Paulson?" World Socialist Web Site. September 23. Accessed April 14, 2012. www.wsws.org/articles/2008/sep2008/paul-s23.shtml.

Eliason, Erik. 2009. "Children's Development Bank: Transforming Street Children Into Entrepreneurs." *Social Earth*, April 2. Accessed September 20, 2011. www.socialearth.org/children'&s-development-bank-transforming-street-children-into-entrepreneurs.

Environmental Protection Agency (EPA). 2011. "3M Lean Six Sigma and Sustainability." Accessed April 23, 2011. www.epa.gov/lean/environment/studies/3m.htm.

Erichsen, Gerald. n.d. "The Chevy Nova That Didn't Go." *About.com: Spanish Language.* Accessed July 24, 2011. http://spanish.about.com/cs/culture/a/chevy_nova_2.htm.

Esser, James. 1998. "Alive and Well after Twenty-Five Years: A Review of Groupthink Research." *Organizational Behavior and Human Decision Processes* 73: 116–41.

Ethics & Compliance Officers' Association (ECOA). n.d.[a]. "History of the ECOA." Accessed April 24, 2012. www.theecoa.org/imis15/ECOA Public/ABOUT_THE_ECOA/History_of_the_ECOA/ECOAPublic/AboutContent/History.aspx?hkey=43ce057e-1870–408c-a6b3-b2f27c5b2950.

Ethics & Compliance Officers' Association (ECOA). n.d.[b]. "ECOA Mission, Vision, and Values." Accessed April 24, 2012. www.theecoa.org/imis15/ECOAPublic/ABOUT_THE_ECOA/Mission__Vision__and_Values/ECOAPublic/AboutContent/Mission_and_Vision.aspx?hkey=d11443d2-fbab-4e78–8dfe-84bd99e3aa3a.

Ethics Resource Center (ERC). 2012. "National Business Ethics Survey: Workplace Ethics in Transition." Accessed April 27, 2012. www.ethics.org/nbes/.

Ferguson, Charles H. 2010. *Inside Job.* 109 min. New York City: Sony Pictures Classics. DVD.

Ferrell, O. C., Fraedrich, John and Ferrell, Linda. 2012. *Business Ethics: Ethical Decision Making and Cases.* Mason, OH: Centage Learning.

Financial Industry Regulatory Authority (FINRA). 2012. n.d. "About FINRA." Accessed February 22, 2012. www.finra.org/AboutFINRA/.

Foot, Philippa. 1978. "The Problem of Abortion and the Doctrine of Double Effect." In *Virtues and Vices,* 19–32. Oxford: Basil Blackwell.

Freed, Dan. 2012. "Banks' Glass-Steagall Walls Quietly Rebuilt." *Forbes,* March 2. Accessed April 13, 2012. www.forbes.com/sites/thestreet/2012/04/02/banks-glass-steagall-walls-quietly-rebuilt/2/.

"French TV Contestants Made to Inflict 'Torture.'" 2010. *BBC News.* Accessed May 6, 2012. http://news.bbc.co.uk/2/hi/8571929.stm.

Fukuyama, Francis. 1995. *Trust: The Social Virtues and the Creation of Prosperity.* New York: Free Press.

Fuller, Sally Riggs, and Aldag, Ramon J. 1998. "Organizational Tonypandy: Lessons from a Quarter Century of the Groupthink Phenomenon." *Organizational Behavior and Human Decision Processes* 73: 163–84.

Galef, B. G., Jr. 1976. "Social Transmission of Acquired Behavior: A Discussion of Tradition and Social Learning in Vertebrates." In *Advances in the Study of Behavior,* Vol. 6, edited by J. S. Rosenblatt, R. A. Hinde, E. Shaw and C. Beer, 77–100. New York: Academic Press.

Gaventa, John. 1982. *Power and Powerlessness: Quiescence and Rebellion in an Appalachian Valley.* Urbana, IL: University of Chicago Press.

Gentner, D. and Whitley, E. W. 1997. "Mental Models of Population Growth." In *Environment, Ethics and Behavior,* edited by Max H. Bazerman, David M. Messick, Anne E. Tenbrunsel, and Kimberly A. Wade-Benzoni, 209–33. San Francisco: New Lexington Press.

Ghoshal, S. and Bartlett, C. A. 1995. "Building the Entrepreneurial Corporation: New Organizational Processes, New Managerial Tasks." *European Management Journal* 13 (2): 139–55.

Gilbert, Margaret. 1996. *Living Together: Rationality, Sociality, and Obligation.* Lanham, MD: Rowman and Littlefield.

Gilbert, Steven J. 1981. "Another Look at the Milgram Obedience Studies: The Role of the Gradated Series of Shocks." *Personality and Social Psychology Bulletin* 7: 690–5.

Gill, Dee. 2005. "Dealing with Diversity." *Inc. Magazine* (November): 37–40.

Gino, F. and Bazerman, M. H. 2006. "Slippery Slopes and Misconduct: The Effect of Gradual Degradation on the Failure to Notice Others' Unethical Behavior." Harvard Business School Working Paper (#06–007). Accessed September 13, 2011. www.people.hbs.edu/mbazerman/Papers/Gino-Baz-06-007-Slippery Slopes.pdf.

Gino, Francesca, Moore, Don A. and Bazerman, M. H. 2009. "See No Evil: Why We Fail to Notice Unethical Behavior." In *Social Decision Making: Social Dilemmas, Social Values, and Ethical Judgments,* edited by R. M. Kramer, A. E. Tenbrunsel and M. H. Bazerman, 241–63. New York: Routledge.

Gioia, Dennis. 1992. "Pinto Fires and Personal Ethics: A Script Analysis of Missed Opportunities." *Journal of Business Ethics* 11: 379–89.

Global-Tech Appliances, Inc. v. SEB S.A. 2011. 131 S.Ct. 2060.

Goldin, Claudia and Rouse, Cecilia. 2000. "Orchestrating Impartiality: The Impact of 'Blind' Auditions on Female Musicians." *The American Economic Review* 4 (90): 715–41.

Goldman, Alvin. 2010. "Social Epistemology." In *The Stanford Encyclopedia of Philosophy,* edited by Edward N. Zalta. Summer Edition. Accessed September 22, 2011. http://plato.stanford.edu/archives/win2003/entries/davidson/.

"Goldman Sachs Group Inc." 2012. *New York Times,* Business Day: Companies, April 17. Accessed May 21, 2012. http://topics.nytimes.com/top/news/business/companies/goldman_sachs_group_inc/index.html.

"Goldman Sachs spent \$800K on 3Q lobbying." 2011. *Bloomberg Businessweek,* December 16. Accessed May 23, 2012. www.businessweek.com/ap/financialnews/D9RLRI1G0.htm.

Gorman, Michael E. 1992. *Simulating Science*. Bloomington, IN: Indiana University Press.

Gorman, Michael E., Werhane, Patricia H., Mehalik, Matthew M. and Standish, Myles. 1998. "Unilever (a-d)." Darden Business Publishing. UVA-E-1053 through UVA-E-1056.

Grameen Bank. 2011. "GB at a Glance." October. Accessed June 5, 2012. www.grameen.com/index.php?option=com_content&task=view&id=26&Itemid=175.

"Greenspan Admits 'Mistake' That Helped Crisis." 2008. MSNBC/Associated Press. October 23. Accessed on August 26, 2011. www.msnbc.msn.com/id/27335454/ns/business-stocks-and-economy/t/greenspan-admits-mistake-helped-crisis/.

"Greenspan Says I Still Don't Fully Understand What Happened." 2008. Uploaded to YouTube.com by Propublica.org. Video. Accessed September 11, 2012. www.youtube.com/watch?v=R5lZPWNFizQ.

Greenwald, A. G., McGhee, D. E. and Schwartz, J. K. L. 1998. "Measuring Individual Differences in Implicit Cognition: The Implicit Association Test." *Journal of Personality and Social Psychology* 74 (6): 1464–80.

Gunia, Briana C., Li Huang, Long Wang, Wang, Juinwen and Murnighan, Keith J. 2012. "Contemplation and Conversation: Subtle Influences on Moral Decision Making." *Academy of Management Journal* 5: 13–34.

Hacking, Ian. 1999. *The Social Construction of What?* Cambridge: Harvard University Press.

Haney, Craig, Banks, Curtis and Zimbardo, Philip. 1973. "Interpersonal Dynamics in a Simulated Prison." *International Journal of Criminology and Penology* 1: 69–97.

Harman, Gilbert. 1977. *The Nature of Morality*. New York: Oxford University Press.

Hartman, Laura P. and Desjardins, Joseph. 2008. *Business Ethics: Decision-Making for Personal Integrity and Social Responsibility*. Burr Ridge, IL: McGraw-Hill.

Haverston, Heidi. 2010. "In Failure, We Are All Alan Greenspan." *Psychology Today: The Science of Success*, April 24. Accessed July 15, 2011. www.psychologytoday.com/blog/the-science-success/201004/in-failure-we-are-all-alan-greenspan.

Hawksley, Humphrey. 2012. "India's Exploited Child Cotton Workers." *BBC News*, January 19. Accessed June 5, 2012. www.bbc.co.uk/news/world-asia-16639391.

Heffernan, Margaret. 2011. *Willful Blindness*. New York: Walker and Company.

Heisenberg, Werner. 1959. *Physics and Philosophy*. London: George Allen & Unwin, Ltd.

Hindle, Tim. 2009. "Triple-Bottom Line." In *The Economist: Guide to Management Ideas and Gurus*, 193–5. London: Profile Books.

Hiroto, Donald S. and Seligman, Martin E. 1975. "Generality of Learned Helplessness in Man." *Journal of Personality and Social Psychology* 31 (2): 311–27.

Hirshleifer, David, Lim, Sonya Seongyeon and Hong Teoh, Siew. 2009. "Driven to Distraction: Extraneous Events and Underreaction to Earnings News." *Journal of Finance* 64 (5): 2289–325.

Hoffman, Michael W. 2010. "Repositioning the Corporate Ethics Officer." *Business Ethics Quarterly* 20 (4): 744–5.

Hollister, Steve. 2012. "Raymond James." Personal e-mail message to Elaine Englehardt, March 1.

Hudson, James M. and Bruckman, Amy S. 2004. "The Bystander Effect: A Lens for Understanding Patterns of Participation." *The Journal of the Learning Sciences* 13 (2): 165–95.

Hume, David. [1777] 1975. *Enquiries Concerning Human Understanding and Concerning the Principles of Morals*, 3rd edn, edited by L. A. Selby-Bigge and P. H. Nidditch. Oxford: Clarendon Press.

Hutton, Robert and Morales, Alex. 2011. "Rupert Murdoch Denies Knowledge of Phone-Hacking, Vows to 'Clean This Up.'" *Bloomberg*, July 19. Accessed September 19, 2011. www.bloomberg.com/news/2011-07-19/rupert-murdoch-has-most-humble-day-in-u-k-testimony-over-hacking-probe.html.

Institute for Transportation Research and Education (ITRE). 2012. "Blind Pedestrians Access to Roundabouts and Other Complex Intersections." Accessed April 20, 2012. www.itre.ncsu.edu/ITRE/research/Pedestrian-Accessibility/index.html.

James, Scott. 2011. "From Oakland to the World, Words of Warning: Time's Up." *The New York Times*, May 20. Accessed September 13, 2011. www.nytimes.com/2011/05/20/us/20bcjames.html.

Janis, Irving. 1982. *Groupthink*. 2nd edn. Boston: Houghton-Mifflin.

Jenkins, Sally. 2012. "Jon Paterno's Last Interview." *The Washington Post*, January 14. Accessed April 9, 2012. www.washingtonpost.com/sports/colleges/joe-paternos-first-interview-since-the-penn-state-sandusky-scandal/2012/01/13/gIQA08e4yP_story.html.

Johansson, P., Hall, L., Sikstrom, S. and Olsson, A. 2005. "Failure to Detect Mismatches Between Intention and Outcome in a Simple Decision Task." *Science* 310: 116–9.

Johnson, C. E. 2009. *Meeting the Ethical Challenges of Leadership: Casting Light or Shadow*. 3rd edn. San Francisco: Sage.

Johnson, Kevin and Whiteside, Kelly. 2011. "Penn State President Wants to Put Less Emphasis on Football." *USA Today*, December 6.

Accessed April 12, 2012. www.usatoday.com/sports/college/football/
bigten/story/2011–12-06/penn-state-rodney-erickson-interview-
football-emphasis/51686080/1.

Johnson, Mark. 1993. *Moral Imagination*. Chicago: University of Chicago
Press.

Jones, Ashby. 2009. "Madoff Speaks: The Plea Allocution." *Wall Street
Journal Blogs: The Law Blog*, March 12. Accessed August 27,
2011. http://blogs.wsj.com/law/2009/03/12/madoff-speaks-the-plea-
allocution/.

Jonsen, Albert R. and Toulmin, Stephan. 1988. *The Abuse of Casuistry: A
History of Moral Reasoning*. Berkeley: University of California Press.

Kalichman, Michael. 2001. "Whistleblowing." Resources for Research
Ethics Education. Accessed February 6, 2012. http://research-ethics.
net/topics/whistleblowing.

Kant, Immanuel. [1787] 1965. *Critique of Pure Reason*. Translated by Norman Kemp Smith. New York: Bedford/St. Martins Press.

Karavidas, M., Lim, N. K. and Katsikas, S. L. 2005. "The Effects of Computers on Older Adult Users." *Computers in Human Behavior* 21 (5):
697–711.

Karnitschnig, Matthew, Solomon, Deborah, Pleven, Liam and Hilsenrath,
Jon E. 2008. "U.S. to Take Over AIG in $85 Billion Bailout; Cen-
tral Banks Inject Cash as Credit Dries Up." *Wall Street Journal*,
September 16. Accessed June 5, 2012. http://online.wsj.com/article/
SB122156561931242905.html.

Kay, Ira and Putten, Steven Van. 2007. *Myths and Realities of Executive
Pay*. New York: Cambridge University Press.

Kempen, Eric B. and Bakaj, Andrew. 2009. "Marshaling Whistleblower
Protection: Protecting the Whistleblower Process Is One of the Most
Important Duties of an Inspector General." *Journal of Public Inquiry*
(Spring Summer): 6–8.

Kilham, Wesley and Mann, Leon. 1974. "Level of Destructive Obedience
as a Function of Transmitter and Executant Roles in the Milgram Obedience Paradigm." *Journal of Personality and Social Psychology* 29:
696–702.

Kobus, K. and Henry, D. 2010. "Interplay of Network Position and Peer
Substance Use in Early Adolescent Cigarette, Alcohol, and Marijuana
Use." *Journal of Early Adolescence* 30 (2): 225–45.

Konish, Lorie and McMorris, Frances A. 2012. "Raymond James Rising." *On Wall Street*, February 1. Accessed April 14, 2012. www.
onwallstreet.com/ows_issues/2012_2/raymond-james-rising-2676975-
1.html?pg=3.

Krell, Eric. 2010. "How to Conduct an Ethics Audit." *HR Magazine* (April):
48–51.

Kristof, Nicholas. 2009. "Would You Slap Your Father? If So, You're a Liberal." *The New York Times*, May 27. Accessed June 5, 2012. www.nytimes.com/2009/05/28/opinion/28kristof.html.

Krugman, Paul. 2009. "Boiling the Frog." *The New York Times*, July 12. Accessed May 6, 2012. www.nytimes.com/2009/07/13/opinion/13krugman.html.

Labaton, Stephen. 2008. "S.E.C. Concedes Oversight Flaws Fueled Collapse." *The New York Times*, September 26.

Lacayo, Richard and Ripley, Amanda. 2002. "Persons of the Year 2002: The Whistleblowers." *Time Magazine*, December 30. Accessed May 6, 2012. www.time.com/time/printout/0,8816,1003998,00.html.

Landrigan, Christopher P., Rothschild, Jeffrey M., Cronin, John W., Kaushal, Rainu, Burdick, Elisabeth, Katz, Joel T., Lilly, Craig M., Stone, Peter H., Lockley, Steven W., Bates, David W. and Czeisler, Charles A., for the Harvard Work Hours, Health and Safety Group. 2004. "Effect of Reducing Interns' Work Hours on Serious Medical Errors in Intensive Care Units." *The New England Journal of Medicine* 351: 1838–48.

Latané, Bibb and Darley, John M. 1969. "Bystander 'Apathy.'" *American Scientist* 57 (2): 244–68.

Latané, Bibb and Nina, S. 1981. "Ten Years of Research on Group Size and Helping." *Psychological Bulletin* 89 (2): 308–24.

Lawrence, Joanne T. and Beamish, Paul W. 2013. *Globally Responsible Leadership: Managing According to the UN Global Compact*. Los Angeles: Sage Publishing.

"The Letter by Lehman Whistle-Blower Matthew Lee." 2010. *The New York Times*, March 19. Accessed May 23, 2012. http://dealbook.nytimes.com/2010/03/19/the-letter-by-lehman-whistle-blower-matthew-lee/.

Levin, Bess. 2010. "Lloyd Blankfein, Jamie Dimon Keep the Yuks Coming." *Dealbreaker*, May 24. Accessed September 7, 2012. http://dealbreaker.com/2010/05/lloyd-blankfein-jamie-dimon-keep-the-yuks-coming/.

Levin, D. T. and Simons, D. J. 1997. "Failure to Detect Changes to Attended Objects in Motion Pictures." *Psychonomic Bulletin and Review* 4: 501–6.

Lewis, Michael. 2010. *The Big Short*. New York: W.W. Norton.

Litt, A., Reich, T., Maymin, S. and Shiv, B. 2011. "Pressure and Perverse Flights to Familiarity." *Psychological Science* 22 (4): 523–31. doi: 10.1177/0956797611400095.

Loftus, Peter. 2011. "J&J CEO Total 2010 Compensation Down 7% vs 2009." *Fox Business*, March 16. Accessed March 27, 2011. www.foxbusiness.com/industries/2011/03/16/jj-ceo-total-2010-compensation-7-vs-200/.

Los Alamos National Laboratory. 1995. "The Karen Silkwood Story." PBS.org. Accessed June 5, 2012. www.pbs.org/wgbh/pages/frontline/shows/reaction/interact/silkwood.html.

Lowenstein, Roger. 2010. *The End of Wall Street*. New York: Penguin Press.

Lowenstein, Roger. 2012. "The Villain." *Atlantic* (April): 49–60.

MacIntyre, Alasdair. 1981. *After Virtue*. Notre Dame University Press.

Mack, A. and Rock, I. 1998. *Inattentional Blindness*. Cambridge: MIT Press.

Maloney, R. 2001. "Authenticity and Contact with Youth." *Review for Religious* 60: 262.

Marcus, Jonathan L. 1993. "Model Penal Code Section 2.02(7) and Willful Blindness." *The Yale Law Journal* 102 (8): 2231–57.

Markus, Hazel Rose and Kitayama, Shinobu. 1991. "Culture and the Self: Implications for Cognition, Emotion, and Motivation." *Psychological Review* 98 (2): 224–53.

Martin, Jacquelyn. 2011. "Supreme Court Rules in Wal-Mart's Favor: How the Sides are Reacting." *Christian Science Monitor*, June 20. Accessed July 27, 2011. www.csmonitor.com/USA/Justice?2011/0620/.

Matanda, M., Jenvey, V. B. and Phillips, J. G. 2004. "Internet Use in Adulthood: Loneliness, Computer Anxiety and Education." *Behaviour Change* 21 (2): 103–14.

May, William S. 1988. "Professional Virtue and Self-Regulation." In *Ethical Issues in Professional Life*, edited by Joan Callahan, 404–11. New York: Oxford University Press.

McKinley, Jesse. 2011. "An Autumn Date for the Apocalypse," *The New York Times*, May 23. Accessed September 12, 2011. www.nytimes.com/2011/05/24/us/24rapture.html.

McLean, Bethany. 2010. "The Bank Job." *Vanity Fair* (January). Accessed April 12, 2012. www.vanityfair.com/business/features/2010/01/goldman-sachs-200101.

Mead, Jenny, Werhane, Patricia H. and Wicks, Andrew. 2005. "Cynthia Cooper and WorldCom." Charlottesville, VA: Darden Business Publishing. UVA E 279.

Meyer, Jeremy P. 2010. "Students' Cheating Takes a High Tech Turn." *Denver Post*, May 26. Accessed August 18, 2011. www.denverpost.com/news/ci_15170333.

Milgram, Stanley 1970. "The Experience of Living in Cities." *Science* 167: 1461–8.

Milgram, Stanley 1973. "The Perils of Obedience." *Harper's Magazine* (December): 62–77.

Milgram, Stanley 1974. *Obedience to Authority*. New York: Harper & Row.

Mitler, Merrill M., Carskadon, Mary A., Czeisler, Charles A., Dement, William C., Dinges, David F. and Graeber, R. Curtis. 1988. "Catastrophes, Sleep, and Public Policy: Consensus Report." *Sleep* 11: 100–9.

Mnookin, Seth. 2004. *Hard News: The Scandals at the* New York Times *and Their Meaning for American Media.* New York: Random House.

Moberg, Dennis J. 2000. "Role Models and Moral Exemplars." *Business Ethics Quarterly* 10: 675–96.

Moberg, Dennis J. 2006. "Ethics Blind Spots in Organizations: How Systematic Errors in Person Perception Undermine Moral Agency." *Organizational Studies* 27 (3): 413–28.

National Institutes of Health (NIH). 1979. *The Belmont Report: Ethical Principles and Guidelines for the Protection of Human Subjects of Research.* Office of Human Subjects Research. April 18. Accessed March 16, 2012. http://ohsr.od.nih.gov/guidelines/Belmont.html.

Packer, D. J. 2008. "Identifying Systematic Disobedience in Milgram's Obedience Experiments: A Meta-Analytic Review." *Perspectives on Psychological Science* 3: 301–4.

Parmar, Bidhan. 2011. *The Role of Ethics, Sensemaking, and Discourse in Enacting Authority Relationships.* PhD. Dissertation, University of Virginia.

"Pfizer's Ex-Chief to Get Full Retirement Package." 2006. *The New York Times*, December 22.

Phillips, Katherine W., Mannix, Elizabeth A., Neale, Margaret A. and Gruenfeld, Deborah H. 2004. "Diverse Groups and Information Sharing: The Effects of Congruent Ties." *Journal of Experimental Social Psychology* 40 (4): 497–510.

Pina e Cuha, Miguel, Rego, Armenio and Clegg, Stewart R. 2010. "Obedience and Evil: From Milgram and Kampuchea to Normal Organizations." *Journal of Business Ethics* 97: 291–309.

Plato. 1974. *The Republic.* Translated by G. M. A. Grube. Indianapolis: Hackett Publishing.

Plumb, C. and Wilchins, D. 2008. "Lehman CEO Fuld's Hubris Contributed to Meltdown." *Reuters*, September 14. Accessed April 30, 2011. www.reuters.com/article/2008/09/14/us-lehman-backstory-idUSN1341059120080914.

Porter, Michael E. and Kramer, Mark R. 2011. "Creating Shared Value: How to Reinvent Capitalism – and Unleash a Wave of Innovation and Growth." *Harvard Business Review* (January/February): 63–70.

Presidential Commission on the Space Shuttle Challenger Accident. 1986. *Report*, Vol. I-II. Accessed September 12, 2011. http://science.ksc.nasa.gov/shuttle/missions/51-l/docs/rogers-commission/table-of-contents.html.

Pritchard, Michael S. and Holtzapple, Mark. 1997. "Responsible Engineering: Gilbane Gold Revisited." *Science and Engineering Ethics* 3 (2): 217–31.

Pulliam, Susan. 2003. "Wrong Numbers." *The Wall Street Journal: Classroom Edition* (November). Accessed August 31, 2011. www.wsjclassroomedition.com/archive/03nov/bibg_worldcom.htm.

Putnam, Hilary. 1990. *Realism with a Human Face*. Cambridge, MA: Harvard University Press.

Rawls, John. 1971. *A Theory of Justice*. Cambridge, MA: Harvard University Press.

Reich, Robert B. 2007. "CEOs Deserve Their Pay." *The Wall Street Journal*, September 14.

"Report of the Board of Trustees Concerning Nov. 9 Decisions." 2012. *Penn State Live*, March 12. Accessed May 25, 2012. http://live.psu.edu/story/58341.

Rest, James and Narvaez, Narcia (eds). 1994. *Moral Development in the Professions*. Hillsdale, NJ: Lawrence Erlbaum Associates.

Richtel, Matt. 2009. "Promoting the Care Phone, Despite Risks." *The New York Times*. December 6.

Roberts, Allen B. 2011. "Dodd–Frank Bounty Awards and Protections Change: Whistleblower Stakes – Will Opportunity for Personal Gain Frustrate Corporate Compliance?" *Bloomberg Law Reports* 5 (23): 1–7. Reprint. Accessed September 7, 2012. www.ebglaw.com/showarticle.aspx?show=14528.

Rorty, Richard. 1993. "Putnam and the Relativist Menace." *Journal of Philosophy* 90: 443–561.

Rosenzweig, Phil. 2007. *The Halo Effect*. New York: Free Press.

Rouse, William B. and Morris, Nancy M. 1986. "On Looking into the Black Box: Prospects and Limits in the Search for Mental Models." *Psychological Bulletin* 100: 349–63.

Rudman, Laura A. and Heppen, Jessica B. 2003. "Implicit Romantic Fantasies and Women's Interest in Personal Power: A Glass Slipper Effect?" *Personality and Social Psychology Bulletin* 29 (11): 1357–70.

Sack, Robert, Wicks, Andrew, Werhane, Patricia H. and Mead, Emily. 2009. "World Com: Keeping the Planes in the Air." Darden Business Publishing. UVA-E-335.

Sanati, Cyrus. 2009. "10 Years Later, Looking at the Repeal of Glass-Steagall." *The New York Times*. Dealbook. November 12. http://dealbook.nytimes.com/2009/11/12/10-years-later-looking-at-repeal-of-glass-steagall/.

Santiso, Javier. 2010a. "Cognitive Dissonance and the Financial Crisis." *The Globalist*, August 9. Accessed October 24, 2010. www.theglobalist.com/storyid.aspx?StoryId=8638.

Santiso, Javier. 2010b. "Emerging Markets and the Shifting Wealth of Nations." Presentation to The European Association Of Business And Society (EABIS), September 21. St. Petersburg, Russia.

Saphi, Ann. 2010. "Lehman Brothers' Whistleblower Was Ousted: Report." *Reuters*, March 16. Accessed September 7, 2012. www.reuters.com/article/2010/03/16/us-lehman-whistleblower-idUSTRE62F0XP 20100316.

Sartre, Jean-Paul. 1956. *Being and Nothingness*. Translated by Hazel Barnes. New York: Philosophical Library.

Schneiderman, R. M. 2011. "Flawed Titan of the Fed." *NewsWeek*, June 12. Accessed September 14, 2011. www.newsweek.com/2011/06/12/new-documentary-looks-at-greenspan-s-flaw.html.

Scott, R. W. [1995] 2001. *Institutions and Organizations*. Thousand Oaks, CA: Sage Publications.

Schwartz, Nelson D. 2012. "Public Exit From Goldman Raises Doubt Over a New Ethic." *The New York Times*, March 14.

Securities and Exchange Commission (SEC). n.d. "The Laws That Govern the Securities Industry." Accessed April 24, 2012. www.sec.gov/about/laws.shtml#sox2002.

Securities and Exchange Commission, Office of Investigations (SEC). 2009. "Investigation of Failure of the SEC to Uncover Bernard Madoff's Ponzi Scheme." Accessed March 21, 2012. www.sec.gov/news/studies/2009/oig-509.pdf.

Seligman, M. E. P. and Maier, S. F. 1967. "Failure to Escape Traumatic Shock." *Journal of Experimental Psychology* 74: 1–9.

Sen, Amartya. 1993. "Positional Objectivity." *Philosophy and Public Affairs* 22: 119–30.

Senge, Peter. 1990. *The Fifth Discipline*. New York: Doubleday.

"Shareholder Interest in Triple Bottom Line 'Increasing.'" 2012. *Environmental Leader*, April 5. Accessed April 24, 2012. www.environmentalleader.com/2012/04/05/shareholder-interest-in-triple-bottom-line-increasing/.

Simons, D. 2010. "Movie Perception Test." The Invisible Gorilla. Video. Accessed May 2, 2011. www.theinvisiblegorilla.com/videos.html.

Simons, D. J. and Chabris, C. F. 1999. "Gorillas in Our Midst: Sustained Inattentional Blindness for Dynamic Events." *Perception* 28: 1059–74.

Sinha, Meenakshi. 2008. "Street-Smart Bankers." *The Times of India*, March 2.

Sittenfeld, Curtis. 1998. "He's No Fool (But He Plays One Inside Companies)." *Fast Company*, October 31. Accessed September 2, 2011. www.fastcompany.com/magazine/19/nofool.html.

Smith, Adam. [1776] 1981. "An Inquiry Into the Nature and Causes of the Wealth of Nations." In *The Glasgow Edition of the Works and*

Correspondence of Adam Smith, edited by R. H. Campbell and A. S. Skinner. Indianapolis: Liberty Fund, Inc.

Smith, Adam. [1790] 1984. *The Theory of Moral Sentiments*. Edited by D. D. Raphael and A. L. Macfie. Indianapolis: Liberty Fund, Inc.

Smith, Greg. 2012. "Why I am Leaving Goldman Sachs." *New York Times*, March 14.

Sorkin, Andrew Ross. 2008. "Lehman Files for Bankruptcy; Merrill Is Sold." *The New York Times*. September 14.

Sorkin, Andrew Ross and Craig, Susanne. 2011. "Goldman Said to Get Subpoena Over Its Role in Crisis." *The New York Times*, June 2.

Soshnick, Scott and Novy-Williams, Eben. 2011. "How Paterno Put His Penn State Money above Full Disclosure of Child Abuse." *Bloomburg*, December 26. Accessed June 5, 2012. www.bloomberg.com/news/2011–12-27/paterno-put-his-penn-state-money-above-disclosure-of-child-abuse.html.

Spurgeon, Anne, Harrington, J. Malcolm and Cooper, Cary L. 1997. "Health and Safety Problems Associated with Long Working Hours: A Review of the Current Position." *Occupational and Environmental Medicine* 54 (6): 367–75.

Stephenson, G. R. 1967. "Cultural Acquisition of a Specific Learned Response Among Rhesus Monkeys." In *Progress in Primatology*, edited by D. Starek, R. Schneider and H. J. Kuhn, 279–88. Stuttgart: Fischer.

Stiglitz, Joseph E. 2011. "Of the 1%, by the 1% and for the 1%." *Vanity Fair* (May). Accessed April 12, 2012. www.vanityfair.com/society/features/2011/05/top-one-percent-201105.

Strayer, David L., Drews, Frank A. and Crouch, Dennis J. 2006. "A Comparison of the Cell Phone Driver and the Drunk Driver." *Human Factors: The Journal of the Human Factors and Ergonomics Society* 48 (2): 381–91.

Subramanian, S., Dhanaraj, C. and Branzei, O. 2010a. "Bayer CropScience in India (A): Against Child Labor." Richard Ivey School of Business Foundation. Case #910M61-PDF-ENG.

Subramanian, S., Dhanaraj, C. and Branzei, O. 2010b. "Bayer CropScience in India (B): Values and Strategy." Richard Ivey School of Business Foundation. Case #910M62-PDF-ENG.

Sunstein, Cass. 2009. *Going to Extremes: How Like Minds Unite and Divide*. Oxford University Press.

Suri, R., Lee, J. A., Manchanda, R. V. and Monroe, K. B. 2003. "The Effect of Computer Anxiety on Price Value Trade-Off in the On-line Environment." *Psychology & Marketing* 20 (6): 515–36.

Suttell, S. 2011. "Greenspan, Bernanke Share in Blame for Financial Market Collapse." *Crain's Cleveland Business*, January 28. Accessed September 12, 2011. www.crainscleveland.com/article/20110128/BLOGS03/110129796.

Tenbrunsel, Ann E., Diekmann, Kristina A., Wade-Benzoni, Kimberly A., and Bazerman, Max H. 2007. "The Ethical Mirage: A Temporal Explanation as to Why We Aren't as Ethical as We Think We Are." Harvard NOM Working Paper No. 08–012. Accessed September 13, 2011. http://ssrn.com/abstract=1010385.

Tepper, Bennett. 2010. "When Managers Pressure Employees to Behave Badly: Toward a Comprehensive Response." *Business Horizons* 53: 591–8.

Thaler, Robert H. and Sunstein, Cass R. 2009. *Nudge: Improving Decisions About Health, Wealth, and Happiness.* Revised and Expanded Edition. New York: Penguin Books.

Thornton, R. G. 2010. "Responsibility for the Acts of Others." *Baylor University Medical Center Proceedings* 23 (3): 313–5. Accessed May 3, 2011. www.ncbi.nlm.nih.gov/pmc/articles/PMC2900989/.

Tocqueville, Alexis de. 2000. *Democracy in America*, translated by George Lawrence, edited by J. P. Mayer. NY: HarperCollins/Perennial Classics.

Toulmin, Stephan R. 1981. "The Tyranny of Principles." *The Hastings Center Report*, 11 (6): 31–9.

Transparency International. 2011. "2011 Corruption Perceptions Index." Accessed June 1, 2012. http://cpi.transparency.org/cpi2011/results/.

United Nations. 1950. "Principles of International Law Recognized in the Charter of the Nürnberg Tribunal and in the Judgment of the Tribunal." Accessed May 3, 2011. http://untreaty.un.org/ilc/texts/instruments/english/draft%20articles/7_1_1950.pdf.

United States Chemical Safety Board (US CSB). 2007. "Investigation Report: Refinery Explosion and Fire." Accessed September 25, 2011. www.csb.gov/assets/document/CSBfinalreportBP.pdf.

United States House of Representatives. 2009. Committee on Financial Services. *Testimony of Lloyd C. Blankfein, Chairman and CEO, The Goldman Sachs Group, Inc.* February 11. Accessed June 5, 2012. www.house.gov/apps/list/hearing/financialsvcs_dem/lloyd_blankfein_sachs_goup.pdf.

United States Sentencing Commission (USSC). 2010. "2010 Federal Sentencing Guideline Manual." Accessed April 24, 2012. www.ussc.gov/guidelines/2010_guidelines/.

Van Beest, Ilja and Williams, Kipling D. 2006. "When Inclusion Costs and Ostracism Pays, Ostracism Still Hurts." *Journal of Personality and Social Psychology* 91 (5): 918–28.

Van de Ven, Andrew H. and Hargrave, Timothy J. 2004. "Social, Technical, and Institutional Change: Literature Review and Synthesis." In *Handbook of Organizational Change and Innovation*, edited by Marshall Scott Poole and Andrew H. Van de Ven, 259–303. New York: Oxford University Press.

Van Voris, Bob. 2011. "Citigroup, SEC Defend $285 Million CDO Accord as US Judge Questions Deal." *Bloomberg*, November 9. Accessed June 5, 2012. http://mobile.bloomberg.com/news/2011–11–09/citigroup-sec-tell-judge-285-million-cdo-accord-is-fair-1-.

Veenendaal, Paul van. 2008. "Case Study: Transport For London – Do the Test." *Viral Blog*. Accessed September 17, 2011. www.viralblog.com/viral-cases/case-study-transport-for-london-do-the-test/.

Verschoor, Curtis C. 2010. "Increased Motivation for Whistleblowing." *Strategic Finance* (November): 60–2.

Vogell, Heather. 2011. "Investigation Into APS Cheating Finds Unethical Behavior Across Every Level." *Atlanta Journal-Constitution*, July 6. Accessed August 18, 2011. www.ajc.com/news/investigation-into-aps-cheating-1001375.html.

Vohs, Kathleen D., Mead, N. L. and Goode, Miranda R. 2006. "The Psychological Consequences of Money." *Science* 314 (5802): 1154–6.

Vos, Jacob. 2009. "Actions Speak Louder than Words: Greenwashing in Corporate America." *Notre Dame Journal of Law, Ethics, and Public Policy* 23: 673–97.

Weaver, Gary and Trevino, Linda K. 1999. "Compliance and Values Oriented Ethics Programs: Influences on Employees' Attitudes and Behavior." *Business Ethics Quarterly* 9 (2): 312–35.

Weick, Karl, Sutcliffe, Kathleen and Obstfeld, David. 1995. *Sensemaking in Organizations*. Thousand Oaks, CA: Sage Publications.

Weick, Karl, Sutcliffe, Kathleen and Obstfeld, David. 2005. "Organizing and the Process of Sensemaking." *Organizational Science* 16: 409–21.

Welby, Justin. 1997. "The Ethics of Derivatives and Risk Management." *Ethical Perspectives* 4 (2): 84–92.

Werhane, Patricia H. 1999. *Moral Imagination and Management Decision-Making*. New York: Oxford University Press.

Werhane, Patricia H. 2005. "Why Good People Do Bad Things?" In *New Challenges for Business Schools and Corporate Leaders*, edited by

Robert A. Peterson and O. C. Ferrell, 38–55. Armonk, NY: M.E. Sharp.

Werhane, Patricia H. 2007. "A Place for Philosophers in Applied Ethics and the Role of Moral Reasoning in Moral Imagination: A Response to Richard Rorty." *Business Ethics Quarterly* 16 (3): 401–8.

Werhane, Patricia H. 2008. "Mental Models, Moral Imagination and System Thinking in the Age of Globalization." *Journal of Business Ethics* 78: 463–74.

Werhane, Patricia, Hartman, Laura, Moberg, Dennis, Englehardt, Elaine, Pritchard, Michael and Parmar, Bidhan. 2011[a]. "Social Constructivism, Mental Models, and Problems of Obedience." *Journal of Business Ethics* 100: 103–18.

Werhane, Patricia, Hartman, Laura, Archer, Crina, Bevan, David and Clark, Kim. 2011[b]. "Trust After the Global Financial Crisis." *Business and Society Review* 16 (4): 403–33.

Werhane, Patricia and Moriarty, Brian. 2009. "Moral Imagination and Management Decision Making." *Business Roundtable: Institute for Corporate Ethics.* Accessed September 13, 2011. www.corporate-ethics.org/pdf/moral_imagination.pdf.

"Whistleblowers' Stories: Wityczak." n.d. Accessed September 15, 2011. www.all-about-qui-tam.org/stories_wityczak.shtml.

Wilfong, J. D. 2006. "Computer Anxiety and Anger: The Impact of Computer Use, Computer Experience, and Self-Efficacy Beliefs." *Computers in Human Behavior* 22 (6): 1001–11.

Williamson, Dianne. 2011. "Murdoch Scandal Taints All Journalists." *Worcester Telegram & Gazette*, July 24. Accessed September 19, 2011. www.telegram.com/article/20110724/COLUMN01/107249834/1101/.

Wimsatt, Alison Ross. 2005. "The Struggles of Being Ernest: A. Ernest Fitzgerald, Management Systems Deputy in the Office of the Asst. Sec of the Air Force." *Industrial Management*, July 28.

Wittgenstein, Ludwig. 1953. *Philosophical Investigations.* Translated by G. E. M. Anscombe. New York: Macmillan.

Wojciszka, Bogdan. 1997. "Parallels Between Competence Versus Morality-Related Traits and Individualistic Versus Collectivist Values." *European Journal of Social Psychology* 27: 245–56.

Wright, Martin. 2012. "Reinventing Consumption: An Exclusive Interview with the CEO of Unilever." *Green Futures Magazine* 83: 20.

Wyatt, Edward. 2011. "Judge Blocks Citigroup's Settlement with S.E.C." *The New York Times*, November 28.

Yeo, Michael. 1988. "Marketing Ethics: The Bottom Line?" *Journal of Business Ethics* 7 (12): 929–32.

York, Jeffrey G. 2009. "Pragmatic Sustainability: Translating Environmental Ethics into Competitive Advantage." *Journal of Business Ethics* 85 (1): 97–109.

Young, Greg and Hasler, David S. 2010. "Managing Reputational Risks: Using Risk Management for Business Ethics and Reputational Capital." *Strategic Finance* (November): 37–46.

Yunus, Muhammad. [1999] 2003. *Banker to the Poor: Microlending and the Battle Against World Poverty*. New York: PublicAffairs.

Zimbardo, Philip. 1973. "A Pirandelian Prison." *The New York Times Magazine*, 38ff. April 8.

Zimbardo, Philip G. 2007. *The Lucifer Effect*. New York: Random House.

Author index

Subject index

Fuld, Richard, 4, 100, *See also*
    Lehman Brothers bankruptcy

Game of Death, 49, *See also* French
    television experiment
gangs, 74–5
gatekeepers, 53, 56
gender discrimination, 36
General Electric, 25, 199, *See also*
    ecoimagination
Genovese, Catherine, 87
Gilbane Gold (film), 162
Ginsberg, Ruth Bader, 36
Gioia, Dennis, 22, 23
Glass-Steagall Act of 1933, 183
global financial crisis, 26
Global-Tech Inc. v. Sebs S.A., 122
Goldman Sachs, 1, 6, 152, 164, 181,
    185, 189, *See also* Blankfein,
    Lloyd
Government Accountability Project,
    75
gradualistic moral disengagement, 79
Grameen Bank, 31, 32
Grameen Industries, 31
Great Depression, 183
green movement, 25
Greenspan, Alan, 82, 179
greenwashing, 155
Grisham, John, 80
group dynamics, 132, 134
group polarization, 133
groupthink, 132, *See also* Janis, Irving
Gulf oil spill, 34, *See also* British
    Petroleum (BP)
gut reactions, 96
Gyges, ring of, 116

habit, 65, 77, 97, 146
Hacking, Ian, 20, 21
Haidt, Jonathan, 5
halo effect, 24
Harrington, Noreen, 193
Harvard Work Hours, Health and
    Safety Group, 86
Hastings Center, 145
Hawksley, Humphrey, 210
Heffernan, Margaret, 35, *See also*
    willful blindness
Heisenberg uncertainty principle, 19

hip implant, 24
homogeneity, 93, 109, 111, *See also*
    flight to the familiar
House Committee of Oversight and
    Government Reform, 179
Hume, David, 139
Hurricane Katrina, 99

ideologue, 81
ideology, 81, *See also* ethical obstacles
impartial spectator, 125, 127, 128, *See
    also* ethical obstacles
Implicit Association Test, 110
implicit learning, 98
inattentional blindness, 83, *See also*
    focusing failure
incrementalism, 56
India, 27
    child labor, 210
    children bankers in, 30
    microfinance scandal in, 32
    Thomson Reuters' information
        service in, 200
Institute for Transportation Research
    and Education (ITRE), 146–7
Institutional Review Board (IRB), 206
International Labor Organization, 210
intrinsic motivation, 155
intuition, 96, 146
investor distraction hypothesis, 86
invisibility, myth of, 116
Iraq, 54

J. P. Morgan Chase, 181
Janis, Irving, 132
Johnson & Johnson, 3, 23, 55–6

Kant, Immanuel, 17
Karp, Brad, 191
Kelly Martin, 182
Kennedy, John F., 133
Kenya, 200
Kerr-McGee Plant, 194
Ketcham, Richard G., 201
knowledge, 18, 122, 135
Ku Klux Klan, 113

language, 19, 20
Lay, Kenneth, 43, 70, *See also* Enron
leader-and-follower, 28